Neuropsychology of Language, Reading, and Spelling

EDUCATIONAL PSYCHOLOGY

Allen J. Edwards, Series Editor
Department of Psychology
Southwest Missouri State University
Springfield, Missouri

Published

Ursula Kirk (ed.). Neuropsychology of Language, Reading, and Spelling

Judith Worell (ed.). Psychological Development in the Elementary Years

Wayne Otto and Sandra White (eds.). Reading Expository Material

John B. Biggs and Kevin F. Collis. Evaluating the Quality of Learning: The Solo Taxonomy (Structure of the Observed Learning Outcome)

Gilbert R. Austin and Herbert Garber (eds.). The Rise and Fall of National Test Scores

Lynne Feagans and Dale C. Farran (eds.). The Language of Children Reared in Poverty: Implications for Evaluation and Intervention

Patricia A. Schmuck, W. W. Charters, Jr., and Richard O. Carlson (eds.). Educational Policy and Management: Sex Differentials

Phillip S. Strain and Mary Margaret Kerr. Mainstreaming of Children in Schools: Research and Programmatic Issues

Maureen L-Pope and Terence R. Keen. Personal Construct Psychology and Education

Ronald W. Henderson (ed.). Parent–Child Interaction: Theory, Research, and Prospects

W. Ray Rhine (ed.). Making Schools More Effective: New Directions from Follow Through

Herbert J. Klausmeier and Thomas S. Sipple. Learning and Teaching Concepts: A Strategy for Testing Applications of Theory

James H. McMillan (ed.). The Social Psychology of School Learning

M. C. Wittrock (ed.). The Brain and Psychology

Marvin J. Fine (ed.). Handbook on Parent Education

Dale G. Range, James R. Layton, and Darrell L. Roubinek (eds.). Aspects of Early Childhood Education: Theory to Research to Practice

The list of titles in this series continues on the last page of this volume.

Neuropsychology of Language, Reading, and Spelling

EDITED BY

Ursula Kirk

Department of Psychology
Program in Neurosciences and Education
Teachers College
Columbia University
New York, New York

 1983

ACADEMIC PRESS
A Subsidiary of Harcourt Brace Jovanovich, Publishers
New York   London
Paris   San Diego   San Francisco   São Paulo   Sydney   Tokyo   Toronto

ACADEMIC PRESS, INC.
111 Fifth Avenue, New York, New York 10003

United Kingdom Edition published by
ACADEMIC PRESS, INC. (LONDON) LTD.
24/28 Oval Road, London NW1 7DX

Library of Congress Cataloging in Publication Data
Main entry under title:

Neuropsychology of language, reading, and spelling.

(Educational psychology)
Includes bibliographical references and index.
1. Neurolinguistics. 2. Language disorders in
children. I. Kirk, Ursula. II. Series. [DNLM:
1. Language. 2. Language development. 3. Learning
--Physiology. 4. Higher nervous activity. 5. Language
disorders. WL 102 N5055]
QP399.N49 1982   153.6   82-11365
ISBN 0-12-409680-8

PRINTED IN THE UNITED STATES OF AMERICA

83 84 85 86   9 8 7 6 5 4 3 2 1

To Florence Roswell

Contents

NEURODEVELOPMENTAL FACTORS

II

PERIPHERAL MECHANISMS

5 Perceptual Prerequisites for Language Development

PAULA TALLAL
RACHEL STARK

97

III

CENTRAL MECHANISMS

6 Neural Mechanisms Underlying the Processing of Speech Information in Infants and Adults: Suggestion of Differences in Development and Structure from Electrophysiological Research

DENNIS L. MOLFESE

109

7 Interrelationships in the Brain Organization of Language-Related Behaviors: Evidence from Electrical Stimulation Mapping

GEORGE A. OJEMANN

129

IV _____

DEVELOPMENTAL DISORDERS

11 The Organization of Visual, Phonological, and Motor Strategies in Learning to Read and to Spell   235

LYNETTE BRADLEY

V

CONCLUSION

12 Language and the Brain: Implications for Education   257

URSULA KIRK

Contributors

Numbers in parentheses indicate the pages on which the author's contributions begin.

DORIS A. ALLEN (155), Division of Child Psychiatry, Department of Psychiatry, Albert Einstein College of Medicine, Bronx, New York 10461

RONALD J. BAKEN (83), Department of Speech Pathology and Audiology, Teachers College, Columbia University, New York, New York 10027

LYNETTE BRADLEY (235), Department of Experimental Psychology, University of Oxford, Oxford, England

MARTHA BRIDGE DENCKLA (33), 4405 East-West Highway, Bethesda, Maryland 20814

MAUREEN DENNIS (185), The Hospital for Sick Children, Toronto Ontario, Canada

URSULA KIRK (3, 257), Department of Psychology, Program in Neurosciences and Education, Teachers College, Columbia University, New York, New York 10027

DENNIS L. MOLFESE (109), Department of Psychology, Southern Illinois University, Carbondale, Illinois 62901

GEORGE A. OJEMANN (129), Department of Neurological Surgery, University of Washington, Seattle, Washington 98195

ISABELLE RAPIN (155), Saul R. Korey Department of Neurology, Department of Pediatrics, and Rose F. Kennedy Center for Research in Mental Retardation and Human Development, Albert Einstein College of Medicine, Bronx, New York 10461

BYRON P. ROURKE (209), Department of Psychology, University of Windsor, Windsor, Ontario, Canada N9B 3P4

RACHEL STARK (97), John F. Kennedy Institute, Johns Hopkins School of Medicine, Baltimore, Maryland 21205

PAULA TALLAL (97), Department of Psychiatry, University of California, San Diego, La Jolla, California 92037

COLWYN TREVARTHEN (45), Department of Psychology, University of Edinburgh, Edinburgh, Scotland

Preface

The focus of this book is the neural basis of language, reading, and spelling—skills considered to be "higher cortical functions" (Luria, 1966, 1980). Because the purpose of the book is to examine the many neural systems and subsystems that contribute to the production and comprehension of oral and written language, neither the well-documented view that the dominant hemisphere is specialized for linguistic functions nor the question of cerebral dominance is addressed. Without denying that cortical activity is critical to the emergence and proficient expression of these capabilities, the central concern of this volume is the complex interplay of neural structures—be they cortical or subcortical, central or peripheral, lateralized to the left or to the right—that subserve spoken and written language. To this end, the research selected for presentation here highlights, both neurologically and behaviorally, the interrelatedness of language, reading, and spelling.

An equally important purpose of this book is to explore the relevance of research within the neurosciences to problems and issues in education and clinical practice. It would seem reasonable to suppose that insight into the structure and function of the systems that underlie normal and abnormal linguistic behavior could offer the practitioner a vantage point from which to explore efficient and deficient performance. Conversely, it would seem that a careful delineation of the psychological, linguistic, and educational components of oral and written language could provide the neuroscientist with a perspective from which to ask: How does the brain do this? Hence, this book is addressed to all those whose thought and endeavor locates them at the interface between brain and behavior.

The impetus for this volume was an international conference on the neuropsychology of language, reading, and spelling sponsored by the Program in Neurosciences and Education at Teachers College, Columbia University. The conference, held in the spring of 1980, was organized to provide a forum for exchange among researchers who diverge widely in the scope of their investigations and in the technological tools they employ. It was hoped that a new and more adequate understanding of brain–behavior relationships might emerge from interaction among the speakers, and between speakers and participants. The chapters that form this volume are not a record of the conference; instead they represent a new integration of research findings concerning the neural bases of language. When the chapters are considered together, what stands out is not the divergence, but the convergence of their thought.

The first chapter provides a framework for the chapters that follow. In it, Kirk discusses cognitive development and language development, learning to read and to spell as instances of acquiring skill. Commonalities across these domains and differences among them are explored. The adequacy of current concepts of brain–behavior relationships to account for the acquisition and proficient use of these skills is addressed.

The focus of the next two chapters is on the activity of the learner in the development of skill. Denckla (Chapter 2) suggests that it is the efficient learner who develops fluent language, and she cites evidence that the level of linguistic ability that is attained enhances or retards the child's capacity to learn, to read, and to spell. She speculates about frontal lobe contributions to children's growing capacity to learn how to learn. Trevarthen (Chapter 3) points out that interacting forces influence the developing nervous system. To a certain extent, infants and young children actively structure and control their environment. At the same time, the environment imposes constraints which affect the way the system develops. The importance of both factors in the emergence of language is discussed.

Chapters 4 and 5 examine the role of peripheral mechanisms in the development of speech and language. Baken (Chapter 4) presents evidence that it is the progressive maturation of the articulatory system which makes language production possible. Tallal and Stark (Chapter 5) review evidence that an inability to process brief and rapidly changing acoustic information interferes with language learning. Both chapters highlight the importance of peripheral mechanisms in the acquisition and use of complex skills.

Central integrative mechanisms are explored in Chapters 6 and 7. Molfese (Chapter 6) offers evidence from electrophysiological research with infants that language perception depends on multidimensional, complex processes and cannot be described solely as a left- or right-hemisphere task. He points out that lateral and bilateral electrophysiological responses to different cues for speech perception occur at different points in development and mature at different rates. Ojemann's work (Chapter 7) involves electrical stimulation mapping of language-related functions during neurosurgical operations for relief of intractable epilepsy. His findings provide evidence of discrete localization of language processes within the dominant hemisphere at both cortical and subcortical levels. That the precise anatomic location varies from individual to individual may explain some of the differences that can be observed in overall verbal behavior both prior to and as a consequence of damage. Mechanisms at cortical and thalamic levels common to language processes and sequential motor activity are described.

The final group of chapters is devoted to an analysis of developmental disorders from the varied perspectives of neurology, linguistics, neuropsychology, and education. Using linguistic deficits as a guide, Rapin and Allen (Chapter 8) delineate three groups of children who fail to acquire speech and other language-related skills. The known and conjectured pathology of the neural substrates are discussed. Dennis (Chapter 9) cites the all too prevalent tendency among neuropsychologists to study correlates of reading without identifying and distinguishing between the operations involved in learning to read and those that underlie fluent reading. Drawing on the findings of experimental and cognitive psychologists on the one hand, and her study of children who learned to read with only one hemisphere on the other, she urges that a process analysis of the reading capabilities of children with known damage be undertaken. She maintains that research of this nature could be more effective in generating an understanding of the neural concomitants of deficient reading among children who show no demonstrable cerebral insult than continued reliance on analogies drawn from brain-damaged adults.

Rourke (Chapter 10) focuses on the results of cross-sectional and longitudinal studies of children with reading and spelling disabilities. He relates the marked differences among children who exhibit equally impaired performance on academic tasks to differences in brain-related, information-processing capacities. He urges that individualized evaluation of central-processing deficiencies be the guide to individualized educational planning. The focus of Bradley's work (Chapter 11) complements that of Dennis and Rourke. Her investigations of the strategies involved in the way normal and delayed readers learn to read, to write, and to spell document the role of organizational processes in the transition from skill acquisition to proficiency.

Her findings attest to the importance of Dennis's suggestion that research address task performance and of Rourke's proposal that individual diagnosis serve as a guide for intervention.

Finally, Chapter 12 (Kirk) develops convergent lines of thought arising from the investigations presented in this book and explores implications for instruction, remediation, and future research. The overall conclusion is drawn that an understanding of the neuropsychology of language, reading, and spelling calls for the study of multileveled systems from multiple perspectives.

NEURODEVELOPMENTAL FACTORS

1 Introduction: Toward an Understanding of the Neuropsychology of Language, Reading, and Spelling

URSULA KIRK

The neural basis of language, reading, and spelling has been the focus of research for over a hundred years. Why is it that, in spite of the proliferation of research, an adequate understanding of the neural processes underlying these capabilities continues to elude us? In part, the answer to this question can be traced to the complexity of the skills under investigation; in part, the answer lies in the complexity of the nervous system and its relative inaccessibility to direct observation; in part, the answer is related to the fact that research has proceeded more often along parallel than along convergent lines.

This division of effort has made it possible to study various aspects of language in great detail. As a result, research has added to our understanding of the processes involved in learning to talk and proficient language use, learning to read and skilled reading, learning to spell and proficient spelling. Aberrant or problematic development of these skills, in the absence of demonstrable damage to the nervous system, has been described. Both the disruption of skill and the delayed or deficient acquisition of skill that result from brain damage have been delineated. In addition, a body of information about the emerging, mature, and aging nervous system has begun to develop.

3

In spite of these benefits, this division of effort has not been without negative effects. Of necessity, when research findings within one area of study are interpreted without reference to insights derived from another related area, the effect can only be to delimit the understanding that is attained within each domain. Because we can only investigate the neural bases of behaviors that we know how to describe and because the constructs with which we work shape both the questions that can be asked and the conclusions that can be drawn, the way that language, reading, and spelling are conceptualized will constrain our capacity to look for and to understand the neural mechanisms that subserve these capabilities.

Over the last 20 years, there has been a gradual shift away from a compartmentalized approach to research to one that is interdisciplinary and collaborative. The information derived from separate areas of inquiry has begun to challenge, complement, and modify the nature of the questions that are asked and the inferences that are drawn. The position that is advanced in this chapter is consistent with this recent trend. This chapter brings together research findings that suggest that cognitive development, language development, learning to read and to spell can be viewed as instances of skill acquisition. Evidence is presented that cognitive development and the process of acquiring language skills involve problem-solving activity, the progressive reorganization of component parts of a task in terms of larger and larger working units, and the attainment of two kinds of knowledge: a growing understanding of complex relations and strategies for learning and doing. When language, reading, and spelling are explored within this framework, commonalities across these domains as well as critical differences among them become apparent. Moreover, a number of factors that contribute to the attainment of variable levels of competence can be identified.

It would seem essential to our understanding of structure–function relationships that the complexities inherent in this view of language development and language use be taken into consideration. For this reason, this chapter discusses first, the complex processes that are involved in becoming a skilled language user and then examines the degree to which current models of brain–behavior relationships are capable of accounting for the acquisition and proficient expression of these skills.

COGNITION, PROBLEM SOLVING, AND ACQUIRING SKILL

Cognition

Broadly defined, cognition refers to "the act or process of knowing" and to "something that is known by this process [Webster's New Student Dictionary, 1976, p. 157]." Understood in this way, a number of distinct but interrelated processes can be described as aspects of cognition: attention, perception, memory, thinking, and problem solving. When for example, the term "perception" is used to describe the way knowledge is derived from the environment, interest is focused on the source and mode of information processing. The contributions of other factors, however, such as attention, memory, thinking and problem-solving activity are not excluded (Gibson & Levin, 1975). In effect, the emphasis given to one aspect of cognition appears to specify the relative contributions of the other cognitive components (Gleitman, 1981). This suggests that the complex activity of acquiring knowledge involves shifting relationships among distinct but interrelated processes.

Cognitive Development

What is common to the many ways in which knowledge is attained? What characterizes the knowledge that is acquired? How does prior experience affect the way that new knowledge is gained? The evidence suggests first, that problem-solving activity is central to cognitive development and second, that this ability emerges in ordered stages (Piaget, 1969). Each stage is marked by qualitative changes in the way the underlying orderliness and regularities that structure the world are detected, in the way these invariants are interpreted in terms of organizational principles or systems of rules (Gibson & Levin, 1975), and in the way that structure is imposed on the world to render it meaningful. Evidence of successive change derives from analysis of the way children of different ages recognize and make use of inherent complex relations when they are presented with a problem to be solved. For example, when very young children are asked to sort objects, they tend to form groups on some nontaxonomic, noncategorical basis such as a graphic or spatial characteristic of the stimuli (Markman, 1981). Older children group objects according to hierarchically organized, class-inclusion, class-exclusion relationships (Gibson & Levin, 1975; Markman, 1981).

Similarly, children of different ages demonstrate qualitatively different approaches to remembering sets of objects or lists of words. Preschool children show no indications of advance planning; they simply name or point to items in the display without recourse to a purposeful strategy for remembering. In addition to naming or pointing, 6-year-olds rehearse the items, which suggests that an intentional strategy is beginning to emerge. Although the use of meaningful grouping as a strategy for remembering is evident in the performance of 10-year-olds, rehearsal is still used at this age, despite the fact that it is less efficient and precludes the use of categorizing as a strategy (Appel, Cooper, McCarrell, Sims-Knight, Yussen, & Flavell, 1972; Smirnov & Zinchencko, 1969). Among older children, conceptual organization becomes the preferred strategy for remembering (Neimark, Slotnick, & Ulrich, 1971). This type of evidence suggests that young children are unaware of the advantage that can be conferred by categorizing what they want to remember but that older children recognize categorical information in the array of items and make effective use of it in order to remember (Tenney, 1975).

Some conclusions about the way children acquire knowledge can be drawn from this brief excursion into the literature. It seems clear that at each stage of development, children become more adept at solving problems. Three factors appear to contribute to this increasing efficiency: planfulness, chunking, and automatization. As children become aware of the inherent requirements of tasks, they begin to organize their method of approach and develop a master plan (Gleitman, 1981). The degree to which children catagorize or "chunk" information, that is, subsume many details into conceptually larger wholes, affects the way they plan. To the degree that chunking becomes automatic, problems are solved in fewer but larger steps.

What conclusions can be drawn about the knowledge that is acquired by means of this process? It would appear that two kinds of knowledge are attained. First, children learn more effective ways of solving problems. As a result of their interaction with a world composed of complex relations, they become progressively more efficient in their ability to discover and make use of higher-order structures, organizational principles, or sets of rule systems. In this sense, what is learned can be described as more efficient strategies for learning (Boll & Barth, 1981; Denckla, Chapter 2, this volume; Gibson & Levin, 1975). Second, children build up a store of knowledge. New information becomes part of an existing system of knowledge, not so much by adding to it, as by shifting previously established relationships, thereby increasing the scope of what is known (Gibson & Levin, 1975). Understanding or knowledge of the world grows as children "generate structured patterns of information which are meaningful and meaning-filled gestalts [Turvey, 1977, p. 279]."

Problem Solving and Acquiring Skill

What is the relationship between problem solving and the acquisition of skill? To what extent can skilled behavior be considered an expression of problem-solving activity? To answer these questions, consideration must be given to the way in which both tasks are accomplished.

Gleitman (1981) describes *problem solving* as an active process consisting of a series of internal steps organized around or directed toward a desired outcome, the solution of the problem. Typically, the first step is to identify the relevent dimensions of the problem and to reformulate it in items of an overall plan. Possible solutions are then proposed, evaluated, and finally accepted, rejected, or revised in the light of the provisional master plan. Eventually, when appropriate means to the end are specified, the problem can be solved. Differences between the beginner and the experienced problem solver are most evident in the way problems are conceptualized or organized. Initially, each aspect of the problem demands attention and decision making. An algorithmic approach, which specifies and evaluates each step toward the solution, may be adopted. With time and experience, as subcomponents of the problem are restructured into broad strategic concepts, single "chunks" begin to subsume many particulars. At this point, a heuristic- or hypothesis-testing approach to problem solving becomes possible. Solutions can be derived by working backward from the goal to intermediate subgoals, to the selection of appropriate means.

From the perspective of skill acquisition, the goal to be attained or the task to be accomplished is the equivalent of a problem to be solved (Bruner, 1970, 1973; Gentile, 1972; Gleitman, 1981; Kirk, 1978). In solving the problem, the learner must identify and take into consideration the specific requirements of the task if a plan of action capable of attaining the intended outcome is to be developed. In this sense, the task specifies what must be done; an hypothesis about how a particular intention can be carried out is inherent within the task itself. That this type of problem-solving activity underlies the acquisition of skill is evident from the studies of the organization of movement (Bruner, 1973b; Gentile, 1972), the use of movement to attain a goal (Kirk, 1981; Koslowski & Bruner, 1972) and the process of learning "the rules of the game [Gleitman, 1981]."

Acquiring Motor Skill

Learning How

When the task involves the acquisition of motor skill, two problems must be resolved: The beginner must determine not only what to do and devise an appropriate plan of action, but also how to organize a movement that will carry out the plan (Gentile, 1972). During the first stage of learning, the beginner develops hypotheses about both aspects of the problem and subsequently evaluates these hypotheses in the light of information derived from the actual outcome, knowledge of results; and from the movement that was produced, knowledge of performance (Gentile, 1972). At this stage, attention is often directed toward separate components of the task. Once the relationships among the various components are appreciated, however, the learner begins to develop a set of rules or strategies that leads to success, to attainment of the goal. Practice allows the beginner to solve the problem over and over (Bernstein, 1967), and in so doing, to confirm or modify preliminary hypotheses about goal attainment (Gentile, 1972; Gentile & Nacson, 1976; Kirk, 1981). Confirmation of both hypotheses marks the transition to the second stage of learning: the consolidation of skill.

This process is exemplified in the way that young infants learn to reach and grasp an object (Bruner, 1973b). At first, components of the movement such as hand opening, closing, reaching, and patting are loosely ordered. With repeated attempts, the movement components begin to take on a serial organization. During this period, infants tend to interrupt the flow of movement. They stop in the middle of the act to look at their hands, at the desired object, or back and forth between the two before making another attempt to reach and grasp. Once an infant is successful, the overall structure of the movement is altered. It becomes progressively more economical in terms of time and energy expenditure as well as more successful in attaining the goal. It appears that having solved the problem or gotten "the idea of the movement" required to reach and grasp an object, the infant refines the movement so that it becomes a more effective means of achieving the goal (Bruner, 1973b; Gentile, 1972).

A somewhat similar process can be observed in the behavior of adults who are learning to play golf or tennis or to drive a car. There is a preliminary stage during which the beginner learns what must be done and how it is to be done. Once these "problems" are solved, the beginner moves to the second stage of learning, the consolidation of skill (Gentile, 1972). In spite of these similarities, important differences characterize the problem that faces the infant and the problem that confronts the beginning golfer, tennis player, or driver. First, the infant brings to the task very little prior experience of organizing movement to attain a goal; the adult has a wealth of experience on which to rely. Second, the source of the "rules of the game" and the medium through which they are acquired differs. It is not possible to describe an appropriate plan of action to an infant. The plan must be discovered by self-directed problem-solving activity. The rules of golf, tennis, or the road reflect established conventions that are made available to the beginner by means of instruction. Components of the appropriate movements can be specified. Despite these differences in the way plans of action are acquired, both the infant and the beginning player or driver must learn to organize their movements if they are to attain their respective goals. It is only after both aspects of the problem are resolved that the process of consolidating skill can begin.

Becoming Proficient

Whether the goal of practice is to perfect a movement pattern or to deploy movement as a means to an end, becoming skillful is characterized by discernible steps organized around and directed toward an intended outcome (Bruner, 1973a, b; Gentile, 1972; Gentile & Nacson, 1976; Gleitman, 1981; Koslowski & Bruner, 1972). For both types of skill, consolidation appears to result in a qualitative change in the way the task is performed (Gleitman, 1981). Bruner (1973b) attributes this change to a process of reorganization that he calls *modularization*. Movement is modularized or progressively reorganized in three ways: (*a*) by repeating the successful movement, as for example, one practices a golf swing; (*b*) by incorporating it into a larger act with a more remote goal, as one introduces a tennis stroke into a game on the court; and (*c*) by regrouping the components into a new pattern, as one integrates bits and pieces of familiar movements into a new pattern required to drive a car. The effect of modularization is to free attention for further task analysis, information processing, and problem-solving activity. As a result, the learner can begin to anticipate and adapt to changes in the environment such as wind velocity on the golf course, movements of the opposing player on the tennis court, and shifting patterns of traffic on the road. It would seem, then, that modularization contributes to movement organization the advantage that chunking and automatization confer within a variety of cognitive domains.

Acquiring the Rules of the Game

It should be noted that becoming skilled is not restricted solely to tasks that involve motor learning. On the contrary, a similar process has been documented across a wide range of activities (Gleitman, 1981). Chess playing and telegraphy, for example, represent two very different classes of skill. To become proficient in either area, the beginner must learn the rules of the game first and then begin to consolidate skill through practice. The learning process is not characterized by a gradual but continuous increase in efficiency over time; rather, the process is cyclical. Periods of rapid gain are followed by periods during which performance levels off or reaches a plateau. These are, in turn, succeeded by new periods of rapid improvement (Bryan & Harter, 1897, 1899; Gleitman, 1981). This stepwise progression is thought to reflect a gradual transformation of the task into larger and larger organizational units. Thus, the ability to chunk or to automatize elements that were initially treated in isolation proves to be critical to the attainment of these skills. According to Gleitman (1981), mastership reflects "an organization of the relevant subcomponents that allows fewer but vastly larger steps [p. 323]."

Summary

For the most part, cognitive development and the acquisition of skill are treated as unrelated domains. Nevertheless, the evidence suggests that both involve problem solving and rule-governed, constructive activity. In both cases, what is acquired is increased understanding of complex relations and more efficient strategies for learning and doing. In both cases, the transition from the beginning stage to that of proficiency occurs in ordered steps that are characterized by qualitative changes in the ability to conceptualize the problem or the task in terms of larger working units. In both cases, becoming skilled involves cumulative learning. The acquisition of a new skill builds on a background of preexisting skills (Fitts, 1964); proficiency depends on mastery of earlier steps along with way. In either domain, the degree of competence that is attained falls on a continuum ranging from the achievement of the beginner to that of the master.

COGNITION, LANGUAGE, AND ACQUIRING SKILL

Cognition and Language: Instances of Skill

What is the relationship between language learning and cognitive development? On the one hand, cognition and language learning appear to be hierarchically related. Initially, cognitive development precedes language development; becoming proficient in oral language precedes the acquisition of written language (Denckla, Chapter 2, this volume; Vellutino, 1978). On the other hand, the attainment of competence in one realm does not guarantee mastery in the other domains. Children with an adequate command of language may have difficulty in learning to read; good readers are not always good spellers (Bradley, Chapter 11, this volume; Gibson & Levin, 1975; Rourke, Chapter 10, this volume). Moreover, the fact that retarded individuals differ from normals more in *what* they talk about than in the way they talk (Gleitman & Gleitman, 1981) indicates that even in the face of extreme cognitive deficits, language can be acquired. It would appear, then, that a hierarchical concept is inadequate, by itself, to describe the relationships that exist across these domains.

What explains the hierarchical character of progressive development on the one hand and the uneven distribution of achievement on the other? Must the conclusion be drawn that cognition, language, reading, and spelling are separate realms within which mastery can be attained independent of the level of competence achieved in the other domains? A new and more complex concept appears to be required to account for this apparent discrepancy. A step in this direction might be to consider cognitive development and language development with learning to read and to spell as instances of skill acquisition. When cognition and language are viewed from this perspective, it becomes possible to delineate commonalities across these domains and critical differences among them.

Commonalities: The How and What of Learning

Commonalities are most evident when consideration is given to the learning process per se and to the nature of what is learned. Within each domain, learning proceeds in ordered and identifiable steps. A period of apprenticeship during which the basics, mechanics, or rules of the game are acquired precedes periods of consolidation during which new understandings derived from ongoing experience are integrated and automatized. Within each domain, transitions from one step to the next reflect the learner's growing ability to seek out, to process, and to make use of information in larger, more conceptually complex, working units. Within each domain, learning is cumulative. Ultimately, two types of knowledge are attained: first, the learner learns how to learn and efficient strategies of learning are acquired; second, the *data base* or store of available information proper to each domain is increased. Thus, both the process of learning and the outcome of the process are similar whether the child is mastering a skill, mastering a world of complex relations, or becoming proficient in language, reading, or spelling (Bradley, Chapter 11, this volume; Denckla, Chapter 2, this volume; Gleitman, 1981).

Differences: The Data Base

Differences among these skills become evident when the data base proper to each and the means of access to the rule system that is to be acquired are analyzed. In some cases, as when infants learn to reach and grasp an object (Bruner, 1973b) or learn to use a lever (Koslowski & Bruner, 1972), the data base consists of the properties of objects and events and the relationships among objects and events that make up the infants' personal and extra-personal environment. Access to the rules is mediated by self-directed, problem-solving, hypothesis-testing activity. As has already been shown, it is precisely this type of activity that characterizes early cognitive development. Ordinarily, exposure to and the opportunity to interact with the environment is sufficient for children to acquire the basics or building blocks of representational thought.

Similarly, to derive the rules for the use of words and for joining words into sentences (*language basics*), only the opportunity to communicate is required (Gleitman & Gleitman, 1981). That language basics emerge even in the absence of a model has been demonstrated by the invention of "home sign" among deaf children who had no contact with adult or child signers (Gleitman & Gleitman, 1981; Goldin-Meadow, 1979). On the other hand, to master language elaborations, which Gleitman and Gleitman (1981) describe as the use of *functors*, exposure to a well-developed oral or sign language system is necessary (Goldin-Meadow, 1979). In either event, children attain an implicit knowledge of the complex rule systems that govern the phonological, morphological, syntactic, and pragmatic aspects of language. This occurs without instruction and, it would seem, even in spite of instruction (Brown & Hanlon, 1970; McNeill, 1966).

A distinction should be drawn here between learning to talk and proficient language use. Children in all parts of the world begin to use words and to arrange them sequentially into sentences in much the same way and at much the same time (Bloom, 1970; Bowerman, 1973; Brown, R., 1973; Gibson & Levin, 1975; Gleitman & Gleitman, 1981; Lenneberg, 1967; Slobin, 1973). Although most children are prolific talkers by the age of 4 or 5, mastery of the phonological, syntactic, and semantic components of language develops gradually. Throughout childhood and adolescence, children's implicit knowledge of language becomes progressively more extensive and more explicit (Chomsky, 1969, 1972; Liberman, Shankweiler, Fischer, & Carter, 1974; Loban, 1963; Menyuk, 1963, 1964; Vellutino, 1978). What appears to constrain the development of proficient language use is the degree to which children can appreciate and make use of the underlying structural complexity in the sentences that they hear (Bloom, 1970). To a certain extent, then, language development is governed by, depends on, and reflects cognitive development (Piaget, 1969). Once mastered, language becomes both an expression of thought and a medium of thought (Bruner, 1964; Gibson & Levin, 1975).

Acquiring Complex Skills

Chess Playing and Telegraphy

The task for a beginning chess player or an apprentice telegrapher is quite different from that of an infant learning to reach and grasp or that of the young child learning to talk. First, the data base for these complex skills includes not only the specific rule systems proper to each but also the sum total of knowledge derived from prior experience: previously acquired learning-to-learn skills; an understanding of gamesmanship; a history of sending and receiving messages in code. Second, the rules of the game that underlie these skills are not, in the ordinary course of events, immediately accessible to self-directed, problem-solving activity. In most cases, explicit instruction is the medium through which the underlying organizational principles basic to chess and to telegraphy are communicated.

Because of the complex nature of these skills, becoming proficient requires time and practice. A period of apprenticeship during which the rules and strategies proper to one or other skill are acquired is succeeded by a longer period of progressive reorganization and consolidation. Once the learner has mastered the basics, the nature of the task changes. On the one hand, chess playing involves solving problems. As proficiency increases, the chess player engages in predictive, hypothesis-testing, heuristic activity (Gleitman, 1981). Playing the game becomes more and more like thinking. On the other hand, when the telegrapher becomes proficient, attention is directed away from the original focus on encoding and decoding and toward the message that is being communicated. The skilled telegrapher is free to consider both the content of the message itself and the effect that a different version of the message might have on the one who receives it. This type of skill becomes, then, a tool for thought rather than a medium of thought (Gleitman, 1981).

Reading and Spelling

The task that confronts the school age child who is introduced to reading and spelling is similar to that posed to a beginning chess player or an apprentice telegrapher. The data base for these written language skills includes a considerable store of information derived from the child's prior experience: an implicit knowledge of the language system (Weiner, 1980); an expectation that meaning can be obtained from and expressed in written form; a history of searching for meaningful information within the visual environment; the capacity not only to detect patterns in the environment but also to make use of structure and to impose order where it is absent (Gibson

& Levin, 1975). Thus, the child's cumulative knowledge about the world and competence in learning from the world are critical components of the data base that are essential to learning to read and to spell. In addition, the data base includes new and complex rule systems that must be mastered: the rules and strategies for extracting information from the written page in order to read; the rules for reconstructing the spoken word in order to spell (Blank, 1978; Gibson & Levin, 1975).

Another point of similarity is related to the means of access to the appropriate rule systems. Ordinarily, simple exposure to other readers is not sufficient to enable children to derive the rules of the game by means of self-directed, problem-solving activity. Just as learning to play chess and mastering telegraphy require instruction, so too, instruction is the means by which the rules and strategies proper to reading and spelling are made available. Learning to spell may differ from learning to read in that, for some children, reading instruction and exposure to print may be sufficient to afford access to the rule systems required for spelling. For others, explicit instruction in the rules of spelling appears to be necessary. In spite of this difference, each skill requires a period of initial learning and a long period of progressive consolidation. In each instance, the transition from apprenticeship to proficiency is marked by a shift in the nature of the task once the basics of each skill become automatic.

To the degree that the mechanics of reading are automatized, the learner is free to attend to and make use of the syntactic and semantic structures that render discursive text meaningful. With time and experience, the learner begins to read for a variety of purposes. The goal may be to seek new understandings, to add to one's store of information, or simply to read for enjoyment. Like the proficient chess player, the skilled reader is a problem solver. The organization inherent in the text—its style, content, and syntactic structures—combine to provide a relational framework that can be exploited to enhance comprehension. Thus, proficient reading is akin to thinking; current knowledge is used in order to acquire new understandings (Gibson & Levin, 1975). Although the purpose of spelling differs from that of reading, it is similar to that of telegraphy. Once spelling becomes automatic, little or no attention is directed toward the coding process. Attention can be devoted to the formulation of thought in its written form. Like telegraphy, skilled spelling is not a medium of thought, but is at the service of thought.

Differential Acquisition of Skill

Variable Achievement

In any group of aspiring chess players and telegraphers, some beginners may remain at the level of a beginner while others become proficient.

Variability in the level of competence that is attained is a predictable outcome. Moreover, because each task makes specific but different demands on the learner, mastery in one domain is no guarantee of mastery in another. If reading and spelling are viewed as instances of skilled behavior, differential acquisition of skill can also be predicted both within and across domains. This perspective affords a twofold advantage. First, it provides a framework within which the multiple factors that contribute to variable achievement can be identified and investigated. Second, it distinguishes between acquisition and proficiency and clarifies the requirements of the task at each stage.

This perspective does not resolve or even raise many of the questions that are related to why competency levels differ. It presupposes the integrity of the systems through which information about the world is obtained. Clearly, deficiencies in one or more of these fundamental capacities will affect both the way that skill is acquired and the degree of competence that can be attained (Tallal & Stark, Chapter 5, this volume). Because most of the research on skill acquisition has focused on normal development, conditions that contribute to aberrant or delayed development are not discussed. Nevertheless, insight into what makes skilled behavior possible may lead to an understanding of what impedes progress. More important, precise specification of the source and level at which learning is deficient could lead to the development of effective intervention strategies.

Contributing Factors

The many interrelated factors that contribute to either differential or deficient acquisition of skill can be grouped within three broad categories: some relate to the data base that is appropriate to each skill; some pertain to the means of access to the data base; others involve the learner as a learner. Within each category, there are factors that are common across skills and factors that are specific to particular skills.

The Data Base. With regard to reading and spelling, some aspects of the data base are common to both skills. The beginner brings to both tasks an implicit knowledge of the language system, a cumulative understanding of complex relations, and some degree of "know how" or acquired learning to learn strategies. Different sets of rule systems, which call for different learning strategies, must be mastered. The evidence indicates that a lack of competence in one or more of the components that are common to both skills interferes with and may limit the beginner's ability to learn one or both of the new rule systems (Blank & Bridges, 1966, 1978; Chomsky, 1972; Cromer, 1970; Denckla, 1978, Chapter 2, this volume; Fry, Johnson, & Muehl, 1970; Morehead & Ingram, 1976; Vogel, 1974). For example, children with subtle language deficits (Denckla, Chapter 2, this volume; Rourke, Chapter

10, this volume; Vellutino, 1978) or those who are language delayed or language impaired (Rapin & Allen, Chapter 8, this volume) have difficulty in learning to read and spell. Indeed, when the deficits are extreme, children may never acquire these skills. In addition, the fact that some children learn the basics quite readily but begin to flounder when the task requires inferential thinking, attests to the critical contribution of cognitive factors to the reading process (Denckla, Chapter 2, this volume; Gibson & Levin, 1977).

Learning to read precedes learning to spell, and the knowledge that has been gained from reading constitutes part of the data base that is specific to spelling. Although many successful readers become successful spellers, there are proficient readers who fail to become good spellers. This discrepancy in performance may be the result of "too much, too soon." Some children may need more time than others to consolidate their learning in one area before attempting to integrate a new set of rule systems. On the other hand, the discrepancy may reflect the fact that spelling and reading are very different skills (Bradley, Chapter 11, this volume). Gibson and Levin (1975) suggest that a major difference between these skills relates to memory. They point out that reading calls on recognition memory but that spelling relies on the ability to recall. The conclusion is drawn that the necessity to recall and reconstruct words in the absence of any cues from the environment is the factor that makes spelling a skill that is particularly difficult to acquire. Because spelling has received much less attention from research than reading, there may be other components, as yet unknown, that can account for the difficulties associated with learning to spell (see Bradley, Chapter 11, this volume; Rourke, Chapter 10, this volume).

Access to the Data Base. The rule systems that underlie reading and spelling represent established conventions. For this reason, the contribution of environmental factors is critical to the attainment of competency. Among the many factors that could be considered, two will be singled out for comment: instructional procedures and the conditions for practice. Because instruction provides access to the rule systems for reading and spelling, the appropriateness, the amount, and the timing of instruction are particularly critical variables. Children with good linguistic, cognitive, and learning-to-learn skills are well prepared to undertake the tasks of learning to read and to spell. They can benefit from a variety of procedures. Although inadequate or inconsistent instruction can make the beginning stages more difficult for them to master, such children can call on their own resources to compensate for this deficiency. On the other hand, faulty instruction may actively impede the learning of children whose preparatory skills are inadequate or barely adequate. At best, the consequence may be to slow down the learning process; at worst, the outcome may involve persistent difficulties with reading and spelling. Research has shown that such children can learn to read and to spell when information is presented systematically, in small organized units (Bryant, Drabin, & Gettinger, 1981; Bryant, Kelly, Hathaway, & Rubin, 1981). This type of evidence underscores the importance of appropriate instruction for the acquisition of reading skill.

Conditions for practice differ at each stage of learning to read. At the initial stage, instruction and practice may be more or less synonymous. For the skilled reader, the appropriate "practice" for reading is reading itself (Gibson & Levin, 1975). Most of the questions that arise involve the type of practice that is useful and the amount of time that should be devoted to either guided or self-directed practice during the long period of progressive consolidation of skill. Gibson and Levin recommend that practice emphasize both the purpose of reading—deriving meaning from the written word—and the requirement for reading, the flexible use of all sources of information: phonological, graphemic, semantic, and syntactic. Although they recognize that some students and some subskills require more practice than others, Gibson and Levin argue that drill on separate subcomponents of the process serves to create a new problem: how to go about integrating component parts into a smoothly functioning skill. They propose a multilevel approach and suggest that specific subskills be practiced only within a meaningful context. In this way, special attention can be given to troublesome levels but always in relation to, and never separate from, other levels.

Although the type of practice advocated by Gibson and Levin (1975) may be appropriate for most children, for some, this approach could constitute an information overload. Perhaps the procedure could be modified somewhat for these children by locating small bits of information within a meaningful context. This would reduce the level of complexity and, at the same time, keep the purpose of reading in view. Very little is known about optimal conditions for practicing written language skills. Because practice is so essential to the development of any skill, this aspect of learning to read and to spell ought to be the subject of further investigation.

The Learner as Learner

The last set of factors, those that relate to the learner as a learner, may well be among the most critical for the acquisition of skill (Denckla, Chapter 2, this volume). To a certain extent, the linguistic and conceptual understandings that constitute part of the data base for learning to read and spell reflect the child's problem-solving and learning capabilities. Although reading and spelling are complex skills that are based on rule systems that can be taught, communication of the rules is not sufficient to ensure the attainment of skill. The beginner must not only use previously acquired learning to learn strategies but also develop new and reliable ways of obtaining information from the text in order to read (Blank, 1978) and of making use of the structure that exists within words in order to spell. Instruction can make children aware of the importance of looking for invariant cues; time and experience of the written word can provide the opportunity for the learner to become actively involved in the learning process. To become skilled, however, "the learner must discover the useful structure for himself [Gibson & Levin, 1975, p. 333]."

Lack of interest or motivation, for whatever reason, tends to diminish the level of competence that is attained. Attentional or memory deficits may result in an accumulation of partial learnings that will prove to be insufficient to meet the demands of the written text as it increases in length or complexity or calls for inferential thinking. Thus, the store of knowledge already attained, the capacity to select and attend to salient information, the degree of interest in and motivation for learning to read and to spell, and the ability to organize and integrate new knowledge into working memory contribute to and affect the ultimate level of competence that is attained. Deficiencies in one or other of these crucial components of learning will not only delay the process or learning but also limit the degree of mastery that can be reached.

There are advantages to be gained from considering language development, learning to read and to spell as instances of skill acquisition. First, thinking about language, reading, and spelling in relation to, and not separate from, the many other skills that children master, can contribute to our understanding of these complex, interrelated skills. Second, this perspective provides a framework within which new questions can be asked and deficient or delayed acquisition can be investigated. By taking into consideration the cumulative nature of skill acquisition, the importance of learning to learn skills, the data base and the means of access to it that are appropriate to different skills, a more precise specification of the source and/or level at which learning is deficient may be possible. Third, this perspective differentiates the processes involved in skill acquisition from those that underlie proficient performance. Whereas skill is attained in ordered, predictable steps, each of which is the outcome of multiple external and internal factors, proficiency reflects flexibility both in the deployment of previously acquired strategies and in the way that new problems can be defined and resolved.

When language, reading, and spelling are viewed as instances of skill, it becomes evident that explanations of brain–behavior relationships must be such that they allow for the complexity that this perspective affords. Two questions arise. First, to what extent do current understandings of brain–behavior relationships consider the complex, interactive, constructive processes that underlie language, reading, and spelling? Second, are current models of brain–behavior relationships adequate to account for the acquisition and proficient use of oral and written language? These questions are addressed in the final section of this chapter.

BRAIN–BEHAVIOR RELATIONSHIPS

Current concepts of brain–behavior relationships have evolved primarily from animal research and from investigations of altered behavior observed among adult, brain-damaged patients. A number of explanations have been advanced to account for the relationship between areas of focal damage and loss of function. Specific neural structures have been described variously as the site or locus of function (see Filskov, Grimm, and Lewis, 1981); as equipotential components of a system that, when it is intact, permits the adoption of an abstract attitude (Goldstein, 1936, 1944; Lashley, 1923, 1950); as regions in which particular components or levels of a more complex function are localized (Brown, 1977; Geschwind, 1965, 1970, 1979); or as making an essential contribution to a complex function that is, itself, distributed among a number of neural systems (Luria, 1973, 1980). Neither the first, mosaic view, which localizes function to discrete brain centers, nor the second, globalist, mass action view have proved to be tenable (Filskov, Grimm, & Lewis, 1981; Luria, 1980). Different versions of the other concepts are currently employed to explain the emergence of a number of cognitive, emotional, personality, and movement disorders as a consequence of brain damage. Three representative models will be examined: the disconnection model (Geschwind, 1965, 1979); the structural model (Brown, 1977); and Luria's (1973, 1980) concept of the *working brain*.

The Disconnection Model

The disconnection model proposed by Geschwind (1965, 1979) represents an extension or elaboration of the localizationist position. According to this perspective, function is located within specific, primarily cortical, interconnected zones or regions. Information processed in one region is forwarded to other regions for additional processing in a linear, sequential fashion. Some functions are localized to the left hemisphere whereas others fall within the domain of right hemisphere specialization. Symptoms are attributed to an interruption in the information flow. Damage to the specialized cortical zones themselves or to the fiber tracts that link them serves to disconnect parts of the system thereby disrupting its normal function. Recovery is attributed to the adequacy with which remaining, undamaged tissue can sustain function, to the activation of hitherto unused pathways, or to the transfer of function to other potentially competent regions.

This model has provided a useful framework within which to identify and cluster symptoms that characterize specific types of aphasias, alexias, and agraphias. Nevertheless, it represents a rather restricted view of normal language use. The constructive, problem-solving, cognitive capacities that are evident in the performance of the fluent speaker, reader, and writer are not addressed. Because the focus of attention is on the disruption of acquired skills as a consequence of focal damage, the question of skill acquisition is not examined. Distinctions are not drawn between the task for the beginner and that for the master. Differences between the developing and the matured neural substrates are not considered. Even when the model is extended to include developmental disorders, reference is made to, but no explanation is offered for these differences (Aaron, 1981; Aaron, Baxter, and Lucenti, 1980). Moreover, this model does not take into account the concurrent processing of information within the nervous system. Little or no reference is made to the role of multiple and reciprocal cortico-cortical, cortico-subcortical connections, to the redundancy that exists within the system, or to the simultaneity that characterizes neural activation. However useful this model may be to specify the symptoms of adult brain damaged patients, it does not appear to account for the way that children acquire and make proficient use of oral and written language.

The Structural Model

The structural model proposed by Brown (1977) views the human brain as the outcome of a long evolutionary process of encephalization. Stages in the process are characterized by the emergence of new and more complex structures capable of subserving new and more complex behaviors. Four structural levels or distributed systems are thought to underlie human behavior. Three of these levels (the subcortical, limbic, and neocortical) are considered to be phylogenetic and correspond to stages of encephalization in the evolution of the Triune Brain (MacLean, 1978). The fourth, an asymmetric, neocortical level, develops ontogenetically. Each stage is thought to represent the emergence of a new level of cognition. Although each level derives from the earlier one, this development is not considered to be additive. Rather, each level reflects a progressive and qualitative change in the way the whole system subserves more and more differentiated cognitive functions. At the neocortical level, this change is reflected first, in the elaboration of frontal and temporo–parietal zones and then in the appearance of cerebral dominance or lateralization.

> Asymmetry is a prolongation of encephalization into ontogenetic development . . . .
> Hemispheric dominance or lateralization is one expression of this "asymmetrizing"
> process. Fundamentally, there is no difference between lateralization and locali-
> zation; these are different aspects or phases of an unitary process. In fact,
> lateralization or cerebral dominance is achieved through localization, as a (left)
> intrahemispheric specification of language [Brown, 1977, pp. 21–22].

Within this perspective, cognition does not refer to ideas alone. Rather,   it consists of a constellation of perceptual, motoric, affective, and linguistic elements that together constitute a mental act. In the course of development, cognition and its constituent parts recapitulate the achievements proper to each phylogenetic and ontogenetic level. Successive stages represent a transformation of previous levels; at each stage, a new level of cognition is achieved. According to Brown (1977), the effect of damage is to disorganize the system and to produce a regressive change to an earlier level of organization that, under normal circumstances, would have been a prelim- inary stage. Accordingly, particular psychological functions are not localized to specific brain mechanisms. Stages of cognitive development are localized to a particular structural level (Brown, 1977).

This model provides a framework within which normally developing skill and the dissolution of acquired skill as a consequence of damage can be understood. The many components of cognition and cognitive activity are delineated and the complex relationships between language and thought are explored. Nevertheless, a number of issues are left unresolved. Among these are the effects of damage on the emerging system, the role of environmental factors in the development of skill and in recovery of function, and the varying degrees of plasticity characteristic of different levels of the system at different stages of development. Moreover, differential achievement is not addressed. Both progressive and regressive change appear to be "all or none" rather than "more or less" phenomena. As a result, problems associated with delayed, deviant, or inadequate development of skill as well as those related to variable loss of skill are not considered. Thus, the structural model accounts for some, but not all of the complexities involved in the acquisition and proficient use of oral and written language skills.

The Working Brain

Luria's (1973, 1980) model of the *working brain* represents a respecifi- cation of both the localization and mass action theories of brain function. Function is described as "a complex and plastic system performing a particular adaptive task and composed of a highly differentiated group of interchangeable elements [Luria, 1980, p. 26]." This redefinition is the pivotal element around which this view of brain–behavior relationships is constructed. According to Luria (1980), both psychological functions and the neural substrates that subserve them are organized, complex, dynamic systems. At the cortical level, cognitive abilities are thought to be distributed across a system of synchronously working zones that are differentiated both anatomically and functionally. Each zone makes a unique contribution to the overall organization and thus, to the dynamic localization of function. Behavior is not attributed to cortical activity alone, however. Whatever the task, the conjoint activity of cortical and subcortical structures at all levels of the brain is required. Reciprocity, feedback, and concurrent processing characterize the working brain (Luria, 1973).

This view of brain–behavior relationships leads to an explanation of the consequences of damage and of recovery of function that differs from that proposed by advocates of the disconnection or structural models of brain function. Because a given function is widely distributed throughout the system at both cortical and subcortical levels, damage to any level of the system will have a differential effect on performance. This concept explains two puzzling clinical findings that are frequently noted: the disruption of a particular function as a result of a focal lesion in different areas of cortex; the disruption of a cluster of seemingly unrelated functions following damage to circumscribed cortical areas. Because the effect of damage is to disorganize a working system, recovery of function is not attributed to either regression to an earlier level of organization or to a "transfer of function to a new vicarious center but rather, to a structured reorganization into a new and dynamic system widely dispersed in the cerebral cortex and lower formations [Luria, 1980, p. 29]."

With regard to the question of cerebral dominance or lateralized function, Luria does not ask what functions are localized to the left or right hemisphere. He asks, instead, "What specific contribution is made by each hemisphere to the performance of higher psychological processes [Luria, 1980, p. 375]?" After careful analysis of the disruption of language, reading, and writing that can be observed following damage to either hemisphere, Luria concludes that these capabilities cannot be localized to a single hemisphere. Rather, they "depend upon functional interaction between the two hemispheres but that in a lesion of each hemisphere these processes (including speech) are affected differently [Luria, 1980, p. 376]." This view obviates the need to explain the specialized function of each hemisphere by means of dominance that requires the inhibition of one hemisphere by the other (Gazzaniga, 1970; Selnes, 1974), or by positing an equipotential and progressively lateralized neural substrate (Lenneberg, 1967), or by equating lateralization with localization (Brown, 1977). For Luria, the two hemispheres, and specific regions within each hemisphere, are components of the dynamic and differentiated system that constitutes the working brain.

Although the major emphasis of Luria's (1980) work centers around the loss of acquired skills, the emergence of functional neural systems in the developing brain is also addressed. He points out that the systems of synchronously working zones that underlie complex cognitive activity are not present, ready made, at birth. Their formation is attributed to the child's experience of and interaction with the environment during the ontogenesis of cognition and the gradual acquisition of skills such as language, reading, and writing. These higher mental functions emerge in successive stages. Because each stage is characterized by progressive consolidation and by a shift from reliance on external supports to dependence on internal organizing cues, Luria concludes that the neural organization underlying these emerging capabilities must also change.

> The structural variation of the higher mental functions at different stages of ontogenetic (and, in some cases, functional) development means that their cortical organization likewise does not remain unchanged and that at different stages of development they are carried out by different constellations of cortical zones [Luria, 1980, pp. 34–35].

This concept is critical to Luria's understanding of the consequences of damage to the developing system. Because the foundations for higher mental functions are laid down during development, early damage that alters the emerging neural substrate will affect the level of functional competence that can be attained. Because the pattern of cerebral organization changes with time and experience, the outcome of damage will be different at different stages of development (Luria, 1980).

Luria's view of the working brain as a system of concertedly working zones appears to come closer than either the disconnection or structural model to explaining the consistency and variability that characterize the developing system, the matured system, and the system that is recovering from damage. His analysis of psychological functions takes into consideration the complexities of various skills and the differences in the nature of the task facing the beginner and the proficient performer. The construct of distributed function, in both the psychological and neuroanatomical sense, can account for specific loss of function as a consequence of focal damage. The concept of systemic reorganization can help to explain recovery of function. Although comparatively little attention is given to the developing system, the bulk of recent evidence with regard to sparing and recovery of function after early damage is consistent with his views. A selective review of the effects of early damage and the influence of environmental factors on the developing brain will conclude this chapter.

Sparing and Recovery of Function

Early Damage: The Altered System

Sparing of function or recovery of function after early damage is a complex issue. By and large, evidence drawn from animal studies and from the study of children with known damage shows that the degree of impairment is a function of many factors: the nature of the damage and the age at which it occurs; testing procedures and the age at which function is evaluated; the sex of the animal or the child; exposure to the environment both before and after damage (Boll & Barth, 1981; Dennis, Chapter 9, this volume; Goldman, 1972, 1975, 1976a, b; Goldman-Rakic 1981; Rudel, 1978; Rudel, Teuber, & Twitchell, 1971; Schneider, 1970, 1973, 1974). Two principles seem to underlie the degree to which function is spared or impaired: first, "the earlier the lesion, the greater the degree of functional recovery [Rudel, 1978, p. 284]," and second, "sparing is least in evidence the more complex the function tested [Rudel, 1978, p. 281]." Specific examples that illustrate these findings are discussed in the following section.

On the one hand, early damage to the central nervous system tends to spare elementary sensory functions but to impair more complex functions as, for example, those involving the integration and interpretation of somesthetic information required for stereognosis, route finding, and awareness of the body's position in space (Rudel et al., 1966). On the other hand, the inability to process brief and rapidly changing acoustic information (a peripheral loss) can result in deficient language acquisition (Tallal & Stark, Chapter 5, this volume). Whereas children with callosal agenesis do not show the behavioral signs of disconnection that can be observed in adult, split-brain patients, the level of general intelligence that they attain tends to be somewhat reduced (Rudel, 1978). Moreover, although children can acquire adequate cognitive, language, and spatial skills in the face of early hemispherectomy, a single hemisphere is limited in the extent to which complex skills can be mediated. Children with a single left hemisphere prove to be more proficient in language tasks and less adept at nonlanguage tasks; the opposite result occurs when children have only a right hemisphere (Dennis, Chapter 9, this volume).

It would appear from these examples that although there can be remarkable functional recovery after early damage, the recovered system does not acquire the full complement of skills. Moreover, peripheral deficiencies that distort incoming information (Tallal & Stark, Chapter 5, this volume) may interfere with the development of function more than some forms of central damage (Dennis, Chapter 9, this volume). The mechanisms underlying recovery are not well understood. It may be that the system reorganizes itself as development proceeds (Luria, 1980; Ojemann, Chapter 7, this volume), or that intact areas "take over" the function of damaged areas (Geschwind, 1970), or that, as structures mature, children develop new strategies to compensate for their difficulties (Denckla, 1978; Rudel, 1978). Whatever the mechanism, the process of recovery appears to be both lawful and progressive.

External Conditions: The Altered Environment

What evidence is there that environmental factors can affect the structural development of the brain and alter function? Animal research demonstrates that exposure to an enriched environment results in an increase in size of cortical and subcortical structures (Rosenzweig & Bennett, 1976) and that interaction with the environment contributes both to the gradual elaboration of neural elements (Lansdell, 1980) and to the alteration of neural pathways (Goldman-Rakic, 1981; Kandell, 1977). Similarly, exposure to the environment that is restricted selectively can modify both behavior and cortical organization (Bauer & Held, 1975; Goldman, 1976; Held & Bauer, 1967). This type of evidence suggests that rather than being fixed and predetermined, neural mechanisms are responsive to and capable of being shaped by a variety of external factors.

To understand the effect of environmental factors on neural organization in human beings, it is important to recall that, under normal circumstances, the nervous system becomes progressively elaborated and coordinated as the infant interacts with and responds to persons, objects, and events in the environment (Luria, 1980; Trevarthen, Chapter 3, this volume). Even though very young infants have the capacity to respond selectively to speech sounds (Molfese, Chapter 6, this volume) and, in time, changes occur in the structural relationships of components of the articulatory apparatus that permit children to produce speech (Baken, Chapter 4, this volume), interaction with other speakers or signers is essential for children to acquire and make use of language.

A small but significant body of information shows that when children grow up without an opportunity to communicate with other people, both cognitive and linguistic development is impaired (Brown, 1958; Curtiss, 1977; Davis, 1947; Gleitman & Gleitman, 1981). Even though ongoing language therapy is instituted once such children are found, they do not become normal language users. There is only one report of an isolated child who, after treatment, attained a normal IQ and developed adequate language functions. Isabelle was discovered at age 6, having never heard a human voice. After only one year spent in a normal linguistic environment, her command of language improved dramatically (Davis, 1947; Gleitman & Gleitman, 1981). It may be that despite the absence of language in the environment, the care provided by her deaf–mute mother was sufficient to permit Isabelle to acquire the cognitive competencies that appear to be prerequisites for speech. Perhaps, given normal cognitive development, exposure to language was sufficent for Isabelle to acquire linguistic skill. The other isolated children grew up in environments in which the opportunity to communicate on social, emotional, and linguistic levels was lacking. The fact that these children did not show gains comparable to Isabelle's may be due to the more complete deprivation that characterized their early environment. Alternatively, there may be "critical periods" for language acquisition. Isabelle was discovered at age 6; the other children were older when they were found.

A striking example of the influence of environmental factors on neural and behavioral development is the severe impairment that results from malnutrition. There is considerable evidence that early malnutrition contributes to reduced brain size: The number of cells is reduced; myelination is deficient (Davison & Dobbing, 1966; Dobbing, 1963; Winnick, 1970; Winnick & Rosso, 1969). In addition, cognitive development is drastically and irreparably retarded in children suffering from early malnutrition. It is not possible to assign causality to malnutrition alone because other environmental deprivations may have contributed to altering both structure and function. Thus, evidence of this nature indicates that environmental conditions should not be overlooked when structural or functional deficiencies are being investigated.

CONCLUSION

The difficulties inherent in explaining brain–behavior relationships should be apparent from the research that has been presented in this chapter. Models constructed to account for the effects of damage are limited to a certain extent by the clusters of symptoms that arise. Moreover, what the system can no longer do in the absence of or with the diminished contribution of particular structures need not be predictive of how the intact system mediates function. To understand the neuropsychology of language, reading, and spelling, consideration must be given (a) to the multiple, interactive processes that are involved on both the psychological and neurological level; (b) to the differential levels of competence attained under normal conditions and during recovery of function after brain damage; and (c) to the potential of the environment to influence both the structure and function of the brain. When these factors are recognized and incorporated into our understanding of language, reading, and spelling, we can seek new answers to the question: How does the brain do this?

The notion that behavior represents the outcome of the integrated functioning of multiple neural systems is not new. What is new is that today's technology permits us to look not only within the system but also beneath the surface to subcortical levels. We can observe, if not yet explain, some of the neural events that are coincident with specific activities. Perhaps the technology of the future will enable us to understand more fully both how the system functions after sustaining damage and also how the intact working brain mediates language, reading, and spelling.

REFERENCES

Aaron, P. G. Diagnosis and remediation of learning disabilities in children–A neuropsychological key approach. In G. W. Hynd & J. E. Obrzut (Eds.), *Neuropsychological assessment and the school-age child*. New York: Grune & Stratton, 1981. Pp. 303–333.

Aaron, P. G., Baxter, C. F., & Lucenti, J. Developmental dyslexia and acquired aphasia: Two sides of the same coin? *Brain and Language*, 1980, *11*, 1–11.

Appel, L. F., Cooper, R. G., McCarrell, N., Sims-Knight, J., Yussen, S. R., & Flavell, J. H. The development and acquisition of the distinction between perceiving and memorizing. *Child Development*, 1972, *43*, 1365–1381.

Bauer, J., & Held, R. Comparisons of visually guided reading in normal and deprived infant monkeys. *Journal of Experimental Psychology: Animal Behavior Processes*, 1975, *1*, 298–308.

Bernstein, N. *The coordination and regulation of movement*, Oxford: Pergamon, 1967.

Blank, M. Review of "Toward an understanding of dyslexia: Psychological factors in specific reading disability." In A. L. Benton & D. Pearl (Eds.), *Dyslexia—An appraisal of current knowledge*. New York: Oxford University Press, 1978. Pp. 113–122.

Blank, M., & Bridges, W. H. Deficiencies in verbal labeling in retarded readers. *American Journal of Orthopsychiatry*, 1966, *36*, 840–847.

Bloom, L. *Language development: Form and function in emerging grammars*. Cambridge: MIT Press, 1970.

Boll, T. J., & Barth, J. T. Neuropsychology of brain damage in children. In S. B. Filskov & T. J. Boll (Eds.), *Handbook of clinical neuropsychology*. New York: Wiley, 1981. Pp. 418–452

Bowerman, M. *Early syntactic development: A cross-linguistic study with special reference to Finnish*. London: Cambridge University Press, 1973.

Brown, J. *Mind, brain, and consciousness: The neuropsychology of cognition*. New York: Academic Press, 1977.

Brown, R. *Words and things*. New York: Free Press, MacMillan, 1958.

Brown, R. *A first language: The early stages*. Cambridge: Harvard University Press, 1973.

Brown, R., & Hanlon, C. Derivational complexity and order of acquisition in child speech. In J. R. Hayes (Ed.), *Cognition and the development of language*. New York: Wiley, 1970. Pp. 11–53.

Bruner, J. S. The course of cognitive growth. *American Psychologist*, 1964, *19*, 1–15.

Bruner, J. S. The growth and structure of skill. In K. Connolly (Ed.), *Mechanisms of motor development*. New York: Academic Press, 1970. Pp. 63–94.

Bruner, J. S. Organization of early skilled action. *Child Development*, 1973, *44*, 1–11. (a)

Bruner, J. S. Competence in infants. In J. M. Anglin (Ed.), *Beyond the information given.* New York: W. W. Norton, 1973. Pp. 297–308. (b)

Bryan, W. L., & Harter, W. Studies in physiology and psychology of telegraphic language. *Psychological Review,* 1897, *4,* 27–53.

Bryan, W. L., & Harter, N. Studies on the telegraphic language. The acquisition of a hierarchy of habits. *Psychology Review,* 1899, *6,* 345–375.

Bryant, N. D., Drabin, I. R., & Gettinger, M. Effects of varying unit size on spelling achievement in learning disabled children. *Journal of Learning Disabilities,* 1981, *14,* 200–203.

Bryant, N. D., Kelly, M. S., Hathaway, K., & Rubin, E. A Summary of directions for the "LD-efficient" teaching manual. *Research Institute for the Study of Learning Disabilities.* Teachers College, Columbia University, 1981.

Chomsky, C. *The acquisition of syntax in children from 5 to 10.* Cambridge: MIT Press, 1969.

Chomsky, C. Stages in language development and reading exposure. *Harvard Educational Review,* 1972, *42,* 1–33.

Cromer, W. The difference model: A new explanation for some reading difficulties. *Journal of Educational Psychology,* 1970, *61,* 471–483.

Curtiss, S. *Genie: A linguistic study of a modern-day "wild child."* New York: Academic Press, 1977.

Davis, K. Final note on a case of extreme social isolation. *American Journal of Sociology,* 1947, *52,* 432–437.

Davison, A. N., & Dobbing, J. Myelination as a vulnerable period in brain development. *British Medical Bulletin,* 1966, *22,* 40–44.

Denckla, M. B. Minimal brain dysfunction. In J. S. Chall & A. F. Mirsky (Eds.), *Education and the brain.* Chicago: University of Chicago Press, 1978. Pp. 223–268.

Dobbing, J. The influence of early nutrition on the development and myelination of the brain. *Proceedings of the Royal Society (London).* 1963, *159,* 503–509.

Filskov, S. B., Grimm, B. H., & Lewis, J. A. Brain–behavior relationships. In S. B. Filskov & T. J. Boll (Eds.), *Handbook of clinical neuropsychology.* New York: Wiley, 1981. Pp. 39–73.

Fitts, P. M. Perceptual–motor skill learning. In A. W. Melton (Ed.), *Categories of Human Learning.* New York: Academic Press, 1964. Pp. 244–285.

Fry, M. A., Johnson, C. S., & Muehl, S. Oral language production in relation to reading achievement among selected second graders. In D. J. Bakker & P. Satz (Eds.), *Specific reading disability: Advances in theory and method.* Rotterdam: Rotterdam University Press, 1970.

Gazzaniga, M. S. *The bisected brain.* New York: Appleton, 1970.

Gentile, A. M. A working model of skill acquisition with application to teaching. *Quest Monograph,* 1972, *17,* 3–23.

Gentile, A. M., & Nacson, J. Organizational processes in motor control. In J. Keogh & R. S. Hulton (Eds.), *Exercise and sports sciences reviews* (Vol. 4). Santa Barbara: Journal Publishing Affiliates, 1976. Pp. 1–33.

Geschwind, N. Disconnexion syndromes in animals and man. *Brain,* 1965, *88,* Part I, 237–294; Part II, 585–644.

Geschwind, N. The organization of language and the brain. *Science,* 1970, *170,* 940–944.

Geschwind, N. Specializations of the human brain. In *The brain.* San Francisco: W. H. Freeman, 1979. Pp. 108–117.

Gibson, E. J., & Levin, H. *The psychology of reading.* Cambridge: MIT Press, 1975.

Gleitman, H. Thinking and cognitive development. In H. Gleitman (Ed.), *Psychology.* New York: W. W. Norton, 1981. Pp. 312–352.

Gleitman, L. R., & Gleitman, H. Language. In H. Gleitman (Ed.), *Psychology*. New York: W. W. Norton, 1981. Pp. 353–411.

Goldin-Meadow, S. Structure in a manual communication system developed without a conventional language model: Language without a helping hand. In H. Whitaker & H. A. Whitaker (Eds.), *Studies in neurolinguistics*. Vol. 4. New York: Academic Press, 1979. Pp. 125–209.

Goldman, P. S. Developmental determinants of cortical plasticity. *Acta Neurobiologica Experimentalis*, 1972, *32*, 495–511.

Goldman, P. S. Age, sex, and experience as related to the neural basis of cognitive development. In N. Buchwald & M. A. B. Brazier (Eds.), *Brain mechanisms in mental retardation*. New York: Academic Press, 1975. Pp. 379–392.

Goldman, P. S. Maturation of the mammalian nervous system and the ontogeny of behavior. In J. S. Rosenblatt, K. A. Hinde, C. Beel, & M. C. Busnel (Eds.), *Advances in the study of behavior*. Vol. 7. New York: Academic Press, 1976. Pp. 1–90. (a)

Goldman, P. S. The role of experience in recovery of function following orbital prefrontal lesions in infant monkeys. *Neuropsychologia*, 1976, *14*, 401–411. (b)

Goldman-Rakic, P. S. Development and plasticity of primate frontal association cortex. In F. O. Schmidt, F. G. Worden, G. Adelman, & S. G. Dennis (Eds.), *The organization of the cerebral cortex. Proceedings of a neurosciences research program colloquium*. Cambridge: MIT Press, 1981.

Goldstein, K. The mental changes due to frontal lobe damage. *Journal of Psychology, Neurology and Psychiatry*, 1936, *17*, 27–56.

Goldstein, K. The mental changes due to frontal lobe damage. *Journal of Psychology*, 1944, *17*, 187–208.

Held, D., & Bauer, J. Visually guided reading in monkeys after restricted rearing. *Science*, 1967, *155*, 718–720.

Kandell, E. R. Neuronal plasticity and the modification of behavior. In E. R. Kandell (Ed.), *Cellular biology of neurons*, Vol. 1: *The nervous system*, 1977. Pp. 1137–1182.

Kirk, U. Rule-based instruction: A cognitive approach to beginning handwriting instruction (Doctoral dissertation, Teachers College, Columbia University, New York, 1978). *Dissertation Abstracts International*, 1978, *39*, 113A–114A. (University Microfilms No. 066647).

Kirk, U. The development and use of rules in the acquisition of perceptual motor skill. *Child Development*, 1981, *52*, 299–305.

Koslowski, B., & Bruner, J. S. Learning to use a lever. *Child Development*, 1972, *43*, 790–799.

Lansdell, H. C. Theories of brain mechanisms in minimal brain dysfunctions. In H. E. Rie & E. D. Rie (Eds.), *Handbook of minimal brain dysfunctions—A critical view*. New York: Wiley, 1980. Pp. 112–151.

Lashley, K. S. *Brain mechanisms and intelligence*. Chicago: University of Chicago Press, 1923.

Lashley, K. S. In search of the engram. *Symposium Society of Experimental Biology*, 1950, *4*, 454–482.

Lenneberg, E. H. *Biological foundations of language*. New York: Wiley, 1967.

Liberman, I. Y., Shankweiler, D., Fischer, F. W., & Carter, B. Explicit syllable and phoneme segmentation in the young child. *Journal of Experimental Child Psychology*. 1974, *18*, 201–212.

Loban, W. The language of elementary school children. *NCTE Research Report*, No. 1. Urbana, Illinois: National Council of Teachers of English, 1963.

Luria, A. R. *The working brain*. New York: Basic Books, 1973.

Luria, A. R. *Higher cortical functions in man*. (2nd ed.) New York: Basic Books, 1980

MacLean, P. D. A mind of three minds: Educating the triune brain. In J. S. Chall & A. F.

Mirsky (Eds.), *Education and the brain*. Chicago: University of Chicago Press, 1978. Pp. 308–342.

Markman, E. M. Two different principles of conceptual organization. In M. E. Lamb & A. L. Brown (Eds.), *Advances in developmental psychology*. Vol. 1. Hillsdale, N. J.: Lawrence Erlbaum Associates, 1981. Pp. 199–236.

McNeill, D. Developmental psycholinguistics. In F. Smith & G. A. Miller (Eds.), *The genesis of language: A psycholinguistic approach*. Cambridge: MIT Press 1966.

Menyuk, P. Syntactic structures in the language of children. *Child Development*, 1963, *34*, 407–422.

Menyuk, P. Syntactic rules used by children from preschool through first grade. *Child Development*, 1964, *35*, 533–546.

Morehead, D. M., & Ingram, D. The development of base syntax in normal and linguistically deviant children. In D. M. Morehead & A. E. Morehead (Eds.), *Normal and deficient child language*. Baltimore: University Park Press, 1976. Pp. 209–308.

Neimark, E., Slotnick, N. S., & Ulrich, T. Development of memorization strategies. *Developmental Psychology*, 1971, 5, 427–432.

Nielson, J. M. *Agnosia, apraxia, aphasia: Their value in cerebral localization*. (2nd ed.) New York: Hoeber, 1946.

Piaget, J. *Psychology of intelligence*. Totowa, N. J.: Littlefield, 1969.

Rosenzweig, M. R., & Bennett, E. L. Enriched environments: Fact, factors, and fantasies. In L. Petrinovitch & J. L. McGaugh (Eds.), *Knowing, thinking and believing*. New York: Plenum, 1976. Pp. 179–213.

Rudel, R. G. Neuroplasticity: Implications for development and education. In J. S. Chall & A. F. Mirsky (Eds.), *Education and the brain*. Chicago: University of Chicago Press, 1978. Pp. 269–307.

Rudel, R. G., Teuber, H. L., & Twitchell, T. E. Levels of impairment of sensori–motor functions in children with early brain damage. *Neuropsychologia*, 1971, *9*, 351–366.

Schneider, G. E. Mechanisms of functional recovery following lesions of visual cortex or superior colliculus in neonate and adult hamsters. *Brain, Behavior and Evolution*, 1970, *3*, 295–323.

Schneider, G. E. Early lesions of superior colliculus: Factors affecting the formation of abnormal retinal projections. *Brain, Behavior and Evolution*, 1973, *8*, 73–109.

Schneider, G. E. Neuroanatomical correlates of spared or altered function after brain lesions in the newborn hamster. In D. G. Stein, J. J. Rosen, & N. Butters (Eds.), *Plasticity and recovery of function in the central nervous system*. New York: Academic Press, 1974. Pp. 65–109.

Selnes, O. A. The corpus callosum: Some anatomical and functional considerations with special reference to language. *Brain and Language*, 1974, *1*, 111–139.

Slobin, D. I. Cognitive prerequisites for the development of grammar. In C. Ferguson & D. Slobin (Eds.), *Studies of child language development*. New York: Holt, Rinehart & Winston, 1973. Pp. 175–208.

Smirnov, A. A., & Zinchencko, P. I. Problems in the psychology of memory. In M. Cole & J. Maltzman (Eds.), *A handbook of contemporary Soviet psychology*. New York: Basic Books, 1969. Pp. 452–502.

Tenney, Y. J. The child's conception of organization in recall. *Journal of Experimental Child Psychology*, 1975, *19*, 100–114.

Turvey, M. T. Preliminaries to a theory of action with reference to vision. In R. Shaw & J. Bransford (Eds.), *Perceiving, acting, and knowing*. Hillsdale, N.J.: Lawrence Erlbaum Associates, 1977. Pp. 211–265.

Vellutino, F. Toward an understanding of dyslexia: Psychological factors in specific reading disability. In A. L. Benton & D. Pearl (Eds.), *Dyslexia—An appraisal of current knowledge*. New York: Oxford University Press, 1978. Pp. 63–111.

Vogel, S. A. Syntactic abilities in normal and dyslexic children. *Journal of Learning Disabilities*, 1974, *7*, 103–109.

Vogel, S. A. Morphological abilities in normal and dyslexic children. *Journal of Learning Disabilities*, 1977, *10*, 35–43.

Webster's new student dictionary. New York: American Book Co., 1964.

Weiner, P. S. Developmental language disorders. In H. E. Rie & E. D. Rie (Eds.), *Handbook of minimal brain dysfunctions—A critical view*. New York: Wiley, 1980. Pp. 298–323.

Winnick, M. Cellular growth of cerebrum, cerebellum and brain stem in normal and marasmic children. *Experimental Neurology*, 1970, *26*, 393–400.

Winnick, M., & Rosso, P. Head circumference and cellular growth of the brain in normal and marasmic children. *Journal of Pediatrics*, 1969, *74*, 774–778.

2

Learning for Language and Language for Learning

MARTHA BRIDGE DENCKLA

My first obligation to my readers is to explain the circular title of this chapter. I am trying to communicate my growing sense of a "missing link" that is implicit in the relationship between spoken language and the acquisition of reading skills. We are faced with apparent circularity, with a puzzle that resembles a nest of Chinese boxes; having opened one, we find yet another. The results of recent research into reading disability, or dyslexia, have allowed us to disregard certain assumptions as incorrect and also to question some earlier formulations of neurological as well as psychological approaches to learning disabilities. These same recent results have inevitably presented us with new problems in our understanding of the essential nature of "language" and of its significant connections.

The circularity of the language–learning relationship is paralleled in brain processes, as, for example, in the cerebral cortex an output–input—as well as an input–output—circuit appears to occur. The phrase "he learns like a sponge" turns out to be totally inaccurate, for the best learners are not at all passive. They utilize output processes, which although not overtly motor, are nevertheless inextricably linked to what we consider to be perceptual processing. Thus there is no neat "armchair philosophical" dichotomy of

33

NEUROPSYCHOLOGY OF
LANGUAGE, READING, AND SPELLING

absorptive, receptive, decoding or clearly perceptual processes; instead we need to deal with a more complex recursive set of phenomena.

As research into learning and reading disabilities enters the 1980s, we are confronted with the necessity of defining *how* spoken language may function as either a necessary or sufficient precursor for the use of written language, most particularly the reading skills so essential in conventional education. How much does the correlation between poor speech and poor reading reveal causal connection as opposed to common mechanism? I will build a case for the latter: Not only is reading built upon a foundation of spoken language, but those persons who have difficulty learning to speak and to read may suffer from an underlying disability that is "metalinguistic," or at least not linguistic in the usual sense.

Just as famous psychoanalysts have stated that "love is not enough" with respect to mental health, so I believe that spoken language is not enough for the acquisition of written language. "Language" in its usual sense is a psychological construct or, in a neurological perspective, the functional product of a set of skills that depend upon certain circumscribed and interconnected regions of the brain, lesions of which give rise to the disorders of language known as *aphasia*.

WHAT READING REQUIRES

Linguistic Factors

Looking at this matter of oral and recorded (written) language from the autobiographical or anamnestic vantage point of my own involvement over the past 10 years, I recall that most of us (including many involved in the production of this current volume) started out, a decade ago, by trying to distinguish the visual from the auditory or verbal components of the reading process. What we found out can be largely summarized by the apt title of a 1969 article by Kolers, "Reading Is Only Incidentally Visual."

Classically trained neurologists took the model of the visual–verbal disconnection syndrome known as *pure alexia without agraphia* as the basis for investigation of children with reading disability and then proceeded further into the aphaseological context to note the common association of anomia with disorders of reading in the population of adults with "acquired reading problems." The model seemed appropriate enough because in both cases (developmental and acquired) we had to rule out generalized mental or intellectual deficiency, known as "dementia" in the adult population and as "mental retardation" among children.

In non-neurological terms, the linguistic deficit formulation of reading disability has been brilliantly expounded by Vellutino, (1978) who gives a lucid and detailed explication of the role of psycholinguistic components (phonology, syntax, semantics, or the availability of the "lexicon") in learning to read. In other words, a large body of recent research (see *Dyslexia—An Appraisal of Current Knowledge*, edited by Benton and Pearl, 1978) seems to support the notion that language is more often of significance in reading failure than, as previously thought, any perceptual deficit.

According to this view, a highly specific and subtle kind of deficit is considered to be a cause of reading disability. Vellutino suggests that some subtle subdivision of language competence is not contributing sufficiently. Even though spoken language might appear generally well-developed, so that the nonacademic status of the child is clinically far better than that of the aphasic adult, spoken language cannot be fully utilized to support reading in these children. Again, Vellutino (1978) has put it elegantly by referring to the newly competent reader as "a linguistic gymnast." This point of view could be correlated with the clinical literature demonstrating heterogeneity of "dyslexia" (Mattis, French, & Rapin, 1975; Denckla, 1977; Doehring, Hoshko, & Bryans, 1979; Rourke & Finlayson, 1978). A failure in any one of several subtle components of language competence would give rise to one or another specific subset of reading disabilities. All of this seemed very consistent with the model of the adult aphasia syndromes; there was a period when one could readily conclude that the simplistic "visual–perceptual" explanation for reading disability had been laid to rest and that some of the less than rational therapies emanating from this visual–perceptual explanation had been vanquished.

Nonlinguistic Factors

Yes, but . . . ! A few voices cautioned us all not to rest content with the "linguistic deficit" hypothesis. Marion Blank (1978) said "Reading seems to require a type of visual information-processing that is quite different from the usual processing of visual information . . . many of the physically salient dimensions of the printed word must be disregarded and strong, well-established predispositions in the visual sphere must be suppressed or inhibited [p. 120]." Again, moving away from the visual sphere, Blank notes that "in one metalinguistic task—namely rhyming—one has to 'pull back' from the usually signficant meaning properties of the word and instead pay attention to the generally ignored sound property of the word, a conscious effort to refocus our attention to different aspects." The need for explicit analytic awareness of phonemic segmentation in the beginning reader, even one whose command of spoken language reveals implicit knowledge and utilization thereof, has also been pointed out (Liberman, Shankweiler, Fowler, & Fischer, 1976).

Here are warnings to resist the strict emphasis of the early 1970s on psycholinguistic competence and to go on to face the problem as formulated by Rita Rudel (1980). "It is in fact difficult to know where to place 'language' as a factor in learning disability; obviously language development is itself dependent upon learning and various aspects are measured in tests of intellectual functioning." We come up against a set of functions *not* usually included within the psychological construct of "language" (or, neurologically speaking, thought to be based upon brain systems associated with aphasia) as indeed involved in the learning-to-read process: "metalinguistic awareness", selective focus of attention, consciously arbitrary sequencing of stimuli, and rehearsing–encoding components of verbal learning. These functions are probably necessary for acquisition of the "unnatural" written language code in the academic setting.

Paradoxical Factors

Consistent with the concerns of these sophisticated psychological re-searchers (Liberman, Shankweiler, Liberman, Fowler, & Fischer, 1976; Blank, 1979; Rudel, 1980) has been the clinical experience acquired through the follow-up of learning-disabled children in my specialty practice. In the clinical context, something of a paradox was seen: As the children got older, the neuropsychological profiles of some, whom we had initially felt were language-impaired, actually seemed to reverse themselves. Thus, a child presented as *anomic*, that is, having trouble with word finding and picture naming, actually did best in later follow-ups on verbal testing.

This change was evident not only on the overall verbal IQ, but also on the other specific tests of linguistic competence (syntax, naming, sentence repetition, etc.). Only the more subtle, and less taught or drilled, or overlearned aspects of syntax comprehension and the repetition of random digit sequences remained as weak spots in some children who were retested. For example, in one case, a girl had been so anomic at age 6 that the question of progressive brain disease has been raised; when she returned at age 14 for a follow-up, difficulties appeared in mathematics and on the WAIS–IQ performance tests. There was a marked drop in function on the ostensibly "nonverbal" test of Raven's Colored Progressive Matrices (visually pre-sented patterns that represent a variety of relationships). The profile recorded at age 14 appeared to be a complete inversion of the ratio of competencies obtained at age 6. She was not persistently "dysphasic," rather, it seemed that she *was* persistently dependent on teaching and drill to acquire new learning of academic relevance.

Intelligence Factors

In attempting to explain such changes, consider the hypothesis that some children are impaired in a "G" *subset*, wherein "general intellectual functions," ("G" is the general intelligence factor of IQ theory) are intimately *connected* with language function. These children may not be impaired either in the basic building blocks of language or in the entire scope of "G," or general intelligence. Some of the members of this subset of G are meta-linguistic competence, selective attention, sequential organizational ability, and generalization of verbal rules. This subset of G deals largely with verbal material and deficits that are found among children who cannot be described as globally intellectually impaired. The verbal–analytical "sub-G" factor seems to have some anatomical and functional relationship to those frontal or anterior systems of the brain that lie in close apposition to the language-subserving areas in the left hemisphere of most people. Deficits in this factor may, in some overlapping but poorly understood manner, interfere with both the full normal development *and* the later competent *use* of spoken language.

Let me restate this somewhat broad and difficult concept. In some children, there appear to be deficiencies of rehearsal, coding, selective organizing, or learning-to-learn strategies that are confined to the verbal, analytical, and sequential aspects of learning. These weaknesses are somewhere in the middle between G and S factor deficits and do not express themselves either in general (G) panconceptual failure or specific (S) aphasia-like language failure. As the children develop into the teenage years, they may perform poorly even on ostensibly nonverbal or at least silent and visually presented tasks, such as Raven's Progressive Matrices, because of diminished development in these postulated sub-G factors.

Because, for example, the format of the similarities subtest of the Wechsler Intelligence Scale ("what is the same about an apple and a peach?") structures, focuses, and preorganizes the question so effectively, the problem-solving aspect of choosing the answer is eliminated. As a result, the test is difficult only for those chlidren with general mental deficiency or language deficits approaching the level or quality that, in an adult, we would call specifically "aphasic" (Rudel, 1980).

On the other hand, the learning of word lists may require the generally intelligent and linguistically competent student to provide sequential–organizational, verbal–analytic, and encoding–rehearsing strategies. In this sense, a new verbal learning or memory test may be more demanding than the similarities subtest of the WISC, a reasoning test, because the former requires the child to create an order, that is, to "ask the right question."

NEUROPSYCHOLOGICAL IMPLICATIONS

Frontal Systems

Speculating neurospychologically with respect to the functional capacity of frontal systems, learning lists of unrelated words may actually be no lower in the hierarchy of intellectual functions than is providing the accurate "reasoned" responses to "similarities." Among patients seen in the clinical or laboratory setting, the failure to generate learning strategies seems correlated with the limited capacity for generalization described in remedial reading students. These students learn to read one word at a time as taught and drilled, but they do not spontaneously apply learned rules to new tasks or generate strategies independently. How often have we heard from reading teachers that their pupils appear curiously passive to incoming stimulation and do not utilize in subsequent sessions rules that the reading teacher has attempted to get them to generalize and/or analyze, even when the rules themselves have been memorized.

Some unexpected research findings (Duffy, Denckla, & Sandini, 1980) implicate, for the first time, possible differences in a frontal subsystem of the brain among boys presenting behaviorally as "pure dyslexics." It is essential to define this group in order to appreciate the potential conceptual impact of these technologically sophisticated "brain electrical activity mapping" findings. The population that I selected as "pure dyslexic boys" was restricted in age to 10 years ±6 months in order to minimize developmental EEG variance. They were of average to bright-average IQ (WISC–R scores of 90 to 120), free of traditional lateralizing neurological signs, not categorized by behavioral rating scales as hyperactive or conduct-disordered, and yet reading at below the expected level. I generated reading expectancy according to the method of Michael Rutter (1978) by using a regression equation with variables for chronological age and also for the correlation between IQ and reading attainment proper to each child's particular school. Put simply, 13 boys, about 10 years of age, certainly of average intelligence and with average cultural exposure to the acquisition of reading skills, free of traditional neurological stigmata or of the other common learning disability behavioral syndromes (which one might then insist on calling "dyslexia-plus-hyperactivity") underwent sophisticated electroencephalographic recording with computerized analysis and display of data. These boys were compared with a control group of 11 boys selected by all the same criteria, except that no formal IQ measures (due to current local cultural restraints on the testing of normal children) other than the Raven's Colored Progressive Matrices were available.

Alpha rhythm is thought to be the idling state of the brain. On routine EEG, it is characteristically seen over the back-posterior region of the brain but is not recorded from the frontal regions. It shows marked, predictable changes—called alpha-blocking—when some one is engaged in a variety of cognitive activities. The most striking results of this BEAM (brain electrical activity mapping) experiment were the findings that, in large areas, brain waves recorded from the "pure dyslexic" boys remained invariably the alpha type pattern. This occurred even when, behaviorally, these boys participated in cognitive activities such as learning visual patterns, learning to associate visual patterns with nonsense syllables, reading, listening to speech, or listening to music on a tape recorder. Additionally, among BEAM records of dyslexic boys, a great deal of this idling alpha-rhythm pattern was recorded from locations further forward in the brain than is usually thought to be normal in conventional brain wave recording. The predictable alpha-blocking was observed in the BEAM records of the normal controls.

In summary, both the anatomical regions from which alpha rhythms were recorded are larger in the "pure dyslexic" boys and the variation of the recorded type of activity in response to cognitive processing demands is diminished. Since the BEAM technique is new and not widely standardized on normal populations, the reported results on anatomic location and state-unresponsive persistence of the alpha rhythm must be considered exciting but preliminary. We do not know the extent to which the results are developmental in children's frontal alpha-rhythm activity. This is not discernible from the well-studied conventional EEG techniques.

It is neverthless intriguing to speculate on the meaning of these EEG data in connection with data on regional cerebral blood-flow studies (Lassen, Ingvar, & Skinjoj, 1978). Using radioactive Xenon to trace regions of maximal blood flow during performance of various activating tasks, Lassen *et al.* demonstrated the existence of an unappreciated—that is, known but not emphasized—area of activity in the frontal region of the normal brain during tasks that involved speaking and reading. Naturally occurring brain diseases that damage this region are found infrequently so that it is not normally emphasized in descriptions of the circuitry of the brain considered to be necessary and/or sufficient for speaking and reading. There have been occasional reports of persons with strokes in this region of the frontal (left) convexity who have had nonclassical impairments of speech and language, particularly early on in the course of their illness. Reduced performance in picture-naming, limited speech output, more persistent reluctance to write have been noted, but these are rare cases and we do not generally include damage or disease of the upper convexity portions of the frontal areas in teaching the common aphasic syndromes.

The data on regional cerebral blood-flow studies of *normal* persons engaged in speaking, reading aloud, or even more strikingly, reading silently (Lassen *et al.*, 1978), show clearly some repeated activity in the frontal convexity. The increments in frontal blood flow may be analogous to a cognitive "pilot light" (enhanced blood flow within the regions of frontal convexity during mentation). This region appears to be involved in the activation of relevant specific systems, as, for example, while moving either the mouth musculature or the eye musculature during the respective acts of speaking out loud or reading silently.

It seems that we are, indeed, confronting a kind of unresolved reciprocity or circularity in thinking about the relationships between the "silent" frontal convexity of the brain, on the one hand, and the more conventional aphasia-producing regions of the brain, on the other hand. During acts that we think of as specifically linguistic, there appears to be greater activity of these silent frontal systems than we had previously expected. In dyslexic boys, BEAM seems to hint at underactivation of frontal contribution. This new awareness of brain activity correlates well with our clinical and research awareness of nonlinguistic, yet somehow restrictively organizational–analytic capacities, that are important to verbal learning. Data from investigations on the correlates of "dyslexia" typically show impairment of various processes such as the active encoding of new learning particularly under the pressure of time. For example, paired associate learning of nonsense shapes with nonsense syllables (Vellutino, 1977, 1978) or the timed naming and sequential speech patterns prove to be impaired in dyslexics (Denckla & Rudel, 1976a, b). Tasks requiring sequential organization without overt speech are less diagnostic of dyslexic deficits, as compared to other learning disabled status, than tests that are both sequential and also require overt speech (Rudel *et al.*, 1978) such as rapid naming.

Our comfortable "armchair" diagram of perception, decoding, or language reception going on within the system and motor behavior coming out of it, breaks down when we consider that acquiring reading skills during childhood is *not* the passive absorptive process that it appears to be. Even cerebral blood flow in adults unmasks the involvement of premotor areas, actively working during silent reading. A great deal of active ordering of mental processes in a manner similar to overt motor processes appears to be essential (Savin, 1972; Liberman *et al.*, 1976). The great neuroanatomist, Nauta (1978), has remarked that the brain builds its mental activity system either in parallel with or perhaps even with the *same* pathways as its motor systems; Nauta notes that the reported "festination" of thoughts in the Parkinsonian patient seems to parallel the observable festination of gait, and that the flitting scattered mentation in the patient with Huntington's chorea seems analogous to his choreic movement disorder.

I am reminded at this point of the Luria book, *The Role of Speech in the Regulation Of Normal and Abnormal Behavior.* The experiments in behavior among young preschool (3- to 5-year-old) children summarized in this book fit in with the current focus on reciprocal and reinforcing relationships between speaking and learning. Luria emphasizes that previously acquired language becomes the newly stabilizing influence upon the way a 4-year-old performs a simple task such as differential response with the right or left hand to various stimuli. Elsewhere in work on the adult brain-injured patient, Luria has shown that the inability to *harness* speech for the purpose of regulating ongoing new behavior stigmatizes patients with frontal deficit.

Cautions and Predictions

I cannot rush forward into a "frontal" model without mentioning some significant implications of invoking frontal function. I would say that in the field of learning disabilities we may have inadvertently stumbled on an approach to one of the most difficult anatomical issues in neuropsychology: namely, the differences between right and left and between convexity and the more mesiobasal frontal systems. In other words, my bold suggestion is that a pure dyslexic, with no deficit in spoken language, appears to have some *subset* of general verbal learning deficits associated with left convexity frontal lobe. This speculative focus leads us to formulate research that could reveal the regional specialization of that one third of the cortex that is frontal. I have long resisted Kurt Goldstein's (1948) sweeping phrase "loss of abstract attitude," but I have begun to see that we, like Goldstein, lack adequate vocabulary and must utilize categories that either go too far in their implications ("general intelligence—G" or "failure of the abstract attitude") or else seem too restrictively "S" or specific (such as "aphasic but *not* demented"). I predict that the sophisticated technologies of computer-assisted tomography, or computer-assisted brain electrical activity mapping of regional cerebral blood-flow maps, and of positron emission scanning will make possible a more thorough mapping of the functioning of almost-normal, subtly different, and normal brains. These technologies will mean nothing, however, without improved clinical nosology and our pencil-and-paper tests as clinical tools.

Dyslexic patients who come to us adaptively intelligent and capable of using spoken language for their daily nonacademic needs, would, we hope, also make a mighty contribution to unraveling the riddle of the frontal lobes! Necessity being the mother of invention, the fact that we are presented with so many children who appear to have a possible and *pragmatically important* failure of some frontal subsystem should inspire the development of technologies and methodology (hopefully not further inflating the costs of medical or educational institutions). In the long run, such a development would be a benefit not only to the children but also to research. It could lead to new and exciting discoveries in neuropsychology during the latter part of the twentieth century.

REFERENCES

Benton, A. L., & Pearl, D. *Dyslexia—An appraisal of current knowledge*. New York: Oxford University Press, 1978.

Blank, M. Review of "Toward an understanding of dyslexia: Psychological factors in specific reading disaility." In A. L. Benton & D. Pearl (Eds.), *Dyslexia—An appraisal of current knowledge*. New York: Oxford University Press, 1978. Pp. 115–122.

Denckla, M. B. Minimal brain dysfunction and dyslexia: Beyond diagnosis by exclusion. In M. E. Blaw, I. Rapin, & M. Kinsbourne (Eds.), *Child neurology*. New York: Spectrum, 1977.

Denckla, M. B., & Rudel, R. G. Naming of pictured objects by dyslexic and other learning-disabled children. *Brain and Language*, 1976, *3*, 1–15. (a)

Denckla, M. B., & Rudel, R. G. Rapid "automatized" naming: Dyslexia differentiated from other learning disabilities. *Neuropsychologia*, 1976, *14*, 471–479. (b)

Doehring, D. C., Hoshko, I. M., & Bryans, B. N. Statistical classification of children with reading problems. *Journal of Clinical Neuropsychology*, 1979, *1*, 5–16.

Duffy, F. H., Denckla, M. B., Bartels, P. H., Sandini, G., & Kiessling, L. S. Dyslexia: Anatomical diagrams by computerized classification of brain electrical activity. *Annals of Neurology*, 1980, *1*, 421–428.

Duffy, F. H., Denckla, M. B., & Sandini, G. Regional differences in brain electrical activity by topographic mapping. *Annals of Neurology*, 1980, *7*, 412–420.

Goldstein, K. *Language and language disturbances: Aphasic symptom complexes and their significance for medicine and the theory of language*. New York: Grune & Stratton, 1948.

Kolers, P. A. "Reading is only incidentally visual." In K. S. Goodman & J. T. Fleming (Eds.), *Psycholinguistics and the teaching of reading*. Newark, Delaware: International Reading Association, 1969, n. p.

Lassen, N. A., Ingvar, D. H., & Skinjoj, E. Brain function and blood flow. *Scientific American*, 1978, *239*, 62–71.

Liberman, J. Y., Shankweiler, D., Liberman, A. M., Fowler, C., & Fischer, F. W. Phonetic segmentation and reading in the beginning reader. In A. S. Rieber & D. Scarborough (Eds.), *Towards a psychology of reading*. Hillsdale, N. J., 1976.

Luria, A. R. *The role of speech in the regulation of normal and abnormal speech*. New York: Liveright, 1961.

Mattis, S., French, J. H., & Rapin, I. Dyslexia in children and young adults: Three independent neuropsychological syndromes. *Developmental Medicine and Child Neurology*, 1975, *17*, 150–163.

Nauta, W. Personal communication (lecture). 1978.

Rourke, B. P., & Finlayson, M. A. J. Neuropsychological significance of variations in patterns of academic performance: Verbal and visual-spatial abilities. *Journal of Abnormal Child Psychology*, 1978, *6*, 121–133.

Rudel, R. G. Learning disability: Diagnosis by exclusion and discrepancy. *Journal of the American Academy of Child Psychiatry*, 1980, *19*, 547–578.

Rudel, R. G., Denckla, M. B., & Broman, M. Rapid silent response to repeated target symbols by dyslexic and nondyslexic children. *Brain and Language*, 1978, *6*, 52–62.

Rutter, M. Prevalence and types of dyslexia. In A. L. Benton & D. Pearl (Eds.), *Dyslexia—An appraisal of current knowledge*. New York: Oxford University Press, 1978. Pp. 3–28.

Savin, H. B. What the child knows about speech when he begins to read. In J. F. Kavanaugh & I. S. Mattingly (Eds.), *Language by ear and by eye: The relationships between speech and reading*. Cambridge: M.I.T. Press, 1972. Pp. 319–320.

Vellutino, F. R. Alternative conceptualizations of dyslexia: Evidence in support of a verbal deficit hypothesis. *Harvard Educational Review*, 1977, *47*(3), 334–354.

Vellutino, F. Toward an understanding of dyslexia: Psychological factors in specific reading disability. In A. L. Benton & D. Pearl (Eds.), *Dyslexia—An appraisal of current knowledge*. New York: Oxford University Press, 1978. Pp. 61–111.

3

Development of the Cerebral Mechanisms for Language

COLWYN TREVARTHEN

The main difficulty confronting a rational analysis of the development of language systems is our ignorance of the parts of the brain in which language is created. Science of the brain is a little more than a century old and it still has barely penetrated the mysteries of brain tissue. How this tissue sustains the patterning of consciousness, volition, thought, and feeling is almost completely unexplained and the contribution of such processes to language is obscure. But this is not the only difficulty that is encountered. Problems also exist with psychological theory of language—with knowing what is done with language in ordinary life.

All of us are familiar with how speaking and writing develop in childhood, but the literature in linguistics and psycholinguistics is only beginning to formulate systematic theories about the fundamental processes by which language users understand one another. The unconscious events that make even infants able to understand the intentions behind utterances, the staggering capacity we possess to store and retrieve the meanings of words, and the way we impose orderly categorizations of meaning on the haphazard stream of experiences still elude psychological explanation. We do not understand how the sequence of words in language is generated so as to convey the general sense of agency and action on objects or how qualifi-

NEUROPSYCHOLOGY OF
LANGUAGE, READING, AND SPELLING

cations of experience and feeling that define what a particular agent is doing are added. It is understandable, then, why many who study language behavior prefer the microscopic analysis of peripheral steps in speech perception or the physical description of either the sounds of speech or the movements of speech production, and leave the more difficult questions of interior language for future research.

FUNDAMENTAL PRINCIPLES

To gain a broad perspective on the problem of how language develops and how its brain systems are formed, it may help at the start to recall those fundamental principles by which all organic systems are linked to their functions. First, every inherent organic process—and the mental ones are no exception—is a consequence of evolutionary process and of natural selection. Each innate mental organ or habit has an adaptive design with a capacity to control or regulate the course of its own functional development. Second, each form of mental action requires a supportive environment that is similar to that in which its evolution occurred.

With these two fundamental biological rules in hand, let us try to identify how developments in the brain that result in the emergence of language might relate to a theory of the benefits that language communication gives to human life. To do so we shall have to identify the inherent or native adaptations of language. We must remember, however, that the neural system and the psychological functions they sustain in human communication are specifically constituted to profit from interaction with the environment; that is, to learn. We must, therefore, find a reasonable balance between nativist and empiricist explanations of language, recognizing that the inherent control processes will respond to environmental influences. An epigenetic developmental approach that examines actual steps in the formulation of the language system is essential for our task. Finally, we need to take account of the normal environment for language development which is the actions and communication of other human beings.

MECHANISMS FOR LANGUAGE

Modern studies of brain growth reveal a staggering complexity of antenatal processes by which growing nerve cells interconnect, compete, and form intricate arrangements (Jacobson, 1970; Trevarthen, 1979a; 1980a). Neuronal systems can establish the bases for elaborate psychological "motives" by self-sorting growth processes that anticipate experience. Why should we not suppose, therefore, that the human brain might have antenatal specifications for language? We may hypothesize that when children learn a particular language, they discover how to specify meanings in speech to satisfy some more general inherent needs for communication (Trevarthen, 1979b; 1980b). What shape might such inherent language-making and language-requiring brain systems have?

One way of formulating this question is to ask: What peripheral events must the brain networks coordinate when language is used, and how do these coordinations arise? If there are inherent deep motives for language, they will coordinate sensory and motor events from the start of postnatal life; that is, they will mediate rudimentary forms of cognition, action and response specific for linguistic communication and arising in core structures of the brain that are neither sensory nor motor.

The sensory-motor controls in the language of adults may be described as follows. Conversation links sound-making by movements of the mouth and vocal apparatus with hearing and seeing these speech movements. Speakers also understand the reduced and distorted electronic reproductions of sights or sounds of people speaking that are transmitted by telephone, radio, or television. Reading coordinates seeing of conventional symbolic and static marks on a surface with the images in the mind of the hand movements by which the words have been inscribed, or with what was intended in some artificial manufacturing of visible words by typewriter, printing press, or computer. But, should we conclude that language is just an acquired cerebral association of seen or heard stimuli with motor responses of the mouth or hand? Brain mechanisms related to language have been described in terms that imply just this. This sensory–motor or "outside" description does not help us understand the coordinating structures of the brain that carry the language code.

The receptor surfaces and muscle groups of the organs used in language have well-known maps in the brain. We find that the neural "analyzer" territories specific for signal distal receptor or effector structures (the visual cortex, auditory cortex, hand area, cortical map of vocal apparatus) constitute, in total, less than 5% of cortical tissue (Figure 3.1 A). Nearly all the cerebral cortex is, therefore, intermediate, multimodal, coordinative. The bulk of brain tissue has classically been described as "associative" which is to presume that its role is largely passive. If it were so, what then could drive the development of language?

Brain science provides direct evidence that neural activity anticipates comprehending and producing language. Recordings of electrical changes in the cerebral cortex when persons are speaking or listening to words indicate that territories of nonspecific cortex become active either before speech movements occur or one-quarter to one-half a second after a word has been

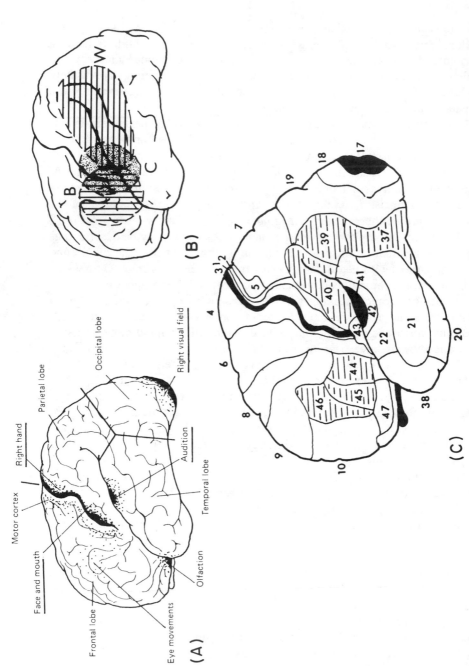

FIGURE 3.1. (A): Special sensory and motor projection areas important in language constitute about 5% of the cerebral cortex. (B): Language systems of the adult brain revealed by neuropsychological examination. Main concentration of lesions. B = Broca's aphasics; C = Conduction aphasics; W = Wernicke's aphasics. (C): Brodmann's cytoarchitectonic map of the human cortex showing primary sensory cortex (black) and regions

48

heard (Grozinger, Kornhuber, & Kriebel, 1977; Kutas & Hillyard, 1980; Marsh & Brown, 1977). In short, the electrical events that correlate best with consciousness of the meaning of words are those generated in territories remote from the primary sensory or motor areas (Trevarthen, 1982). The same regions are identified with disturbances of speech or hallucinations of speech when the exposed cortical territories of awake subjects are electrically stimulated during brain surgery (Ojemann, Chapter 7, this volume; Ojemann & Whitaker, 1980; Penfield & Roberts, 1959), or in the blood flow pattern of a conscious subject having hallucinations of speech (Risberg, 1980). Finally, neuropsychological evidence gained over the past 120 years from observations of the effects of brain lesions reveals a language system that integrates activity between the most intermediate, intrinsic, or homotypical regions of the cerebral cortex of the left hemisphere. It lies at the base of the frontal lobe anteriorly, and at the junction of temporal, parietal, and occipital lobes posteriorly (Hecaen & Albert, 1978; Penfield & Roberts, 1959; Figure 3.1 B).

There are now available techniques for visualizing cerebral lesions without opening the skull which permit us to correlate the site of damage and psychological deficits with increasing reliability. The findings of such investigations correspond broadly with the classical views of language centers advanced by Broca and Wernicke a century ago (Kertesz, Lesk, & McCabe, 1977).

Psychological Components of Language

Turning to psychological performances of adult subjects, we find that functions of mature language are, indeed, far from passive. Categorization of elementary speech sounds, recognition of words, decoding of complex syntactic functions in sentences, appreciation of the messages in conversations and in stories, all require most elaborate motor preparation, cognitive prediction and covert inference regarding the meaning of acts of communication. Both understanding and producing language tax the abilities of the brain to analyze or encode the sequence of events and they put enormous demands on both storage and retrieval functions of memory. Futhermore, the active or creative processes behind language comprehension and language production are extremely versatile or plastic in their connections with peripheral organs. They can readily adopt new combinations of information uptake channels and expressive output machinery. This versatility enables the deaf, for example, to create and transmit between them a visible but silent stream of hand gestures (*signing*), the rich grammatical conventions and vocabulary of which ordinary persons must learn like a full-blown, quite foreign language (Klima & Bellugi, 1979).

While they specify rapidly changing events in the outside world, all languages also satisfy emotional, cognitive, rational, and poetic needs deeply interior to the persons who use them. These needs cannot be explained as just socially conditioned associations between symbolic stimuli and signal gestures. Indeed, developmental studies indicate that they are founded on inborn coordinative or motivational principles that govern intimate communication at a subverbal level. The brain processes for perceiving or emitting language have to determine not only intermodal and usefully categorized contents of individual or solitary consciousness and volition, but also intersubjective transactions. The understandings between language users about objects outside them are specified in relation to what they *share* as conscious and intending subjects. Thus the meaning of language is given within an interpersonal and pragmatic social context. It follows that the neural structures that are necessary for language must include, in addition to the perceptual, motoric, and mnemonic zones of the brain, motivational regions that are capable of mirroring the moods or feelings of persons with whom one is communicating and of defining for each of us what others are experiencing, recognizing, or wanting to do. As we shall show, it is in just these interpersonal functions that infant communicators are most precocious.

All the preceding lines of evidence concur in ascribing crucial cerebral functions for language to an intermodal and coordinative mechanism of the hemispheres that is constrained by hereditary principles in important general features so that it will create an interpersonal understanding. Neither the anatomy of language in the brain nor the psychological power of language to facilitate cooperative awareness of the environment can be explained unless we assume that there exist inherent adaptive neural systems that generate appropriate coordinations between perceived messages and the motives for action. Our task is to try to understand how these systems develop in the child as mastery of language is achieved.

ACTIVE COORDINATION OF LANGUAGE IN THE LEFT HEMISPHERE OF COMMISSUROTOMY PATIENTS

Consciousness

Before examining the developments that lead to language acquisition in childhood, let us first consider one line of scientific inquiry that has brought to light with particular success the spontaneous processes that coordinate linguistic function in the brain. This research involves tests of language use in *commissurotomy patients*—epileptics who have had their cerebral cortices separated by surgical transection of the forebrain commissures in order to control their seizures. Psychological analysis of their mental processes, principally by studies at the California Institute of Technology that were begun by Sperry, Gazzaniga, and Bogen in the late 1950s, has revealed that disconnected hemispheres sustain two independent consciousnesses and two memory stores (Sperry, 1974; Sperry, Gazzaniga, & Bogen, 1969; Trevarthen, 1982). As long as an experience is restricted to one hemisphere, all detailed awareness and recollection of that event or object is confined there; the other hemisphere remains uninformed.

When free to move about, these commissurotomy patients are generally well coordinated and unitary in their purposes, and most of the experiences of the two hemispheres are the same. For activities of the hand and for speech, however, the hemispheres have separate powers for initiating action. The left hemisphere, which is aware of detail only in the right half of space, has

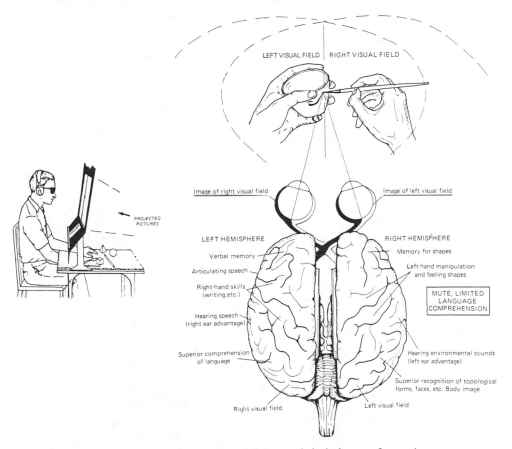

FIGURE 3.2. Hemispheric functions revealed by psychological tests of commissurotomy patients, carried out with orientation controlled as shown on the left (after Sperry, 1970).

complete command of the right hand, but somewhat tenuous control of certain left-hand actions. Correspondingly, the right hemisphere is fully aware of only left space and in full command of the left hand, but not the right. The left hemisphere retains normal powers of expression by speech, but the right hemisphere of a commissurotomy patient is essentially mute (Figure 3.2).

Linguistic Ability

Exploration of the language-related processes of the disconnected right hemisphere, a task that has required considerable ingenuity, reveals that although it cannot speak, this hemisphere can comprehend speech and writing and can perceive the relationship between moderately complex utterances and the objects or pictures of situations that they represent. A considerable syntactic function enables the isolated right half of the brain to decode simple sentences that describe actions and specify positions in time and space. The disconnected left hemisphere, on the other hand, possesses a larger vocabulary, more sophisticated syntactic functions and a much better memory for chains of information in language (Zaidel, 1978a, b). Zaidel's analyses of performances on psycholinguistic tests with crucial stimuli restricted to one half of the brain at a time give us a comprehensive picture of how the left hemisphere of a commissurotomy patient dominates over the right in controlling language.

Cognitive Processing

In testing language and other cognitive processes of commissurotomy patients, Levy and I used a form of tachistoscopically presented double stimulation in which both visual fields contained information relevant to the task questions simultaneously (Levy, Trevarthen, & Sperry, 1972). We wished to examine how the kind of cognitive processing could affect the choice of a hemisphere to respond. We wanted to reveal not what each hemisphere was capable of doing on its own, but how the two reacted when given the opportunity to *choose spontaneously* to take over command of responses in competition. The stimuli were compound pictures. Halves of different drawings or photographs joined down the vertical midline were presented so that the junction was on the vertical meridian of the subject's visual field; that is, the vertical line passed through the fixation point. We called these stimuli "bilateral visual chimeras" (Figure 3.3).

The results were clear. If we asked commissurotomy subjects to name what they saw, the left hemisphere took over and only the right half of the chimera was reported. If, however, we required the subject to indicate by pointing (with either hand) which of a set of pictures put down on the table in front of them matched the picture seen in the tachistoscope, then the left half of the chimera was selected and the right half was ignored. Clearly, visual matching without verbal expression was most effectively or preferentially carried out by the right cerebral hemisphere.

These results of fluent and unhesitating responses with common objects, the names of which were immediately available to the subject, contrasted with a peculiar impediment in performance when nonsense shapes or the faces of unfamiliar persons were presented for naming. The split-brain patients were surprisingly slow in learning to associate names with new faces or arbitrary labels with nonsense shapes. Evidently, they could not distinguish the faces or shapes well enough with the left hemisphere that was seeking to apply the correct verbal tag. The task set up a tussle between the hemispheres and brought out a breakdown in communication. We showed that the right hemisphere could discriminate the stimuli well. but could not generate the verbal label.

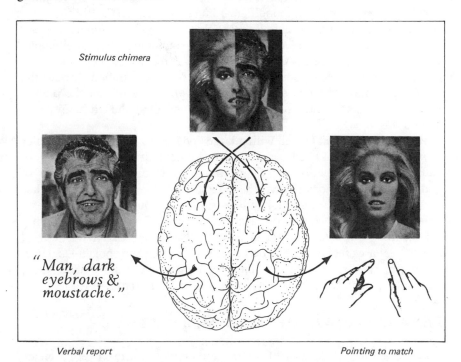

Stimulus chimera

"*Man, dark eyebrows & moustache.*"

Verbal report   *Pointing to match*

FIGURE 3.3. Hemispheric cognitive preferences revealed by use of visual chimeric stimuli. With verbal report the stimulus in the right visual field is identified. With pointing (either hand) to indicate a visual match the left half of the visual chimera is identified (after Levy, Trevarthen, & Sperry, 1972).

When we looked at the details of the subject's behavior during this test, we found evidence that, whereas the right hemisphere could immediately "grasp" the distinctive appearance of each nonsense shape or unfamiliar face as a whole, the left worked with more difficulty and attempted to identify the stimulus by detecting some element of the shape or face that had a familiar or conventional feature, for example, glasses or a moustache (Levy, Trevarthen, & Sperry, 1972). This method of identification by analysis of distinctive familiar features was laborious and proved to be inefficient for the kinds of stimuli we used. That each hemisphere uses a different strategy for recognition is supported by the findings obtained by Levy and others in tests of tactual recognition by the left and right hands of commissurotomy patients. The left hand was more adept at grasping the whole spatial Gestalt of a form, whereas the right tried to detect a set of distinctive features. Other tests indicated that the left hemisphere was better than the right at analyzing serial patterns in order to remember sequences.

A "rhyming in the head" test brought out another one-sided brain factor (Levy & Trevarthen, 1977). The right hemisphere was shown to be virtually incapable of synthesizing a phonological image (speech sound) of the word for a picture–object seen, so as to link this object to another semantically and visually different picture–object with a similiar sounding name, for example, "rose"—"toes," (Figure 3.4). In this test, the subject was prevented from making speech movements or sounds by means of a pad clamped between the teeth to immobilize the lips and tongue. The only way to link the picture correctly was to imagine the sounds of their names. Only the left hemisphere could do this.

These findings correlate well with a large body of data drawn from studies of normal subjects that used cortical-evoked potentials or reaction times to stimuli in left and right visual fields and from studies of the effects of unilateral cerebral lesions (Trevarthen, 1982). The results of these studies indicate that the left cerebral hemisphere has a number of components specialized for the generation or retrieval of words. Some of these components monitor the sounds of speech and others recognize sequences of elements that are crucial to the structure of both written and spoken language. It seems, moreover, that the left hemisphere maintains a store of semantic units and analytically seeks to categorize the world in terms of these.

PRENATAL GROWTH OF THE HEMISPHERES

The extraordinary capacity of infants and children for discovering meaningful objects in a world shared with people must find its origins in the special pattern of human brain growth. In describing this growth, however inadequately, we come closer to the source of human psychic functions that cannot be fully explained by what happens after birth.

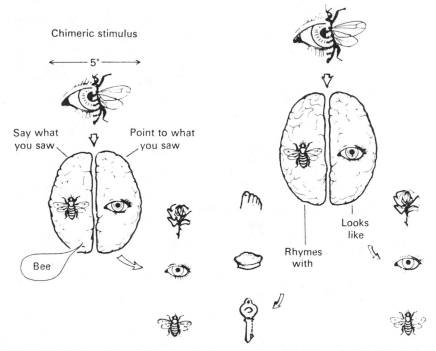

FIGURE 3.4. Use of visual chimeric stimuli to reveal a strongly lateralized left hemisphere process for representing the phonemic characteristics of names for objects and for pairing objects by rhyming (after Levy & Trevarthen, 1977).

The fetus of a bird or mammal is a life stage in which a new more powerful kind of brain is formed, one for which youthfulness has far greater meaning and far greater adaptive potentiality than is to be found in the less-advanced reptile. It may be that humans evolved by selection of characteristics of the young apelike ancestors to extend the period of juvenile curiousity and playful adaptability so that it came to occupy a larger proportion of the life span. Loss of the adult phase, or bringing forward of the process of reproductive maturation, with slowing of development and elaboration of wider potentialities in the less-committed juvenile stages, has been an evolutionary tactic for the start of many major new groups of animals. It is called *neoteny* (De Beer, 1940). Human cooperative intelligence, man's greatest asset, may have evolved neotenically by extending the instincts of young ages to share skills with their peers and elders. Whatever the actual evolutionary steps, the fetal and juvenile stages of human beings must be occupied with novel psychological developments that prepare the way for the revolutionary adaptations of human social life.

In the fetus, the brain expands several times in bulk. It is transformed by

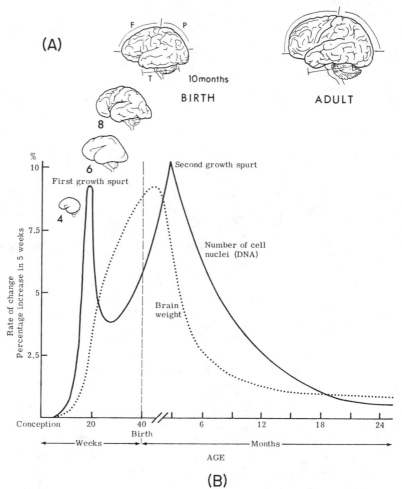

FIGURE 3.5. Growth of the brain in the fetus. (A): Changes in external appearance of the whole brain: Frontal (F), parietal (P) and temporal (T) cortices become folded as the second growth spurt commences, and these areas undergo relative enlargement postnatally (after Larroche, 1966). (B): Phases of cell multiplication as shown by changes in the rate of increase of DNA content of the cortex indicate two spurts of cell production, one midfetal, one postnatal (after Dobbing & Smart, 1974). (C): Cell production and cell migration in the midfetal stage of the human brain. The arrows added to the external view of the cortex are speculative (after Sidman & Rakic, 1973).

the differentiation of many new and varied maps of the body's field of action, some specialized for one modality of perception or refined action of one body part, others integrating them together. The cerebral hemispheres and the cerebellum, which were tiny rudiments in the embryo, become the main tissue masses of the brain (Figure 3.5A). The first of these two comple-mentary double ganglionic structures is concerned with perceptual cognitive

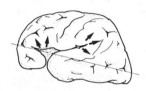

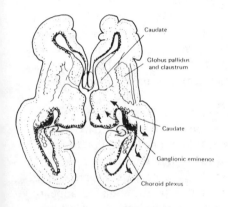

(C)

and volitional aspects of conscious life and with memory; the second, the cerebellum, regulates the flow of forces of a complex and agile body in action and the programs of refined motor skills.

Biochemical measurement of the gene DNA content of the human brain has been used to count nerve cell nuclei. It shows a number of bursts of nerve cell division in months 3–5 of gestation (Dobbing & Smart, 1974; Sidman & Rakic, 1973). A thousand-million new cells are created in this "first growth spurt" of the cortex (Figure 3.5B). These cells migrate into the neocortex from a germinal zone lining the cavity of each cerebral hemisphere and assemble in orderly radiating columns packed side-by-side in a layer called the "cortical cell plate." The plate seems to be of marvellously precise organization, becoming more detailed in its design as its cells meet and interact. It is mapped, as the embryo brain was, in invisible microscopic territories, which represent the body over and over again in relation to the different fields of experience and of action that the body will enter months or years later.

It is possible that the chronology of neuron production and the plan of their migration into the cortex, where they will later join to create an intricate nerve net linking all parts of the brain, retraces the evolutionary history of higher psychological functions. The last produced cortical zones appear to be at the roots of the main cerebral lobes where they grow into the slowly maturing tissue that tends to be asymmetric in psychological function after birth (Sidman & Radic, 1973; Figure 3.5C). In the family tree of the primates, these parts of the cortex have evolved last.

In most of the fetal period the influence on brain morphogenesis of stimuli originating external to the body is kept to a minimum. The brain of the human fetus appears to be elaborately protected until the sixth month of gestation from the few patterned stimuli that penetrate the womb. It is blind and deaf and lacking olfactory or tactual sense because the peripheral receptors are blocked (Trevarthen, 1979a). The greater part of brain growth before birth is probably, therefore, autonomous and independent of sensory input (Oppenheim, 1974).

A second jump in brain size, a fourfold increase from about 100cc to 400cc, takes place in the last months of gestation (Dobbing & Smart, 1974); but this *second growth spurt* is due to differentiation or elaboration of nerve cells, which have declined greatly in rate of multiplication at this stage and may even decrease in number (Figure 3.5 B). As nerve cells grow fine projections, the cerebral cortex thickens and develops the rumpled appearance characteristic of the brain of a highly intelligent animal. Soon it looks unquestionably human (Larroche, 1966; Figure 3.5 A). Within the cortex, dendrites extend to form thickets of enormous delicacy and complexity. Neurons are also growing in the cerebellum, and in those brain stem and reticular formation nuclei that are directly involved with cerebral cortex and cerebellum. The DNA assay technique applied in the later stages of gestation reveals this nerve cell growth indirectly; nonneural glia cells multiply in vast numbers to penetrate the expanding spaces between the nerve cells. Glia cells surround neurons, change the conduction of nerve impulses, and regulate the pattern of treelike growth and formation of nerve cell contacts (*synapses*) on which all integrative functions depend. A mature cortical neuron may have upward of 10,000 synapses with the result that an astronomical number, some 10^{15}, a thousand million million, exist in a single human cortex. (For comparison, the population of humans on the earth is less than 5000 million.) This second brain-growth spurt is the major period of synapse formation during which most of the contacts in main cortical circuits are formed.

Nerve net formation is a much longer process in man than in most other mammals and is far from complete at birth. The rapid phase of cell separation and synaptogenesis continues for 3 months after birth and synaptic patterning occurs in some regions for many years as does myelination of the long association pathways linking cortical regions (Yakovlev & Lecours, 1967). Thus, during the long and complex fetal stage of brain growth, the principal structures that subserve human intelligence are laid down in preparation for large postnatal changes that create many new connective relations.

THE NEWBORN BRAIN AND DEVELOPMENT IN INFANCY AND CHILDHOOD

The brain of a newborn baby has virtually the same external appearance as a half-sized adult brain (Larroche, 1966; Figure 3.5 A). All but a negligible proportion of its cells are in their final positions and all the nuclei, tracts, and cortices are arranged in the adult pattern. From the point of view of what the brain can do and what it will become capable of doing, its appearance is misleading. It does not fit the psychological immaturity of infants. Moreover, it conceals an immense unfinished complexity of nerve circuits that, in some regions, take several decades to reach full maturity and refinement of function. At each stage of development, the brain has a particular functional organization. This is why brain damage at or soon after birth has different consequences than the same damage later in life (Dennis & Whitaker, 1977; Goldman, 1976).

In the newborn, cortical sensory zones are shaped by patterns of stimulation. Two kinds of stimulus effects have been found in studies of growing cortical visual receptor units of kittens and newborn monkeys (Barlow, 1975; Blakemore, 1974; Trevarthen, 1979a). In one, coordination of the eyes as duplicate space-sensing organs with different points of view permits definition of their joint use to measure distance (binocular stereopsis by disparity detection). The evidence does not prove that the binocular disparity detectors are *created* by concurrent stimulation of the two eyes; clearly there is, at least, complex prior specification of conjugate orienting of the eyes and binocular convergence in the cortical circuits. The evidence does show that differentiation of a refined disparity mechanism requires undistorted visual experience during the critical time when the primary binocular circuits are reaching completion, if those units that respond discretely to appropriately small differences of visual stimulation are to be sustained.

A second process of selective retention of connections may be involved in formation of high-acuity form-resolving elements. Scattered cortical connections are weeded out leaving geometrically ordered arrays. Units that respond to given features of stimuli and that are suitable as selective filters for general application in form perception are apparently reinforced by this process soon after birth. Again, the known anatomy favors the view that genetically determined categories of circuits lie behind the formation of feature detectors that result from experience. There could be no other explanation for the systematic ordering of orientation and ocular dominance columns reported in the monkey (Hubel, Wiesel & LeVay, 1977) or for the complex multiple maps of the visual field in all mammals (Zeki, 1974).

Research with kittens shows that during the postnatal period when the synaptic fields of the cortex are being elaborated and patterned, the inter-hemispheric connections between visual and somesthetic zones undergo large-scale plastic changes. At birth, the neurons that project to the opposite hemisphere by way of the corpus callosum, are ubiquitous in sensory cortex. By selective loss of cells, an elaborate pattern emerges: Zones that have callosal connections are interspersed with zones without such links. Experiments show that visual experience can stabilize the callosal neurons and lead to selective retention of connections that integrate the cortical fields in a particular way (Innocenti & Frost, 1979; Innocenti, 1980). This is a clear example of pattern formation in brain tissue by selective loss of unused, redundant connections as a consequence of stimulation.

Behavioral research shows that the basic networks for perception are functional early in infancy and that they mature with great rapidity, probably inside the first year (Bower, 1974; Trevarthen, Murray & Hubley, 1981). There is an intense period of differentiation of the fundamental cortical circuitry of vision in the first 2 months that is fed by the new input of patterned stimulation. By 4 months, an infant has sufficient motor coordination to regulate axial and proximal movements, to shift attention, and to begin prehension. After the growth of controlled focus on local information concerning object structure and identity, a 9-or-10-month old begins to show a marked increase in problem solving and searching behind immediate appearances.

The human brain doubles its volume (to 800cc) during the first year of infancy, and, by the age of 3, attains about 90% of its adult volume. This increase in size must conceal immense and widespread changes in complexity of circuit structure. The process evidently permits increasingly critical analysis of experience even though awareness of objects exists from birth.

Small cycles of nerve cell production occur long after birth in certain parts of the cerebral hemispheres as well as in the cerebellum. Microneurons invade the cortical tissues in vast numbers in late fetal stages and although many later die, the remainder form into small star-shaped cells with short local connections, ideally fitted to modulate the functions of the main

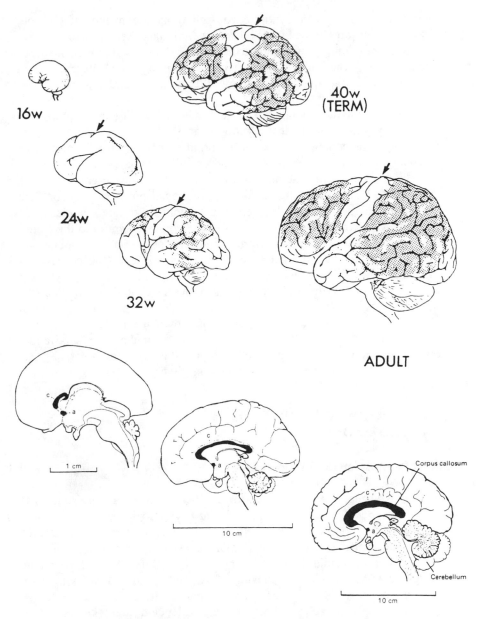

FIGURE 3.6. Relatively late maturation of the integrative tissues of the cortex (stippled), cerebellum, and corpus callosum. Upper figures to same scale.

prewired circuits as their synaptic constellations are formed (Jacobson, 1974). Star cells are thought to be inhibitory and highly sensitive to selective effects of stimulation. They appear to be part of the intricate mechanisms of learning whereby the innate structures of the brain become differentiated in keeping with specific conditions in the world and in the body as it relates to the world.

Postnatal brain development can be traced in outline by plotting the formation by glia cells of fatty myelin sheaths around nerve axons. This refinement of the conducting lines of the brain coincides with maturation of the synaptic arrays at the ends of each nerve cell. The patterns of formation of myelin sheaths in the human brain indicate that the cerebral systems concerned with emotional and instinctual functions (interpersonal) continue to undergo elaborate development over childhood and adolescence (Yakovlev & Lecours, 1967). The parts of the cortex essential to the higher forms of cognitive activity (the frontal and temporoparietal "association" cortices), together with the giant interhemispheric bridge (the corpus callosum that unifies the mechanism of awareness and memory), and the reticular formation of the brain stem (which governs central states of activation of the brain), also develop slowly (Figure 3.6). They differentiate in childhood in step with continuing increase of knowledge, understanding, and the practiced skills of decision making. The mind of the infant and child, though well-equipped with basic tools for intelligent behavior at birth, is restructured by these late maturing functions that progressively enrich the motivations of mental life from within.

DEVELOPMENT OF CORTICAL LANGUAGE ZONES

Clinical and Behavioral Evidence

We have discussed experiments showing that the cerebral hemispheres of humans are specialized to perform different psychological functions. Most evidence for this comes from over 100 years of research on the relationships between hemispheric site of brain injury and particular neurological or psychological abnormalities (Trevarthen, 1982). Disorders of speaking, writing, or understanding of language, as well as inability to perform analytical thought or serial reasoning as in mathematical calculation, follow lesions in the left hemisphere. Accumulated evidence of many kinds leads to the conclusion that, in the adult population, nearly 90% of adults are genotypic right handers, and of these, over 99% are left hemisphere dominant for language. Approximately 10% of the population are left handed or use both hands. Of these, about 56% are left-hemisphere dominant for language (Levy, 1974, 1976).

Clinical and experimental evidence indicates that the higher mental functions become more strongly lateralized as the cerebral hemispheres develop (Trevarthen, 1982). Most information on this process concerns language, but visuospatial abilities also follow a parallel pattern of maturation in the right hemisphere in most boys and girls. Interpretation of studies is difficult because each of the higher psychological functions, as categorized by intelligence tests, perceptual puzzles, or language mastery tests, is regulated by cooperative activity of many cerebral subsystems. Some of these attain maturity quickly, whereas others remain unfinished and still adaptable for years or decades after birth. Recovery from brain trauma in different areas subserving a variety of mechanisms follows a different course depending on the age of onset of the damage (Hecaen, 1976). The pattern of maturation may become misdirected in regions that are still undergoing tissue growth and differentiation causing secondary behavioral anomalies (Schneider, 1979).

Presence of the neocortical commissures appears to be necessary for hemispheric anatomical and functional complementarity to be fully completed. This conclusion is supported by the results of tests on a patient with congenital absence of the corpus callosum—a malformation of the brain that comes about in the late embryonic period (Saul & Sperry, 1968). This subject showed none of the split-brain effects and no evidence of hemispheric specialization of function. It is possible that each hemisphere carried, besides the mechanisms necessary to generate speech, full bilateral representation of the visual field. A higher than average verbal IQ associated with a "mild right hemisphere syndrome [Sperry, 1974]" may indicate that invasion of the minor hemisphere by language functions had preempted circuits that would otherwise have mediated the visuospatial processes. This accords with Levy's view of the evolution and development of lateralized language functions in competition with more primitive visuospatial abilities (Levy, 1969). Dennis (1981; Chapter 9, this volume) reports data that do not support this thesis. It is probable, therefore, that hemispheric specialization of function results from a more complex, balanced pattern of reciprocal inductive effects in which the one-sidedness of language related processes is as much a consequence as a cause of functional complementary specializations in the other hemisphere.

Recent clinical and experimental data suggest that perception of speech is lateralized in the dominant hemisphere within the first 5 years after birth (Trevarthen, 1982). After this, language development expands within the left hemisphere, possibly as a secondary effect but probably by development of primary language systems with longer cycles of differentiation. Receptive semantic function continues to develop in the minor hemisphere, though at a progressively reduced rate relative to the left hemisphere (Zaidel, 1978b). Relocation of speech production in the right hemispheres when the left is removed early in life (Dennis & Whitaker, 1977; Trevarthen, 1982) involves a neural transformation within developing circuits. The process is competitive and resembles that which permits optic terminals from a normally stimulated eye to invade the territory of a stimulus-deprived eye in layer IV of the striate cortex of the newborn monkey (Hubel *et al.*, 1977), or callosal neurons of a cat to disappear from stimulus deprived zones of the visual cortex of a kitten (Innocenti, 1980).

Psychological tests of young babies show that perceptual categorization of speech sounds into entities that correspond with consonants and syllables in the production of mature speakers occurs very early in infancy, probably from birth (Eimas, Sigueland, Jusczyr, & Vigorito, 1971; Fodor, Garrett, & Brill, 1975; Trehub, 1973). Furthermore, EEG records have revealed distinctive evoked potentials for speech sounds in the left hemisphere of neonates as well as adults, as compared to the potentials evoked by melodies or noise (Molfese, Freeman, & Palermo, 1975; Molfese & Molfese, 1979). These findings support the view that complex perceptual mechanisms specialized to regulate speech are innate in man and function at some level in infancy even though the young infant cannot understand the precise information about reality that speech is intended to convey.

The effects of one-sided brain injury at different ages show that the functions of the hemispheres become progressively more distinct over a period of years (Dennis & Whitaker, 1977; Hecaen, 1976). Brain injury before or at birth rarely produces obvious language disorders in later life. The studies of Dennis (Chapter 9, this volume), Dennis and Kohn (1975), Kohn and Dennis (1974), however, clearly demonstrate that the hemispheres are preferentially specialized from birth, and that the right hemisphere can never take over all the functions of language in the event of perinatal loss of the left hemisphere. With injuries at later stages in early childhood, there is a difference: Injury to or removal of the left hemisphere in the first few years causes the child to become mute or to have disordered perception of speech. The effect of partial damage depends on the locus of lesion, whether toward frontal parts of the hemisphere, causing mutism, or exclusively in the temporal area resulting in an auditory perceptual defect (Hecaen, 1976). This pattern of localization of function is similar to but not exactly the same as that of adult. Consistent with the less-well-developed capacities of the child to form words or express ideas in language, brain-injured young children lack fluency, but they do not exhibit uncontrolled word production (*logorrhea*) and they rarely show substitution of words and phrases (*paraphasia*). Subsequent development correlates with the normal course of mastery of language.

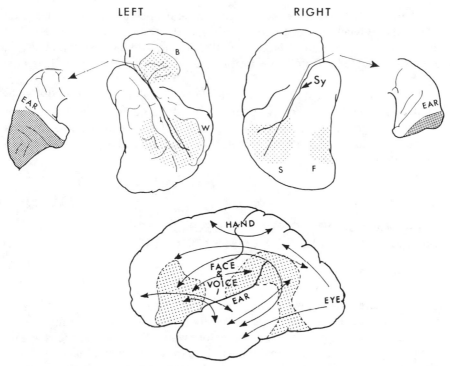

FIGURE 3.7. Anatomical asymmetries of the human cerebral hemispheres and their relationship to the Brodmann territories unique to humans. Sy = Sylvian fissure; B = Broca's speech area; W = Wernicke's language receptive area; S = Visuospatial skills (lesions produce visuoconstructive disorders); F = Facial recognition (lesions produce prosopagnosia) (after Galaburda *et al.*, 1978; Geschwind, 1974; Rubens, 1977).

Morphological Evidence

The anatomical foundations for asymmetrical functions of the hemisphere are established before birth. The hidden upper surface of the temporal lobe inside the Sylvian fissure of the left hemisphere (*planum temporale*), corresponding to Wernicke's area or the auditory association cortex, is visibly larger than the corresponding right hemisphere territory in the majority of adult brains (Galaburda, Le May, Kemper, & Geschwind, 1978; Geschwind, 1974; Geschwind & Levitsky, 1968; Rubens, 1977). This area is also enlarged in most fetuses and newborns (Teszner, Tzavaras, Gruner, & Hecaen, 1972; Wada, Clarke, & Hamm, 1975; Witelson & Pallie, 1973; Figure 3.7).

There are also enlargements of the parietal operculum on the left side above the Sylvian fissure (Rubens, 1977), and a comparable asymmetry has been found in the brain of Neanderthal man and in the orangutan (LeMay, 1976). What the latter indicates for the evolutionary antecedents of language in apes is not clear.

The main anatomical findings concerning regional maturation of the brain while language develops derive principally from studies of myelinization of fiber tracts and intracortical axons. The relationship between these findings and the development of language abilities is summarized in Figure 3.8 based on Lecours (1975).

INFANTS PERCEPTIONS OF PERSONS AND THE PRIMARY MOTIVES FOR COMMUNICATION

The Social Environment

Of all the explorations of experience made by the inexperienced infant, those directed to the social environment are by far the most powerful. Before beginning to test objects by hand and before walking to discover the shape of surroundings, an infant communicates. At barely 2 months of age a baby is alert to, seeks out, and regulates face-to-face interactions with other humans (see Figure 3.9 on page 71). A baby of 2 months exhibits an expressive personality, distinguishes persons from "physical" or inanimate objects, and prefers them (Trevarthen, 1974; 1979c). After showing this clear preference for human care and understanding and after establishing the outlines of conversation-like interaction in the first 3 months, there is a period of several months during which curiosity about what can be seen and heard, and then what can be manipulated and so be seen, felt, and heard better, competes with interest in persons. This exploration of objects and of effects generated through movement is fostered by the response of companions in play. By means of infant-centered games, conflicts in the developing images and purposes of the infant mind are resolved (Trevarthen & Hubley, 1978).

Research on the effects of the separation of infants from their mothers has led to the conclusion that the formation of a bond of affection in the first 6 months of life is both normal and necessary for further psychological growth (Ainsworth, 1973; Bowlby, 1969; Trevarthen, Murray, & Hubley, 1981). When separated from mother or another affectionate caretaker to be taken to the hospital, when the mother is absent or dies, or when cared for without affection, an infant may become emotionally insecure and develop into a socially maladjusted child. Curiosity about surroundings and adaptation to

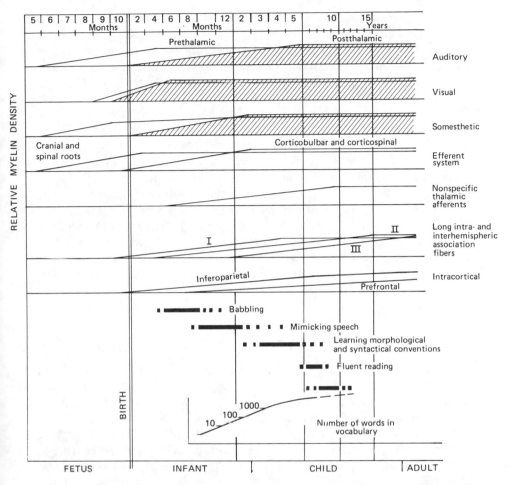

FIGURE 3.8. Relationship of myelin formation in the brain to the development of language. Note maturation of auditory postthalamic pathways while language is acquired and the late maturation of all integrative tissues (after Lecours, 1975).

unfamiliar situations or strange persons toward the end of the first year are taken as measures of the security of an infant's relationship to the mother. Ainsworth (1973) describes various types of mothering, which she believes to be responsible for the different patterns of attachment. Other workers emphasize that most infants develop attachment to several persons, not just the mother. In some cases, the main relationship is with someone else. Nevertheless, security seems to be determined by the closeness and cooperativeness of communication, not any simpler "biological" factor (Rutter, 1972; Schaffer, 1971).

What could be the mechanism and function of this powerful motivation called "attachment"? Research on bonds of immature animals to their parents has not provided an adequate explanation. There is, as yet, little information on what affectionate persons do to foster an infant's attachment, and less on what the infant contributes. Although the assumption commonly made is that, at the start, the infant possesses only a few instinctive reflex demands for care or protection, this belief has not been tested by adequate observation of behaviors leading to attachment. Security in the exploration of objects is described as a byproduct of a relationship to a person, when it could equally be a goal of growing communication. Indeed, infants act as if consistent affectionate companionship from one or a few persons is necessary for their mental development. It is, of course, difficult to obtain direct evidence that the early involvement of infants with other persons has importance for their brain development, but in one case deprivation of normal human care has led, apparently, to a grossly abnormal lateralization of the cerebral mechanisms for language (Curtiss, 1977).

Motives for Communication

The methods used in studies of attachment focus on the emotional and behavioral effects of strange and disturbing events. They tell us little of what goes on between infants and others in spontaneously "happy" situations. Recent work on the development of prelanguage skills opens a wealth of possibilities and suggests that the relationship of infants to their best companions is an incubator for the growth of a shared form of consciousness. Bruner (1976), Bates, Camaioni, and Volterra (1975), and others have emphasized that the social play of infants from about 4 months on allows them to practice and develop patterns of sharing. They become proficient in these at 9 months and begin systematically to seek instructions and coopera-tion from older playmates. Instead of making communication subservient to the immediate guidance of organs for picking up experience and regulating body movement, the infant seeks to share and cooperate with other persons, to accept their ideas openly. For the first time, acts of meaning, instructions, declarations, greetings, and recognitions are performed for their own sake (Trevarthen & Hubley, 1978; Trevarthen, Murray, & Hubley, 1981). The child begins to interact with his companions in a world of agreed interests. A one-year-old child cannot speak but can explicitly make ideas about the world common property with others. Every act is a potential display or demonstration, and what a partner does, shows, or offers is immediately interesting because a person has done it.

In this behavior, the child's expressive "protolanguage," as Halliday, the linguist, calls it, is the essential germ of the transmission of culture and civilization in man (Halliday, 1975, 1978). Its development shows that communication of meanings by vocal signs is an invention of the baby, something synthesized in the young brain. When this baby, too young to say a word, is able to understand the name of a familiar person or thing, he or she is already part of the society's culture and its language. When, at the same age, he or she cooperatively learns how to increase skill in play with a toy by watching what a trusted companion does to vary the possibilities, he or she is starting on the way to cumulative technology (Trevarthen, 1979b). The baby also has suddenly found the trick of showing or giving it to another with obvious pleasure in their acceptance and shares a growing stock of understanding while learning new ideas from others. To understand these features of psychological growth in infancy adequately we will need new techniques and new theoretical frames of reference to study infant social behavior.

Descriptive research with infants using film and television recording has already produced important evidence concerning highly specialized innate mental processes for perceiving the particular interests and intentions of other persons, and for cooperating with them in experience and action. Complementing the infant's growing expressive capacities are elaborate adaptations in the behavior of mothers or other consistent and affectionate caretakers. These complementary behaviors facilitate development of infant powers of expression. The principal developments are described in the following.

Immediately after the neonate period, in the second month, babies orient selectively and preferentially to persons who attend to their vocalizations, facial expressions, gestures, and movements in discriminating ways. Recent imitation experiments (Meltzoff & Moore, 1977) and demonstrations of motor synchronization between very young infants and others (Condon & Sander, 1974) seem to support the idea that in neonates there is a set of fairly automatic responses to perception of others' expressive acts. More complete analysis of the communicative interactions shows, however, that the baby is not just reacting reflexively or performing conditioned responses. The infant is both decoding elaborate facial and vocal signals from the mother and generating complementary communicative movements that are organized into patterns (Alegria & Noirot, 1978; Trevarthen, 1979c). Temporally organized and well-patterned utterance-like emissions of a 2-month-old to a sympathetic listener change radically if the listener fails to respond in the right time and with the right quality of friendliness (Tronick, Als, Adamson, Wise, & Brazelton, 1978).

Experiments by Murray (1980) with this failure of interaction after perturbation of the mother's response have proved that the emotional quality, interpersonal value, or mood of the infant's expression is organized to complement the personal expressions of an intimate caretaker—usually the mother. If treated with affection and happiness, 2-month-olds are happy and spontaneously expressive in facial expressions, vocalization, gesture, and postural attitude. If treated mysteriously or rudely by the same person, they become sad and depressed or agitated and more vocal; by grimace, gesture, and vocalization, they then emit a totally different communicative response. These emotive activities are spontaneously patterned, not imitative (Trevarthen, Murray & Hubley, 1981). Analyses of the behavior of mothers when they are communicating with young infants show that they change all aspects of their expression, which suggests that in doing so, the mother fosters infant motives that have highly specific requirements (Papousek & Papousek, 1977; Stern, 1974). The mother's adaptation to her infant develops steadily as the infant grows (Sylvester-Bradley & Trevarthen, 1978), and by the time speech emerges she is acting as a highly skilled tutor in the uses of language (Snow, 1972).

In the "primary intersubjective" or person–person behavior, infants about 2-months-old emit many gestures in close synchrony with their own facial expressions, which include rudimentary vocalizations (*cooing*) and a pattern of frequently silent lip and tongue movements crudely integrated with a basic breath control (Figure 3.9). We call these oral emissions *prespeech* (Trevarthen, 1979b, c). By prespeech, we mean a particular form of infant expressive behavior that, the evidence suggests, is developmentally related to the act of articulating speech. It is an embryonic or rudimentary speaking not learned by imitating. Sylvester-Bradley (1978) has demonstrated by statistical analysis of particular acts that gestures above shoulder level and prespeech are coupled. They form a variable but coherent expressive mouth–hand motor complex preadapted to conversation. Included in a wide repertoire of organized hand and arm movements of 2- to 3-month-olds, is finger extension that is frequently synchronized with pursing of the lips and possibly raised eyebrows. Index extention may not indicate orientation to a distal goal or target; it may be just a sign of a focal point or climax in the progress of the motive to express. Although in the first 2 months, infants also show highly coordinated cyclical reach and grasp movements that may be aimed to distal objects, they rarely make contact. In these oriented prehensile movements (*prereaching*), frequently the index finger is extended at the climax, and the aim of the finger may be precise (within $10°$). I see no reason to doubt that the adaptive purpose of this indexing is for communication—to show something of interest. Therefore I reject the unsubstantiated theory that an infant's pointing develops out of grasping for objects by conditioning because people

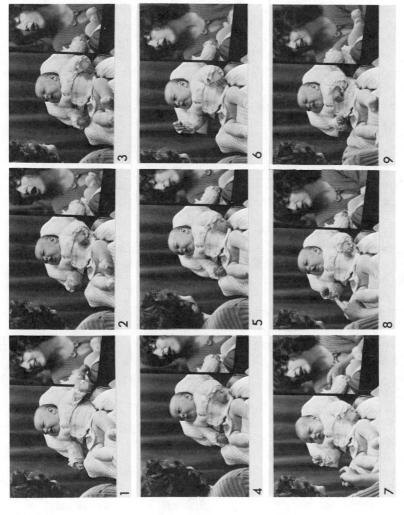

FIGURE 3.9. First stage in development of infant communication: Primary intersubjectivity: A 6-week-old engages in face-to-face communication with her mother. 1. Greeting smiles. Mother says "Come on then." 2 and 3. "Oh aaa. Come on." Baby coos. 4, 5, and 6. Baby coos "Ahgoo." Mother: "Come on. Hoo hoo." 7, 8, 9. As before then, with baby's smile "That's right. Woo, Hoo." (Trevarthen & Hubley, 1978).

infer that grasping means interest. Pointing is already differentiated from grasping at the neonate stage.

The rich repertoire of expressions preadaptive to emotional and linguistic communication that 2-month-olds show becomes organized into significant messages within the first year, before words are produced. We have traced the development of motives as the infant combines object cognition with communication (Trevarthen, 1980b). Establishment of joint temporo–spatial reference and specification of the nature or meaning of an object both appear first in teasing games at about 6 months, as the infant masters efficient object prehension. Humorous interactions in play allow practice of coordinated and reciprocal intentions (Figure 3.10; Hubley & Trevarthen, 1979; Trevarthen & Hubley, 1978; Trevarthen, Murray & Hubley, 1981). Around 10 months, infants usually—and sometimes quite suddenly—begin deliberately to seek to comply with the wishes, interests, instructions, actions, and signs of feeling with a partner (Figure 3.11). Willingness to attend to and obey a request or to follow a lead appears at the same time as the emission of vocalizations that are differentiated from distress cries, etc. They are regulated to signify mutually acknowledged meanings. This kind of vocalization is the essence of Halliday's protolanguage (Halliday, 1975).

The evidence from these descriptive studies of infant communication clearly supports the idea that a central motivational structure for cooperative understanding of objects, actions, goals, etc., has reached proficiency at the end of the first year. It is of great interest that this is the age at which the vocal tract begins to achieve a uniquely human configuration ready for speaking (See Baken, Chapter 4, this volume). It is also a time when the gestural and other expressive acts, studied by Bates *et al.* (1975) and Bruner (1976) appear with increasing frequency in spontaneous communication between infants and their mothers.

I believe that in this research we are beginning to see the general nature of the morphogenetic process leading to human psychological cooperation and to the rich transmission of this cooperation in culturally perfected languages that are passed on to the next generation in the highly receptive stage of early childhood. The behavior of one-year-olds certainly supports the theory that the motives for speaking to other persons about the shared world have elaborate organization before the act of speaking has developed (Macnamara, 1972).

As speech emerges in the second year the child becomes more and more involved in the way things are done by adults familiar to him. By 2 years, toddlers are normally extremely curious imitators and imaginers of roles, tasks, and cooperative adventures. They love to chat about a pretend game and their recently acquired vocabulary is stretched to fit new requirements to talking about what "we" are doing together and for sharing what they think or

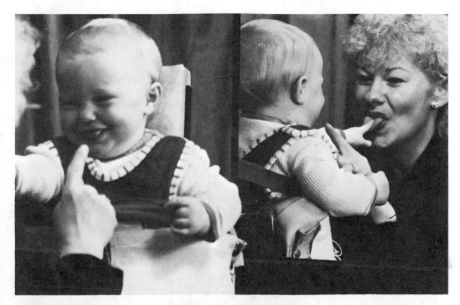

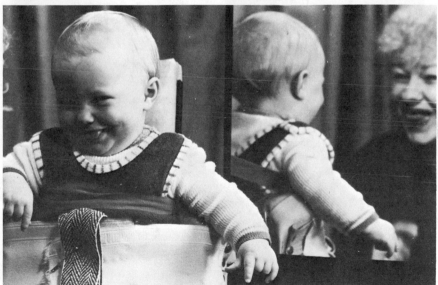

FIGURE 3.10. Playing games: Tongue touching at one year. (Trevarthen & Hubley, 1978)

FIGURE 3.11. Cooperating in a task: A 1-year-old willingly obeys her mother's signs to place wooden dolls in a truck (Hubley & Trevarthen, 1979; Trevarthen, Murray, & Hubley, 1981).

what they want to do. The exciting discovery reported by Bloom (1973) was that first words mean something because the common context is already being used by the child and the mother. It is obvious now that meanings of first words slide easily into the cooperations of protolanguage.

The infantile behaviors, described in the preceding, outline the syntax and semantics of language, as well as its mood and prosody. They foreshadow cooperative work of all kinds and cooperative search for knowledge. They are manifestations of the state of human brain mechanisms in a physically helpless organism so immature that it must be fed, carried about, and protected from environmental stresses and extremes. The strategy of this life history is thus a remarkable inversion of evolution. Being human in essence, the brain can begin the process of human communication before learning any object concept or how to locomote about the world, and can become involved in assimilating and extending the cultural use of experience before talking about it. The human brain is thus an organ of culture that intuitively stimulates the transmission of information from other humans who know the details of the world better. The transfer of wisdom by example and by instruction is a response to a clearly stated need of the child. The inherent language processes are a part of this human need to share experience.

CONCLUSIONS

Although the evidence is far from complete, our quest for information on the growth of brain mechanisms for language leads to the following interesting correlations:

1. Among the slowest maturing cortical zones are the asymmetrically organized tissues at the base of the frontal lobe and at the junction of parietal, occipital, and temporal lobes. They take decades of postnatal life to mature and their asymmetry is correlated with exceptionally rich callosal connections.
2. These same tissues are in cytoarchitectonic zones that Brodmann designated as unique to man. Homologues of other cortical areas appear to exist in monkeys and apes, but not for these territories (Brodmann numbers 44–46, 39, and 40).
3. From the patterns of neuron multiplication and dispersal observed in fetal brains at the close of the first brain growth spurt it seems as though the neurons of these human territories may be produced last. That is, they seem to be the final major component of neurons inserted between cell arrangements established in earlier phases of hemisphere morphogenesis.

4. Neuropsychological research indicates that this most human sector of the neocortex includes systems that are essential to higher forms of consciousness and rational thought in the left hemisphere. They constitute the areas most implicated in regulation of language functions and in analytical reasoning. In the right hemisphere, they mediate perceptuospatial functions that are of great importance in technical activities of man.

5. The above psychological functions are essential to the development of human cultural achievement of all kinds. If they are deficient, participation in cultural life is definitely impaired.

6. It seems a straightforward logical step to a final claim that these special late maturing human tissues, innately specified to have that place in the cerebral system and already asymmetrically arranged between the hemispheres before birth, constitute the cerebral organ of human culture. They create the mental processes on which human communication, human cooperation, and transmission of meaning depend. The functions we call language are the most highly differentiated, most specific of the activities that this set of brain circuits can perform.

Although we cannot specify the anatomy of an "intersubjectivity mechanism," the evidence from infant psychology that was just sketched seems to fit well with the hypothesis of a cerebral system regulating growth of cooperative understanding. There certainly are powerful and specific motives for interpersonal cooperation in an infant. Even before the onset of language, motives emerge in the baby for cooperating with others in using objects and knowing the world. Language allows this initiative to expand. It confers an enormous increase in capacity for specifying particular meanings. The child becomes a talker about what is known and what is done in the world of humans. The result is that mankind is always gaining well-defined knowledge and discussing more and more intricate systems for applying it.

REFERENCES

Ainsworth, M. D., S. The development of infant–mother attachment. In B. M. Caldwell & H. N. Ricciuti (Eds.), *Review of child development research*. Chicago: University of Chicago Press, 1973. Pp. 1–94.

Alegria, J., & Noirot, E. Neonate orientation behaviour towards the human voice. *International Journal of Behavioral Development*, 1978, *1*, 291–312.

Barlow, H. B. Visual experience and cortical development. *Nature*, 1975, *258*, 199–204.

Bates, E., Camaioni, L., & Volterra, V. The acquisition of performatives prior to speech. *Merrill-Palmer Quarterly*, 1975, *21*, 205–226.

Blakemore, C. Development of functional connexions in the mammalian visual system. *British Medical Bulletin*, 1974, *30*, 152–157.

Bloom, L. *One word at a time: The use of single word utterances before syntax.* The Hague: Mouton, 1973.

Bower, T. G. R. *Development in infancy.* San Francisco: Freeman, 1974.

Bowlby, J. *Attachment and loss* (Vol. 1). *Attachment.* New York: Basic Books, 1969.

Bruner, J. S. The ontogenesis of speech acts. *Journal of Child Language*, 1975, *2*, 1–19.

Bruner, J. S. From communication to language—A psychological perspective. *Cognition*, 1976, *3*, 255–287.

Condon, W. S., & Sander, L. W. Neonate movement is synchronized with adult speech: Interactional participation and language acquisition. *Science*, 1974, *183*, 99–101.

Curtiss, S. *Genie: A psycholinguistic study of a modern-day "wild child."* New York: Academic Press, 1977.

De Beer, G. R. *Embryos and ancestors.* Oxford: Oxford University Press, 1940.

Dennis, M. Language in a congenitally acallosal brain. *Brain and Language*, 1981, *12*, 33–53.

Dennis, M., & Kohn, B. Comprehension of syntax in infantile hemiplegics after cerebral hemidecortication: Left hemisphere superiority. *Brain and Language*, 1975, *2*, 472–482.

Dennis, M., & Whitaker, H. A. Hemispheric equipotentiality and language acquisition. In S. Segalowitz & F. Gruber (Eds.), *Language development and neurological theory.* New York: Academic Press, 1977. Pp. 93–106.

Dobbing, J., & Smart, J. L. Vulnerability of developing brain and behaviour. *British Medical Bulletin*, 1974, *30*, 164–168.

Eimas, P., Sigueland, E., Jusczyr, P., & Vigorito, J. Speech perception in infants. *Science*, 1971, *171*, 303–306.

Fodor, J. A., Garrett, M. F., & Brill, S. L. Pi Ka pu: The perception of speech sounds by prelinguistic infants. *Perception and Psychophysics*, 1975, *18*, 74–78.

Galaburda, A. M., Le May, M., Kemper, T. L., & Geschwind, N. Right–left asymmetries in the brain. *Science*, 1978, *199*, 852–856.

Gaze, R. M. *Formation of nerve connections.* New York: Academic Press, 1970.

Geschwind, N. The anatomical basis for hemispheric differentiation. In S. J. Dimond & J. G. Beaumont (Eds.), *Hemisphere function in the human brain.* New York: Halstead, 1974. Pp. 17–24.

Geschwind, N., & Levitsky, W. Human brain, left–right asymmetries in temporal speech regions. *Science*, 1968, *161*, 186–187.

Goldman, P. S. An alternative to developmental plasticity: Heterology of CNS structures in infants and adults. In D. G. Stein, J. J. Rosen, & N. Butters (Eds.), *Plasticity and recovery of function in the central nervous system.* New York: Academic Press, 1976. Pp. 149–174.

Grozinger, B., Kornhuber, H. H., & Kriebel, J. Human cerebral potentials preceding speech production, phonation and movements of the mouth and tongue, with reference to respiratory and extracerebral potentials. In J. E. Desmedt (Ed.), *Language and hemispheric specialization in man: Cerebral event related potentials.* Basel: S. Karger, 1977. Pp. 87–103.

Halliday, M. A. K. *Learning how to mean.* London: Arnold, 1975.

Halliday, M. A. K. Meaning and the construction of reality in early childhood. In H. I. Pick, Jr. & E. Saltzman (Eds.), *Modes of perceiving and processing information.* Hillsdale, N. J.: Lawrence Erlbaum Associates, 1978. Pp. 67–96.

Hecaen, H. Acquired aphasia in children and the ontogenesis of hemispheric functional specification. *Brain and Language*, 1976, *3*, 114–134.

Hecaen, H., & Albert, M. L. *Human neuropsychology.* New York: Wiley, 1978.
Hubel, D. H., Wiesel, T. N., & LeVay, S. Plasticity of ocular dominance columns in monkey striate cortex. *Philosophical Transactions of the Royal Society (London),* Series B., 1977, *278,* 131–163.
Hubley, P., & Trevarthen, C. Sharing a task in infancy. In I. Uzgiris (Ed.,) *Social interaction during infancy, new directions for child development,* 1979, *4,* 57–80.
Innocenti, G. M. Two types of brain plasticity? In M. Cuenod, G. W. Kreutzberg, & F. E. Bloom (Eds.), *Development and chemical specificity of neurones, progress in brain research* (Vol. 5). Amsterdam: Elsevier/North-Holland, 1980. Pp. 479–487.
Innocenti, G. M., & Frost, D. O. Effects of visual experience on the maturation of the efferent system to the corpus callosum. *Nature,* 1979, *280,* 231–234.
Jacobson, M. *Developmental neurobiology.* New York: Holt, 1970.
Jacobson, M. A plenitude of neurones. In G. Gottlieb (Ed.), *Aspects of neurogenesis.* New York: Academic Press, 1974. Pp. 151–166.
Kertesz, A., Lesk, D., & McCabe, P. Isotope localization of infarcts in aphasia. *Archives of Neurology,* 1977, *34,* 590–601.
Klima, E., & Bellugi, U. *The signs of language.* Cambridge: Harvard University Press, 1979.
Kohn, B., & Dennis, M. Selective impairments of visuo–spatial abilities in infantile hemiplegics after right cerebral hemidecortication. *Neuropsychologia,* 1974, *12,* 505–512.
Kutas, M., & Hillyard, S. A. Reading between the lines: Event-related brain potentials during natural sentence processing. *Brain and Language,* 1980, *11,* 354–373.
Larroche, J.-C. The development of the central nervous system during intrauterine life. In F. Falkner (Ed.), *Human Development.* Philadephia: Saunders, 1966. Pp. 257–276.
Le May, M. Morphological cerebral asymmetries of modern man, fossil man, and nonhuman primate. *Annals of the New York Academy of Science,* 1976, *280,* 349–366.
Lecours, A. R. Myelogenetic correlates of the development of speech and language. In E. H. Lenneberg & E. Lenneberg (Eds.), *Foundations of language development: A multidisciplinary approach.* New York: Academic Press, 1975. Pp. 75–94.
Levy, J. Possible basis for the evolution of lateral specialization of the human brain. *Nature,* 1969, *224,* 614–615.
Levy, J. Psychobiological implications of bilateral asymmetry. In S. J. Dimond & J. G. Beaumont (Eds.), *Hemisphere function in the human brain.* New York: Halstead, 1974. Pp. 121–183.
Levy, J. A review of evidence for a genetic component in the determination of handedness. *Behavioral Genetics,* 1976, *6,* 429–453.
Levy, J., & Trevarthen, C. Perceptual, semantic and phonetic aspects of elementary language processes in split-brain patients. *Brain,* 1977, *100,* 105–118.
Levy, J., Trevarthen, C., & Sperry, R. W. Perception of bilateral chimeric figures following hemispheric deconnection. *Brain,* 1972, *95,* 61–78.
Marsh, J. T., & Brown, W. S. Evoked potential correlates of meaning in the perception of language. In J. E. Desmedt (Ed.), *Language and hemispheric specialization in man: Cerebral event related potentials.* Basel: S. Karger, 1977. Pp. 60–72.
Meltzoff, A. N., & Moore, M. K. Imitation of facial and manual gestures by human neonates. *Science,* 1977, *198,* 75–78.
Molfese, D. L., Freeman, R. B., & Palermo, D. S. The ontogeny of brain lateralization for speech and nonspeech stimuli. *Brain and Language,* 1975, *2,* 356–368.
Molfese, D. L., & Molfese, V. J. Hemisphere and stimulus differences as reflected in the cortical responses of newborn infants to speech stimuli. *Developmental Psychology,* 1979, *15,* 505–511.
Murray, L. *The sensitivities and expressive capacities of young infants in communication with*

their mothers. Unpublished doctoral dissertation, University of Edinburgh, 1980.

Ojemann, G. A., & Whitaker, H. A. Language localization and variability. *Brain and Language*, 1980, *6*, 239–260.

Oppenheim, R. W. The ontogeny of behavior in the chick embryo. In D. H. Lehrman et al. (Eds.), *Advances in the study of behavior* (Vol. 5). New York: Academic Press, 1974. Pp. 133–172.

Papousek, H., & Papousek, M. Mothering and the cognitive head start: Psychobiological considerations. In H. R. Schaffer (Ed.), *Studies in mother–infant interaction*. New York and London: Academic Press, 1977. Pp. 63–85.

Penfield, W., & Roberts, L. *Speech and brain mechanisms*. Princeton: Princeton Unviersity Press, 1959.

Risberg, J. Regional cerebral blood flow measurements by 133 Xe-inhalation methodology and applications in neuropsychology and psychiatry. *Brain and Language*, 1980, *9*, 19–34.

Rubens, A. B. Asymmetries of human cerebral cortex. In S. Harnad *et al.* (Eds.), *Lateralization in the nervous system*. New York: Academic Press, 1977. Pp. 503–516.

Rutter, M. *Maternal deprivation reassessed*. Harmondsworth: Penguin, 1972.

Saul, R., & Sperry, R. W. Absence of commissurotomy symptoms with agenesis of the corpus callosum. *Neurology*, 1968, *18*, 307.

Schaffer, H. R. *The growth of sociability*. Harmondsworth: Penguin, 1971.

Schneider, G. E. Is it really better to have your brain lesion early? A revision of the "Kennard Principle." *Neuropsychologia*, 1979, *17*, 557–583.

Sidman, R. L., & Rakic, P. Neuronal migration, with special reference to developing human brain: A review. *Brain Research*, 1973, *62*, 1–35.

Snow, C. E. Mothers' speech to children learning language. *Child Development*, 1972, *43*, 549–565.

Sperry, R. W. Lateral specialization in the surgically separated hemispheres. In F. O. Schmitt & F. G. Worden (Eds.), *The neurosciences: Third study program*. Cambridge,: MIT Press, 1974. Pp. 5–20.

Sperry, R. W., Gazzaniga, M. S., & Bogen, J. E. Interhemispheric relationships: The neocortical commissures; syndromes of hemisphere deconnection. In P. J. Vinken & G. W. Bruyn (Eds.), *Handbook of clinical neurology* (Vol. 4). Amsterdam: North-Holland, 1969. Pp. 273–290.

Stern, D. N. Mother and infant at play: The dyadic interaction involving facial, vocal and gaze behaviors. In M. Lewis & L. Rosenblum (Eds.), *The effect of the infant on its caregiver*. New York and London: Wiley, 1974. Pp. 187–213.

Sylvester-Bradley, B., & Trevarthen, C. Baby talk as an adaptation to the infant's communication. In N. Waterson & C. Snow (Eds.), *The development of communication*. New York: Wiley, 1978. Pp. 75–92.

Teszner, D., Tzavaras, A., Gruner, J., & Hecaen, H. L'asymetrie droite–gauche du planum temporale: Apropos de l'etude anatomique de 100 cerveaux. *Revue de Neurologie*, 1972, *126*, 444–449.

Trehub, S. E. Infants' sensitivity to vowel and tonal contrasts. *Developmental Psychology*, 1973, *9*, 91–96.

Trevarthen, C. The psychobiology of speech development. In E. H. Lenneberg (Ed.), *Language and brain: Developmental aspects neurosciences research program bulletin*, 12. Boston: Neurosciences Research Program, 1974. Pp. 570–585.

Trevarthen, C. Neuroembryology and the development of perception. In F. Falkner & J. M. Tanner (Eds.), *Human growth: A comprehensive treatise*, 3. New York: Plenum, 1979. Pp. 3–96. (a)

Trevarthen, C. Instincts for human understanding and for cultural cooperation: Their development in infancy. In M. von Cranach, K. Foppa, W. Lepenies, & D. Ploog (Eds.), *Human ethology*. Cambridge, England: Cambridge University Press, 1979. Pp. 530–571. (b)

Trevarthen, C. Communication and cooperation in early infancy: A description of primary intersubjectivity. In M. Bullowa (Ed.), *Before speech: The beginnings of human communication*. London: Cambridge University Press, 1979. Pp. 321–346. (c)

Trevarthen, C. Neurological development and the growth of psychological functions. In J. Sants (Ed.), *Developmental psychology and society*. London: Macmillan, 1980. Pp. 46–95. (a)

Trevarthen, C. The foundations of intersubjectivity: Development of interpersonal and cooperative understanding in infants. In D. Olson (Ed.), *The social foundations of language and thought: Essays in honor of J. S. Bruner*. New York: W. W. Norton, 1980. (b)

Trevarthen, C. Hemispheric specialization. In I. Darian-Smith (Ed.), *Handbook of physiology* (Vol. 2). Washington: American Physiological Society, 1982.

Trevarthen, C., & Hubley, P. Secondary intersubjectivity: Confidence, confiding and acts of meaning in the first year. In A. Lock (Ed.), *Action, gesture and symbol: The emergence of language*. London: Academic Press, 1978. Pp. 183–229.

Trevarthen, C., Murray, L., & Hubley, P. Infant psychology. In J. A. Davis & J. Dobbing (Eds.), *Scientific foundations of paediatrics*. London: Heinemann Medical Books, 1981.

Tronick, E., Als, H., Adamson, L., Wise, S., & Brazelton, T. B. The infant's response to entrapment between contradictory messages in face-to-face interaction. *Journal of the American Academy of Child Psychiatry*, 1978, *17*, 1–13.

Wada, J. A., Clarke, R., & Hamm, A. Cerebral hemispheric asymmetry in humans: Cortical speech zones in 100 adult and 100 infant brains. *Archives of Neurology*, 1975, *32*, 239–246.

Witelson, S. F., & Pallie, W. Left hemisphere specialization for language in the newborn: Neuroanatomical evidence of asymmetry. *Brain*, 1973, *96*, 641–646.

Yakovlev, P. I., & Lecours, A. R. The myelogenetic cycles of regional maturation of the brain. In A. Minkowski (Ed.), *Regional development of the brain in early life*. Oxford: Blackwell, 1967. Pp. 3–70.

Zaidel, E. Lexical structure in the right hemisphere. In P. Buser & A. Rougeul-Buser (Eds.), *Cerebral correlates of conscious experience*. Amsterdam: Elsevier, 1978. Pp. 177–197. (a)

Zaidel, E. Auditory language comprehension in the right hemisphere following cerebral commissurotomy and hemispherectomy: A comparison with child language and aphasia. In A. Caramazza & E. B. Zurif (Eds.), *Language acquisition and language breakdown: Parallels and divergences*. Baltimore: Johns Hopkins University Press, 1978. Pp. 229–275. (b)

Zeki, S. M. The Mosaic organization of the visual cortex in the monkey. In R. Bellairs & E. G. Grey (Eds.), *Essays on the nervous system—Festschrift for J. Z. Young*. London: Oxford University Press, 1974. Pp. 327–343.

PERIPHERAL MECHANISMS

4 Getting Ready to Talk: The Infant's Acquisition of Motor Capability for Speech

RONALD J. BAKEN

This chapter will consider speech, rather than language or cognition. It has been argued by some, although not very persuasively, that to consider speech in the absence of underlying psychological processes represents an invalid approach to the study of human verbal communication. This is not really so. As Borden and Harris (1980) have pointed out, "speech, language, and thought are closely related, but they can be considered separately because they are qualitatively different [p. 1]." It is a major thesis of this chapter that consideration of speech as a separate process is not only possible, but is in fact highly desirable in certain circumstances. This disjunction may lead to an expanded understanding of the nature of the development of oral expressive skills.

Speech is the process of using the vocal tract to produce an acoustic signal capable of communicating information. In the normal course of events, communication will result from thought processes and will be structured by linguistic rules, but these are not strictly necessary. "Using the vocal tract to produce an acoustic signal" implies a set of competent structures and precise control over dozens of muscles whose action will generate the requisite air pressure, moderate impedances at critical points in the vocal tract, and alter resonant properties of the system to meet the needs of the instant. In short,

NEUROPSYCHOLOGY OF
LANGUAGE, READING, AND SPELLING

speech is a motor phenomenon. It is, in many ways, "movement made audible [Kent, 1979]." Sometimes this fact is overlooked.

There are important and burning questions about language development that need to be explored and resolved. In the process of focusing on these, we may too often forget that speech—the chief means of linguistic expression—is a product of the somatic periphery. To be sure, the peripheral actions are under CNS control: Language output requires that the spinal cord–brain generate a motor program, the nature of which is in large part a function of the learned linguistic code. But the peripheral actions also have a purely peripheral basis: The so-called speech system has inherent biomechanical properties and acoustic characteristics that interact with centrally propagated motor commands to produce a given output.

On the one hand, then, the purpose of this chapter is to share some of the insights gleaned by the speech scientists into the way in which this enormously complex system works. On the other hand, this is a propaganda piece intended to focus attention on the body that is connected to the left cerebral cortex; to spotlight the scores of muscles, bones, cartilages, tendons, and membrances that are the fabricators of the interpersonal transmission of language.

The case in point is the child's development of phonemic competence, for it is in this area that the role of the periphery is paramount. A lot of thinking in this area during the last several years seems to rest on the assumption that the chief, and perhaps only, problem confronting the child is the mastery of a set of "rules." In other words, the process of speech-sound acquisition is presumed to depend on cognitive maturation. Although most writers recognize the importance of the motor acts involved, usually in the form of tangential remarks about vaguely defined "fine motor coordination," in general, the discussion reverts quite rapidly to rule learning. What is obscured by this approach is the very real likelihood that a major limiting factor in early speech-sound maturation is the physical development of the vocal tract and its motor control system.

PRODUCING THE SPEECH SIGNAL

The Spectrogram

It is useful to begin with an evaluation of some of the salient acoustic features of a speech signal that invest it with meaning. Figure 4.1 is a spectrogram of a simple English utterance: "She put the money back." The

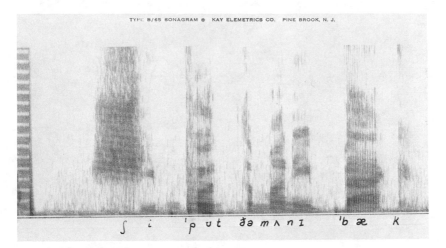

FIGURE 4.1 Spectrogram of the phrase "She put the money back." Horizontal bars at the left are frequency markers spaced 500 Hz apart.

vertical scale is frequency; the horizontal dimension is time. Darker areas represent greater intensity than light areas.

The regions in the spectrogram that show discrete frequency emphases are vowels or vowel-like sounds—in this case /i, U, ə, ʌ, I, æ/.[1] The emphasized frequencies represent formants; their position relative to each other at any point in time causes us to perceive a given vowel. In English, the average formant frequencies of the vowels are those shown in Figure 4.2.

It is important to understand how these formants are produced because it is the mechanics of doing so that children master as they learn to speak their language. A short digression to explore this mechanism is therefore in order.

Voicing

Voicing, or phonation, is one way in which we generate audible speech signals. To produce voice, shelves of tissue (the vocal folds) in the larynx are brought together to occlude the airway. The pressure of the air in the lungs causes the vocal folds to be blown apart, opening the airway just a bit, allowing a small puff of air to escape. As soon as this happens, however, their elastic properties cause the vocal folds to return to the midline, closing the

[1]Throughout this chapter, speech sounds will be referred to by their symbols in the International Phonetic Alphabet.

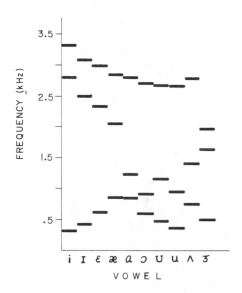

FIGURE 4.2 Average frequencies of first and second formants of vowels spoken by adult women. (Data from Peterson and Barney, 1952)

airway again and setting the stage for them to be blown apart again. The cycle will be repeated as long as the vocal folds are positioned at the midline with enough air pressure below them. The effect of this is to chop the expiratory airstream into a series of small puffs—that is, into a series of complex periodic acoustic waves.

Elementary acoustic theory tells us that this acoustic product must be composed of a fundamental frequency (equal to the rate at which the airstream is interrupted) and a series of related overtones. During speech some of the overtones are attenuated whereas others are emphasized by the resonant characteristics of the vocal tract, which in turn, are primarily determined by the shape into which the tract has been formed by muscle action. The emphasized overtones constitute the formants. This acoustic result is evident in the spectrogram of Figure 4.1, for example during /æ/. Each vertical stripe represents one puff of air through the larynx. Note that only certain frequency components of each pulse are emphasized, forming the vowel's distinctive formants.

Obviously, if different formants are required for different vowels the resonance characteristics of the vocal tract will have to be altered by reposturing the vocal tract every time a vowel is produced. Such alteration requires that the child has learned the target phone to be generated and has mastered the muscular adjustments needed to produce the required resonances. Put more technically, the child must be able to control the laryngeal sound source and the vocal tract transfer function. This assumes that the vocal tract is structurally capable of achieving an adequate shape, an assumption that may not be valid in the young child. This possibility will be explored a little further on.

Not all speech sounds depend on glottal pulsing. Examination of the /ʃ/ portion of the spectrogram of Figure 4.1 shows an absence of vertical striation and formants. Acoustic energy is distributed with comparative uniformity from about 2000 to well over 6000 Hz. The absence of vertical striations indicates quite clearly that the source of this acoustic energy is not the larynx. In the case of /ʃ/ and other voiceless fricatives, sound is produced by forcing expired air through a very narrow constriction to generate a great deal of airstream turbulence, which is perceived as noise. The "quality" of the noise can be altered by forming the constrictions at different places in the vocal tract, which is another way of saying that the turbulence can be generated in different acoustic environments. Sometimes phonation is produced while a turbulence-generating constriction is formed and the result is a voiced fricative, for instance /ð/.

Voice Onset Time

The /p/ in *put* and the /b/ in *back* provide yet another example of a way in which consonant sounds can be produced in English. These phonemes require that the airstream be blocked by a complete closure, in this case, at the lips. This causes the air pressure in the mouth to rise and a small explosion of air results when the lips are then separated. This process is identical for both /p/ and /b/. What distinguishes between the two is shown clearly in the spectrogram. Each syllable, *put* and *back*, begins quite suddenly with the noise produced by the small explosion of air. In the case of /p/, voicing for the following vowel does not begin until a significant amount of time (on the order of 80 msec) has passed, but for /b/, voicing begins very soon after release of air pressure (about 10 msec). This kind of distinction— long voice onset time versus short voice onset time—differentiates the English /p, t, k/ on the one hand from /b, d, g/ on the other, at least before a vowel.

These, then, are a few of the ways in which English phonemes are produced. Our task at the moment is to understand their physiologic bases. The flowchart of Figure 4.3 (adapted from Abbs and Watkin, 1976) will be useful in summarizing the nature of the skills that have been implied in the preceding discussion.

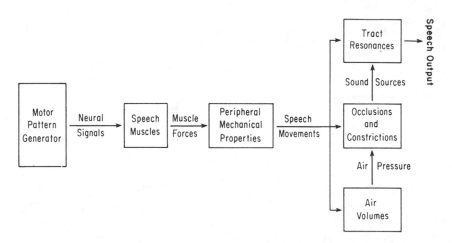

FIGURE 4.3 Conceptualization of the speech production process. (Modified from Abbs and Watkin, 1976.)

REQUIREMENTS FOR SPEECH

What is required for speech is an adequate lung volume that can be used to produce a well-regulated and reliable driving pressure to act on the constrictions formed in the vocal tract so as to produce vocal and turbulent sound sources. These are generated in the resonant spaces created by careful posturing of the vocal tract. All of this results from movements of the structures of the speech system—movements that are the product of muscle forces and the transfer function of the biomechanical properties of the peripheral structures on which those muscle forces are imposed.

Developmental Factors: Physiological

We are finally at the point at which it is useful to ask: How well is the child equipped to do all that is required for speech? One means of exploring the question is to examine several critical variables that will permit us to draw at least gross inferences about the state of the system at different ages.

We may begin toward the left of the flowchart. What do we know of the adequacy of the neural output that underlies speech behavior? Ignoring questions (utterly unresolved) about how the neural patterns are generated or, indeed, wht they are, we can at least look at correlates of motor planning precision and stability. Eguchi and Hirsh (1969) required subjects between the ages of 3 and 13 years, as well as adults, to repeat the sentences "He has a blue pen" and "I am tall" five times each. Analyses were done on the vowels and on the voice onset times of the plosives /b, p, t/. Several of the specific measurements they made are of use in the present discussion.

Fundamental Frequency

First, Eguchi and Hirsh measured the fundamental frequency (F_o) at which each of the vowels in each of the utterances was spoken. Precision of phonatory motor control may be evaluated by measuring the variability of F_o across a subject's repetitions. The mean of the ratios of subjects' standard deviation to mean F_o provides a good measure of how well a speaker can hit the same phonatory target frequency repeatedly, irrespective of the change in mean F_o that is expected with increased age. Table 4.1 shows the results of such an analysis.

Clearly, the child at age 3 shows almost three times the variability of the adult, and most of the improvement in performance occurs by age 7. We may hypothesize that the ability to adjust the vocal folds quickly to achieve a desired fundamental frequency with adult precision is pretty much mastered only at about age 8; before then things are chancy indeed. The fundamental frequency of voicing is a suprasegmental characteristic; it does not, in English, relate directly to the semantic value of the sounds uttered.

TABLE 4.1
Reliability of Repetition of Fundamental Frequency of
Vowels in Eguchi and Hirsh's (1969) Study

Age	Mean $SD/\overline{X}$	Relative value (Adult = 100)
3	.132	293
4	.091	202
5	.079	176
6	.068	151
7	.067	149
8	.054	120
9	.052	116
10	.047	104
11	.051	113
12	.044	98
13	.041	91
Adult	.045	100

Vocal Tract Posturing

Another, perhaps more immediately relevant, measure of motor accuracy is the ability to posture the vocal tract in the same way every time a given vowel is produced. Since different postures result in formants of different frequencies, we may look again at the data of Eguchi and Hirsh for an estimate of precision of vocal tract posturing. Table 4.2 shows the mean of the standard deviation divided by the subject mean for the first formant of /i/ for each age group. Once again, it is clear that the relative variability of the 3 year olds is much greater than of adults. Most of the improvement occurs around the age of 8. Two points should be emphasized: These data are typical of those for all vowels studied; reliability of formant production is important to intelligibility.

Voice Onset Time

A measure of the ability to control sequential timing of speech events is available from the voice onset time. The means of the intrasubject standard deviations for voice onset time of /p/ are presented in Table 4.3 These data are quite consistent with the other measures. Early variability is very high, and adultlike levels of reliability are not achieved until after the age of 7. It should be noted that the improvement is unlikely to be due to improved perceptual skills. There is good reason to believe that phoneme discrimination on the basis of voice onset time is a function of inborn "feature

TABLE 4.2
Reliability of the First Formant of /i/ in Eguchi and Hirsh's (1969) Study

Age	Mean $SD/\bar{X}$	Relative value (Adult = 100)
3	.110	250
4	.093	211
5	.091	207
6	.076	173
7	.070	159
8	.060	136
9	.053	121
10	.048	109
11	.043	98
12	.048	109
13	.043	98
Adult	.044	100

TABLE 4.3
Variability of Voice Onset Time of /p/ in Eguchi and Hirsh's
(1969) Data

Age	SD (msec)	Relative value (Adult = 100)
3	26.1	253
4	19.8	192
5	17.4	169
6	17.1	166
7	11.8	114
8	11.2	109
9	10.8	105
10	10.6	103
11	10.4	101
12	9.9	96
13	10.0	97
Adult	10.3	100

detectors." (See Kuhl, 1979 for a review of this area.) Voice onset time is also important to intelligibility.

The measures just surveyed tell us that motor control is not very good during the early years. Laryngeal adjustment, vocal tract posturing, and their sequencing are not characterized by high reliability. Skill is acquired relatively rapidly, but adultlike performance is not approximated until about age 8. It is not coincidental that this is the age at which a child can be expected to have mastered all of the phonemes of English.

All of this means that development of motor control for speech parallels the general development of fine motor control, as a glance at any child assessment scale will convince you. "Oral language" depends on motor maturation. The child is not likely to be able to produce it accurately, rapidly, fluently, and with high intelligibility until the motor pattern generator schematized in Figure 4.3 has matured and stabilized.

Developmental Factors: Structural

Anatomy of the Vocal Tract

The child's speech production problems are not only—and perhaps not even mainly—those of fine motor control. The structure of the infant's vocal tract is not well suited to reproduce the adult speech that serves as a model. Figure 4.4 shows the vocal tracts of a normal adult and a newborn infant.

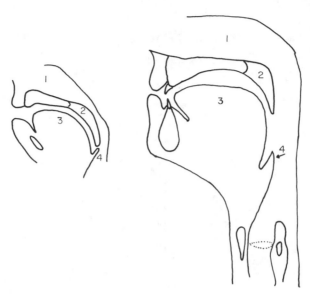

FIGURE 4.4 Diagrammatic representation of adult (right) and neonatal (left) vocal tracts: 1 = nasal cavity; 2 = velum; 3 = tongue; 4 = epiglottis.

Except for teeth, both of these systems are composed of similar structures. The problem is that the component parts differ in absolute and—infinitely more importantly—relative size.

When the two vocal tracts are compared it is clear that the vocal tract is not only shorter but the larynx is very much higher in the infant than in the adult. It is, in fact, so high that the epiglottis lies against the soft palate (Crelin, 1976) as it does in lower mammals. This situation makes the infant a very efficient feeder, but it virtually eliminates the pharyngeal space, a very important resonator (Lieberman, 1975). Furthermore, the tongue of the infant lies completely within the oral cavity, whereas the adult organ has a right-angle bend, its posterior third forming a wall for the extended pharynx. When taken together with the shortening of the pharynx due to an elevated larynx, it is clear that the very young child has only a single (oral) resonant space, compared to the two spaces (oral and pharyngeal) available to the adult (Lieberman, Crelin, & Klatt, 1972).

Since the vocal tract diameter must be kept large enough to provide for effective ventilatory and ingestive function, the infant's vocal tract is also wider in proportion to its length than is the adult's. It is evident, then, that the acoustic space of the adult differs radically (see Figure 4.2). Acoustic analysis of infant cry (Lieberman, Harris, Wolff, & Russell, 1971; Wasz-Truby & Lind, 1965; Wasz-Höckert, Lind, Vourenkoski, Partanen, &

Valanne, 1968) has shown the effects of these structural differences quite clearly. No adult is likely to produce signals that acoustically resemble a baby's cry and, more to the point, no infant will utter adultlike speech sounds, no matter how well linguistic rules could be mastered.

Maturation

The processes of differential growth result in laryngeal lowering and the creation of an acoustically useful pharynx. The later eruption of teeth further shortens the oral cavity. The child still has not only an abnormal vocal tract, from the point of view of the adult norm, but one that continues to change during the years of the child's development. This has signficant consequences for speech development.

Recall that vowels are discriminated by their formants that, in turn, are the product of the resonance characteristics of the vocal tract. Usually these characteristics are controlled and modified by elevation of some portion of the tongue to create a constriction in the vocal tube. This tends to define at least two cavities: one anterior in the oral cavity and one posterior, extending through the back part of the oral cavity and through the pharynx. The nature of the resulting resonances depends on the size of the cavities and their relationship to each other as well as to the overall length of the vocal tube. The impact of growth on the system can be judged by referring once again to the data of Eguchi and Hirsh (1969). In Figure 4.5, the mean of the second formant of /i/ for each age group is plotted against the mean of the first formant. It is clear that the F_2–F_1 relationship, which is critical for intelligibility, continues to shift in a not altogether orderly way as maturation proceeds. Most of the change is accomplished by age 5. At this age, the child's F_2–F_1 ratio lies within 2 standard deviations of the adult mean. This means that change is greatest in the period of most rapid prepubscent growth.

The adult perceptual system is tolerant of significant productive variability, and context also helps the listener. Consequently, adults may think that a child's phonetic repertoire includes a clear /i/ even at age 3 or 4, when production typically lies quite far from the adult norm. The child at these ages patently has the "rule" for /i/. What is lacking is structural adequacy.

Other Structural Considerations

There are other structural considerations. For instance, the infant's tongue is relatively larger than the adult's and essentially fills the oral space. As a result of the geometry of the young child's head–neck region, the orientation of the extrinsic muscles of the tongue differs from that of the adult and limits

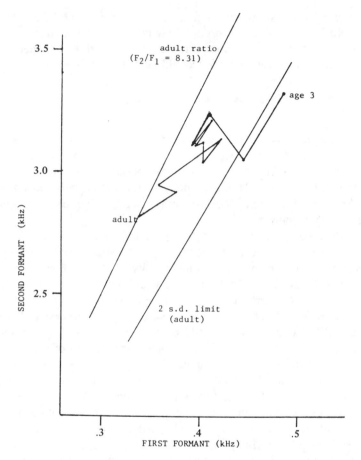

FIGURE 4.5 Change in the F_2–F_1 relationship for /i/ with age, based on the data of Eguchi and Hirsh (1969). The left diagonal represents the (female) adult ratio, whereas the right diagonal indicates the ratio that is 2 standard deviations from the adult mean.

the possibilities for tongue elevation. The tongue is efficient as a feeding tool but not very useful as an acoustic controller. Unlike the adult tongue, it is not very moldable. In light of this, it is not surprising that the earliest phonemes mastered are those that do not require very much tongue control (Arldt & Goodban, 1976). It is likely that phonemes such as /s/ and /ʃ/ are acquired later because there are limits to the demands that can be met by immature structures. Further, as the larynx changes, fundamental frequency drops; as the palatal structures change, control of nasalization appears. Maturation of the respiratory system coincides with increases in length of utterance.

CONCLUSION

Is phonologic development a function of learning the rules of a given language? It is in part, of course, but only in part. In developing adequate speech articulation, the child attempts to generate acoustic signals that conform to fixed rules, but is doing so with a system quite different from the one that models the sounds that are to be imitated. The child uses a progressively changing system. The speech that results reflects both the mastery of a set of rules and the increasing structural and physiologic approximation of the adult form.

In achieving oral expressive skills the child acquires language *and* develops speech. The two are separable and distinct. The former does not subsume the latter and absence of productive capability does not necessarily imply the immaturity of the linguistic system. Memorizing traffic laws does not make one a driver, nor linguistic rules a talker.

REFERENCES

Abbs, J. H., & Watkin, K. L. Instrumentation for the study of speech physiology. In N. J. Lass (Ed.), *Contemporary issues in experimental phonetics.* New York: Academic Press, 1976. Pp. 41–75.

Arldt, P. B., & Goodban, M. T. A comparative study of articulation acquisition as based on a study of 240 normals, aged three to six. *Language, Speech, and Hearing Services in Schools,* 1976, *7,* 173–180.

Borden, G. J., & Harris, K. S. *Speech science primer.* Baltimore: Williams and Wilkins, 1980.

Crelin, E. S. Development of the upper respiratory system. *Clinical Symposia,* 1976, *28,* 3–30.

Eguchi, S., & Hirsh, I. S. Development of speech sounds in children. *Acta Otolaryngologica,* 1969, suppl., *257,* 4–53.

Kent, R. D. *Articulatory–acoustic perspectives on speech development.* Paper presented at the conference on Language Behavior in Infancy and Early Childhood, Santa Barbara, October 1979.

Kuhl, P. K. The perception of speech in early infancy. In N. J. Lass (Ed.), *Speech and language* (Vol. 1). New York: Academic Press, 1979. Pp. 1–47.

Lieberman, P. *On the origins of language.* New York: Macmillan, 1975.

Lieberman, P., Crelin, E. S., & Klatt, D. H. Phonetic ability and related anatomy of the newborn and adult human, Neanderthal man and the chimpanzee. In P. Lieberman (Ed.), *The speech of primates.* The Hague: Mouton, 1972. Pp. 101–133.

Lieberman, P., Harris, K. S., Wolff, P., & Russell, L. H. Newborn infant cry and nonhuman primate vocalization. *Journal of Speech and Hearing Research,* 1971, *14,* 718–727.

Peterson, G. E., & Barney, H. L. Control methods used in a study of the vowels. *Journal of the Acoustical Society* of America, 1952, *24,* 175–184.

Truby, H. M., & Lind, J. Cry sounds of the newborn infant. In J. Lind (Ed.), *Newborn infant cry.* Uppsala: Almqvist and Wiksells, 1965. Pp. 7–59.

Wasz-Höckert, O., Lind, J., Vuorenkoski, V., Partanen, T., & Valanne, E. *The infant cry: A spectrographic and auditory analysis.* London: Spastics International Medical Publications, 1968.

5 Perceptual Prerequisites for Language Development[1]

PAULA TALLAL
RACHEL STARK

Developmental language disorders in children are known to result when one or more prerequisite functions basic to language development are abnormal. The most concrete example of this is in the area of hearing loss where difficulty in detecting the acoustic signal at the sensory level impinges on the child's ability to process the acoustic wave form of speech, and hence to understand language. Impairment of the speech cavity, the oral musculature, or the central motor system may impinge on the child's ability to produce speech and hence impair the development of expressive language. General neurological deficit, resulting in impaired intellect, can also affect the development of normal language function as can severe emotional disturbance.

In addition to children who have specific sensory, motor, and/or neurological deficits that can result in developmental language delay, there is a group of children who fail to develop language normally at or near the expected age, whose language disorder appears to occur in the absence of these described deficits. This group of children has been described by various

[1]The research reported in this chapter was funded in part by an NINCDS contract number NS52 323

NEUROPSYCHOLOGY OF
LANGUAGE, READING, AND SPELLING

authors as developmentally aphasic or dysphasic or specifically language delayed (See Wyke, 1979 for review). Due to the lack of a clear understanding of the etiology underlying this developmental language disability, together with the central role that language is known to play in development, there are both theoretical as well as practical pressing needs for research in this area.

Research into developmental dysphasia has, in general, encompassed two main approaches: that which investigates the linguistic abilities of these children, per se, and that which investigates those abilities presumed to be prerequisite to the development of normal language functioning. This chapter will focus on the investigation of the development of skills presumed to be prerequisite to the normal development of receptive and/or expressive language.

PRELIMINARY INVESTIGATIONS

Auditory perceptual deficits have been reported consistently in the literature pertaining to the study of various groups of children with language disorders (Benton, 1964; Eisenson, 1966; Hardy, 1965; McCroskey & Kasten, 1977; Rosenthall, 1971). This literature has been reviewed in detail elsewhere (Tallal & Piercy, 1979) and therefore will not be repeated here. In 1970, Tallal and Piercy began to study the auditory perceptual abilities of a group of language impaired children in considerable detail. The results of these early studies that have been reported elsewhere (Tallal, 1978, 1980 a; Tallal & Piercy, 1973a, b, 1974, 1975) will be summarized here for the purpose of providing background data necessary for the interpretation of more recent data.

Temporal Cues: Nonverbal Stimuli

In their initial studies, using psychoacoustic techniques, Tallal and Piercy (1973a, b) found the developmentally dysphasic children they studied to be specifically impaired in their ability to respond correctly to rapidly presented nonverbal complex tones. This was the case regardless of the task presented. These children were impaired on tasks of discrimination, sequencing, and serial memory when nonverbal auditory stimuli were presented rapidly. When similar stimuli were presented more slowly (by increasing either duration of the stimulus items or the interval between items), however, the children's performance improved significantly. These results, taken in conjunction with those reported previously in the literature, indicate that some language-impaired children have specific difficulty processing rapidly presented or rapidly changing sequential nonverbal information.

Modality Specificity and Age

The results of our psychophysical studies of nonverbal perception and memory indicate that language-impaired children do *not* have difficulty with all aspects of temporal processing, or that temporal analysis is their only difficulty. These children continue to demonstrate the most difficulty discriminating between stimuli that are presented either simultaneously or rapidly in succession—regardless of whether discrimination, sequencing, or serial memory performance is being assessed. Interestingly, the modality specificity of these perceptual deficits was shown in these studies to be age dependent (Tallal, Stark, Kallaman, & Mellits, 1981). Whereas younger (5- and 6-year-old) language-impaired children as a group were significantly impaired in comparison to the normal controls in responding correctly to stimuli presented in rapid succession, regardless of sensory modality (auditory, visual, tactile, and cross modal), the deficits of the older (7- and 8-year-old) language-impaired children were found to be specific to the auditory modality. The older language-impaired children's performance was *not* significantly different from that of the controls on visual, tactile, or cross-modal perceptual tasks. Significantly different performance between the older subjects in each group only occurred on perceptual and/or memory tasks presented to the auditory modality.

Because of the cross-sectional design of this study, it is not possible to interpret fully the implications of these age-related results. Within the younger (5- and 6-year-old) group, individual data indicates that some language-impaired children have auditory specific deficits, whereas others have multimodality deficits. For the older (7- and 8-year-old) language-impaired subjects, however, only auditory specific deficits were noted. It is possible that those children who demonstrate more serious auditory perceptual deficits early in the their development continue to be seriously language impaired into their seventh and eighth year. A longitudinal developmental study of young language-impaired children is necessary in order that the effect of different patterns of perceptual deficits on the pattern and course of language disability can be assessed. This study is presently underway in Tallal's laboratory.

Temporal Cues: Speech Sounds

Tallal and Piercy (1974) hypothesized that if auditory perceptual deficit were related to the speech perceptual difficulties of these children, it should selectively affect their ability to discriminate among speech sounds that are characterized by rapidly changing acoustic spectra. It was hypothesized that these children would not prove to be impaired in their ability to discriminate among all speech sounds. Rather, their discrimination abilities would depend on the temporal acoustic characteristics of specific classes of speech sounds.

Rapidly Changing versus Steady-State Spectra

To investigate this hypothesis, Tallal and Piercy (1974) assessed the ability of language-impaired children to discriminate between (*a*) speech sounds that are characterized by rapidly changing acoustic spectra (the stop consonant–vowel syllables /ba/ and /da/ and (*b*) speech sounds that are characterized by steady-state formant spectra (the vowels /ε/ and /æ/). The results of this study demonstrated that the developmentally dysphasic children were unimpaired in their ability to discriminate between the steady-state vowels. Thus, merely changing from a nonverbal to verbal processing task did not result in a decrement in performance, as long as the verbal stimuli to be discriminated were characterized by steady-state (nonchanging) acoustic spectra. These same developmentally dysphasic children, however, were grossly impaired in their ability to discriminate between the stop-consonant–vowel syllables, which are characterized by very rapidly changing acoustic spectra that are critical for their discrimination.

Brevity versus Rapid Change

In a subsequent study, Tallal and Piercy (1975) demonstrated that it was the brevity rather than the transitional nature of the formant spectra of these syllables that contributed to these children's specific discrimination difficulties. When the duration of the formant transitions within the stop-consonant–vowel syllables was extended (using a speech synthesizer), the performance of these children signficantly improved. Thus, these children were able to discriminate between speech sounds that they formerly had been unable to discriminate when the rate of change of the critical acoustic cues within the spectra were synthetically extended. This difference in perception resulted from altering the temporal acoustic characteristics (the phonetic label remained unchanged). Based on these findings, Tallal and Piercy (1975) concluded that the speech and language deficits characteristic of developmentally dysphasic children might be related, at least in part, to a more primary deficit in temporal analysis.

These conclusions were based on the results of studies in which relatively few subjects participated and only two classes of speech sounds were investigated. More recently, Tallal and Stark have replicated these findings in a larger group of carefully selected developmentally dysphasic and normal children. Thirty-five language-impaired and 38 normally developing control subjects participated in these studies. The criteria for inclusion of subjects in the study and characteristics of the children in each group have been published elsewhere (Stark & Tallal, 1981). In addition to the previously described tests, a large battery of nonverbal as well as verbal perception and production tasks were presented to these language impaired and normal subjects. The results of these studies have helped us to refine further our hypotheses concerning the role of prerequisite perceptual and production skills in language development and disorders.

FURTHER INVESTIGATIONS OF SPEECH PERCEPTION

Temporal and Spectral Cues

In the area of speech perception, Tallal and Stark (1980) studied several additional classes of speech sound contracts specifically to assess the processing of specific temporal and/or spectral cues occuring within speech.

1. Two pairs of stop-consonant–vowels (CV) syllables were included. One pair of CV syllables /ba/ and /da/ differed only in the rapidly changing second formant transition. The other pair of CV syllables /da/ and /ta/ differed in voice onset time (VOT—the interval between the release of the burst and the onset of voicing).
2. Two pairs of stimuli differed on the basis of a vowel contrast. One pair comprised two very brief duration (40 msec) steady-state vowels /ɛ/ and /æ/. The other pair were CVC syllables that differed only in the medial vowel /dab/ versus /dæb/. Both of these stimulus pairs shared the characteristic that they differed from each other acoustically throughout their entire duration. In the case of the isolated vowels (/ɛ/ and /æ/), this difference was brief, but steady-state in nature. In the case of the vowels in context, (/dab/ versus /dæb/), the difference occurred over a much longer period of time (250 msec), but was transitional in nature.
3. Two stimulus paris incorporating fricatives were also included. One pair /sa/ versus /sta/ differed only in the duration of the silent interval between the consonants and the vowels. The other pair /sa/ versus /ʃa/ differed in the frequency distribution of the initial high fricative noise.

All stimuli were generated on a parallel resonant synthesizer at Haskins Laboratories. For each pair, one of the two stimuli was designated the target stimulus. Subjects' ability to discriminate between syllables in each pair was assessed using a target identification procedure in which subjects pressed a response panel whenever the target stimulus was presented, but did not press the panel when the nontarget stimulus was presented. Subjects received positive reinforcement throughout the study.

Language Impaired and Control Group Differences

The results of the study showed that, as reported previously (Tallal & Piercy, 1974), there was a highly significant difference in the ability of the language impaired and the normally developing subjects to respond correctly to the stop-consonant–vowel syllable pairs /ba/ versus /da/ ($p < .001$). There was also a significant between group difference for the stop-consonant–vowel syllables /da/ versus /ta/ ($p < .01$). The language-impaired subjects made more errors, required more trials to criterion, and failed to reach criterion more often with the /ba/ versus /da/ discrimination than on any other syllable pair studied.

In contrast to the results obtained with the stop CV syllables, there were no significant differences between groups either in the number of errors made or in the trials required to reach criterion on either the brief steady-state vowel stimuli /ɛ/ versus /æ/ or the stimuli contrasting vowels in context /dab/ versus /dæb/. The language-impaired group made the fewest number of errors and required the fewest trials to criterion on these stimuli than on any other contrast studied.

No significant differences were obtained when the groups responded to the syllables /sa/ versus /sta/. Both groups found this to be quite a difficult contrast, however. The control subjects made their highest number of errors on this stimulus pair, with more normal subjects failing to reach criterion on this contrast pair than on any of the other contrasts studied.

There was a minimally signficant difference ($p < .02$) in performance between the language-impaired and control group on the fricative contrast /sa/ versus /ʃa/. The language-impaired group made the same number of errors on this stimulus contrast as they did on the /sa/ versus /sta/ pair. The controls made fewer errors on the /sa/ versus /ʃa/ pair, however, than they did on the /sa/ versus /sta/ pair. Thus, the between group difference found in performance on the /sa/ versus /sta/ and /sa/ versus /ʃa/ pairs can be attributed to change in performance in the normal group.

The language-impaired group made most errors on syllables that were differentiated by consonants and fewest errors on syllables in which only the vowels were different. In contrast, the normally developing children made most errors in discriminating between stimuli that included fricatives and very brief vowels, and fewest errors on stimuli differentiated by stop-consonants and vowels in context.

The performance of the language-impaired group was not significantly different from that of the controls on three pairs of stimuli, demonstrating that they understood the task and were able to respond normally using these procedures on those stimulus contrasts that they were able to discriminate.

Summary

The results of these studies suggest that language-impaired children do not have difficulty with all aspects of temporal processing, or that temporal analysis is their only difficulty. These children continue to demonstrate most difficulty discriminating between syllables that incorporate rapidly changing formant transitions, particularly stop-vowel syllables differentiated by place of articulation (/ba/ versus /da/). They also were signficantly impaired in discriminating between stop-vowel syllables differing in spectral cues (/sa/ versus /ʃa/), however. These results suggest that rather than being impaired in discriminating all temporal cues or even all brief cues, language-impaired children seem to have most difficulty responding correctly to stimuli that both (a) incorporate acoustic cues that are brief, and (b) are followed in rapid succession by other acoustic cues.

The hypothesis that this group of children has specific difficulty processing brief acoustic cues that are followed in rapid succesion by other acoustic cues, is also supported by data from psychoacoustic studies using nonverbal auditory stimuli with language-impaired children. Kornet, Thal, and Maxon (1977) demonstrated that language-impaired children produced normal temporal summation functions, that is, they are able to integrate normally very brief nonverbal auditory stimuli, presented in isolation, as a function of amplitude. Tallal and Piercy (1973) found, however, that language-impaired children were grossly deficient in their ability to discriminate between brief duration tones when they were presented rapidly in succession. Importantly, as was the case with verbal stimuli, performance significantly improved on this nonverbal processing task when the duration of the stimuli was increased, that is, when these stimuli were either made less brief or presented so that the second stimulus followed the first less rapidly in time.

The particular constraints demonstrated by language-impaired children in their nonverbal and verbal processing abilities may be attributable to abnormalities in mechanisms involved in auditory masking. These children seem to have particular difficulty responding to brief acoustic cues presented very rapidly in succession. Studies specifically designed to investigate forward and backward masking functions in language-impaired children may further enhance our understanding of the mechanisms normally involved in auditory masking, and their role in speech perception.

CONCLUSION

Our research has utilized psychophysical and speech synthesis techniques to investigate the perceptual abilities of language-impaired children. The results of these studies demonstrate that language-impaired children's ability to respond correctly to various temporal and spectral cues at the rate at which they normally occur within speech is developing abnormally. If this deficit were linked to the observable clinical symptoms of receptive and/or expressive language delay in this population, it would be expected that the severity of impairment in rapid acoustic analysis would be significantly correlated with the degree of language disorder in this population. Multivariate analysis indicates that this is, indeed, the case.

The variables discussed in the preceding section, which were designed to assess the nonverbal and verbal temporal processing abilities of language-impaired children, were found to correlate very highly and significantly ($r = .85, p < .001$) with the level of receptive language ability (as measured by standardized clinical tests) of language-impaired children. The more deficient language-impaired children are in their ability to process rapidly changing sensory information, the more delayed they are in their development of receptive language skills. This strikingly significant correlation between basic perceptual skills in temporal processing and receptive language development provides strong support for our initial hypothesis that developmental language delay may be related, at least in part, to deficits in lower level processing that may be prerequisite to the normal development of speech and language skills.

In conclusion, the results of these studies suggest that the ability to process rapidly changing acoustic information may be prerequisite to the ability to analyze the rapidly changing acoustic wave form characteristic of ongoing speech. If this were the case, then a reduced rate of processing would interfere with the analysis of the acoustic wave form in ongoing speech, resulting in abnormal speech perception and hence, delayed development of language. It is also possible, however, that difficulties in temporal processing are concomitant with—but not directly related to—impaired language development, both resulting from more general left-hemisphere dysfunction. Temporal processing of the type described in this chapter has been shown to be disrupted by damage to the left cerebral hemisphere (Efron, 1963; Tallal & Newcombe, 1978). Research with normal adult listeners has also indicated that rapid temporal cues are processed more accurately by the left than by the right hemisphere (Mills & Rollman, 1979; Schwartz & Tallal, 1980; Tallal, 1980b, for review). It is possible, therefore, that language-impaired children are signficantly impaired in their development of left hemisphere functions, which include both the analysis of rapidly changing temporal cues and the development of speech and language skills.

This interpretation would suggest that this group of children has a more general left-hemisphere dysfunction, the various components of which are not necessarily causally related. It will be necessary in future studies to investigate the degree to which the severity and pattern of temporal processing deficits in language-impaired children changes developmentally and the extent to which this changing pattern is predictive and/or correlated with changes in language functioning in this population.

REFERENCES

Benton, A. L. Developmental aphasia and brain damage. *Cortex*, 1964, *1*, 40–52.

Efron, R. Temporal perception, aphasia and deja vu. *Brain*, 1963, *86*, 404–424.

Eisenson, J. Perceptual disturbances in children with central nervous dysfunction and implications for language development. *British Journal of Disorders of Communication*, 1966, *1*, 21–32.

Hardy, W. G. On language disorders in young children: A reorganization of thinking. *Journal of Speech and Hearing Disorders*, 1965, *8*, 3–16.

Kornet, R. H., Thal, D., & Maxon, A. Temporal interpretation in dysphasic children. *The Working Papers in Experimental Speech Pathology and Audiology*, 1977, *6*, 73–94.

McCroskey, R. L., & Kasten, R. N. Auditory processing abilities of children in regular and special classrooms. *Audiology: An Audio Journal for Continuing Education*, 1977, *2*.

Mills, L., & Rollman, G. B. Left hemisphere selectivity for processing duration in normal subjects. *Brain and Language*, 1979, *7*, 320–335.

Rosenthal, W. S. *Auditory threshold-duration functions in aphasic subjects: Implications for the interaction of linguistic and auditory processing in aphasics.* Paper delivered at 47th Annual Convention of the American Speech and Hearing Association, Chicago, Illinois, November 1971.

Schwartz, J., & Tallal, P. Rate of acoustic change may underlie hemispheric specialization for speech perception. *Science*, 1980, *207*, 1380–1381.

Stark, R., & Tallal, P. Selection of children with specific language deficits. *Journal of Speech and Hearing Disorders*, 1981, *46*, 114–122.

Tallal, P. An investigation of auditory processing factors in normal and delayed language development. In A. Carmazza & E. Zuriff (Eds.), *Acquisition and breakdown of language, parallels and divergencies.* Baltimore: Johns Hopkins Press, 1978.

Tallal, P. Defects of auditory perception in children with developmental dysphasia. In M. A. Wyke (Ed.), *Developmental dysphasia.* London: Academic Press, 1979.

Tallal, P. Perceptual requisites for language. In R. Schiefelbusch (Ed.), *Non-speech language intervention.* Baltimore: University Park Press, 1980. Pp. 449–467. (a)

Tallal, P. Temporal processing, speech perception and hemispheric asymmetry. *Trends in neurosciences*, 1980. (b)

Tallal, P., & Newcombe, F. Impairment of auditory perception and language comprehension in dysphasia. *Brain and Language*, 1978, *5*, 13–24.

Tallal, P., & Piercy, M. Defects of non-verbal auditory perception in children with developmental aphasia. *Nature*, 1973, *241* (5390), 468–469. (a)

Tallal, P., & Piercy, M. Developmental aphasia: Impaired rate of non-verbal processing as a function of sensory modality. *Neuropsychologia*, 1973, *11*, 389–398. (b)

Tallal, P., & Piercy, M. Developmental aphasia: Rate of auditory processing and selective impairment of consonant perception. *Neuropsychologia*, 1974, *12*, 83–93.

Tallal, P., & Piercy, M. Developmental aphasia: The perception of brief vowels and extended stop consonants. *Neuropsychologia*, 1975, *13*, 67–74.

Tallal, P., & Stark, R. Acoustic analysis of speech discrimination abilities of normally developing and language impaired children. *Journal of the Acoustical Society of America*, 1981, *69*(2): 568–574.

Tallal, P., Stark, R., Kallman, C., & Mellits, D. A re-examination of some non-verbal perceptual abilities of language impaired and normal children as a function of age and sensory modality. *Journal of Speech and Hearing Research*, 1981, *24*, 351–357.

CENTRAL MECHANISMS

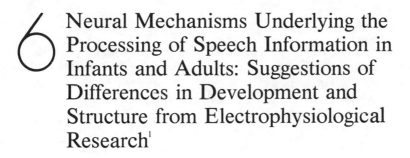

6 Neural Mechanisms Underlying the Processing of Speech Information in Infants and Adults: Suggestions of Differences in Development and Structure from Electrophysiological Research[1]

DENNIS L. MOLFESE

For more than a century it has generally been believed that man's language abilities are controlled by discrete mechanisms that are lateralized to the left hemisphere (LH). This view has been supported by research that has utilized a wide variety of methodologies such as dichotic listening techniques (Kimura, 1967; Shankweiler & Studdert-Kennedy, 1967), split-brain procedures (Gazzaniga, 1970), the study of clinical populations (Geschwind, 1965; Luria, 1966), anatomical procedures (Geschwind & Levitsky, 1968), as well as electroencephalogram and evoked potential recording techniques (Donchin, Kutas & McCarthy, 1977; Molfese, 1979; Morrell & Salamy, 1971). Given the consistency of the findings obtained from such diverse methodologies, the existence of differential hemispheric abilities in adults would appear to be an accepted research fact.

It was not until 1972, however, that such hemisphere differences were found in young infants. Prior to that time, hemisphere differences were

[1] Support for various aspects of the research reported in this chapter was provided in part from grants from the General Clinical Research Centers Program of the Divisions of Research Resources (RR-8), National Institutes of Health, the National Science Foundation (BNS-8004429), the National Foundation–March of Dimes (12-13), and the Office of Research Development and Administration (2-10747), Southern Illinois University at Carbondale.

109

thought to develop only with the onset of productive language abilities, sometime between 2 and 3 years of age (Lenneberg, 1967). The first work to test systematically for the presence of early hemisphere differences utilized auditory evoked potential response (AER) recording procedures in a cross-sectional design with infants (mean age = 0 years and 5.8 months—0:5.8), preschool and elementary school age children (mean age = 6:0), and adults (mean age = 25:9) (Molfese, 1972; Molfese, Freeman, & Palermo, 1975). Noting that the auditory evoked response is a temporally stable, reliable wave form that can be recorded at the scalp and has been found to be generated by mechanisms within the brain in response to specific external stimuli (Regan, 1972), Molfese recorded auditory evoked responses (AER) generated over the left and right scalp regions in response to a series of speech syllables, monosyllabic words, musical chords, and white noise. When differences in the amplitudes of the AERs were measured, the AERs from the left and right hemispheres were found to differ at each age level. Hemispheric differences characterized the cortical responses of even young infants. More recent work involving both behavioral and electrophysiological techniques has continued to support these findings of hemispheric differences early in life (Caplan & Kinsbourne, 1976; Crowell, Jones, Kapuniai, & Nakagawa, 1973; Davis & Wada, 1977; Dennis & Kohn, 1975; Dennis & Whitaker, 1976; Gardiner & Walter, 1977; Glanville, Best, & Levenson, 1977; Molfese & Molfese, 1979a; Molfese, Nunez, Seibert, & Ramanaiah, 1976; Teszner, Tzavaras, Gruner, & Hecaen, 1972; Turkewitz & Creighton, 1974; Wada, Clarke, & Hamm, 1975; Witelson & Pallie, 1973).

Although hemisphere differences have been noted in both infant and adult populations, relatively little work has been undertaken to determine the nature of the cortical mechanisms responsible for such differences or to identify the specific acoustic features that trigger these differences. In part, this failure has been due to the use of relatively gross stimulus features in such studies. As Molfese & Molfese (1979) point out, most speech and nonspeech stimuli utilized in infant laterality studies have differed along many dimensions (differences in formant structure, number of formants, the presence or absence of frequency transitions, and the frequency shifts in such transitions, etc.). Consequently, although the magnitude and direction of hemisphere differences have been found to shift depending on the general type of stimuli presented (speech or nonspeech), the specific stimulus characteristics that are responsible for the hemisphere differences found in such studies could not be identified. Consequently, despite the amount of attention paid to hemisphere differences, little is known about the ways in which the mechanisms responsible for such differences operate, what specific stimulus features they are sensitive to, what the limitations of the cortical mechanisms are, or how they are utilized in cognitive processing.

It is clear that studies need to go beyond a simple demonstration of hemisphere differences at different stages of development in order to assess the relationships that might exist between hemispheric lateralization and cognitive–linguistic development. The research reviewed here attempted to isolate and identify electrophysiological correlates for various speech-related cues in an effort to determine the extent to which such relationships are present in early infancy and to identify how they may change through development into adulthood. In an attempt to address at least some of these issues, our laboratory has focused its attention (within the area of speech perception) on the perception of stop consonants involving voicing contrasts and place of articulation contrasts. A review of this work is outlined in the following.

VOICING CONTRASTS

Adult and Infant Data

Voicing contrasts or voice onset time (VOT) reflects the temporal relationship between *laryngeal pulsing* (vocal chord vibration) and *consonant release* (the separation of lips to release a burst of air from the vocal tract during the production of bilabial stop consonants such as /b, p/). Investigations of this cue have indicated that when VOT was systematically manipulated, adult listeners could discriminate changes in VOT only to the extent that they could assign unique labels to these sounds (Lieberman, Cooper, Shankweiler, & Studdert-Kennedy, 1967). Listeners failed to discriminate between bilabial stop consonants with VOT values of 0 and +20 msec and identified both stimuli as /ba/. Stimuli with +40 and +60 msec VOT were both identified as /pa/, and subjects failed to discriminate between the +40 and +60 msec stimuli. These adults could discriminate between and assign different labels to stimuli with VOT values of +20 and +40 msec, however. These were stimuli from different phoneme categories (/b/ versus /p/). The 20-msec difference in VOT between speech syllables was detected only when the VOT stimuli were from different phoneme categories. Consequently, changes in VOT appeared to be categorical.

Such findings have been consistently reported with adults (Liberman, Delattre, & Cooper, 1958; Lisker & Abramson, 1964, 1970); as well as with young infants in studies that employed high amplitude sucking (HAS) procedures (Eimas, Siqueland, Jusczyk, & Vigorito, 1971; Treub & Rabinovitch, 1972). Findings with infants as young as one month of age indicate that VOT perception is present early in life, long before the emergence of language. This could suggest that at least some of the mechanisms that subserve language functions are innately specified from birth. Given the severe limitations of behavioral techniques, such as HAS, however, with infants less than one or two months of age, no behavioral studies to date have successfully addressed the question of when the mechanisms for VOT perception first appear in development.

Additional questions that have not been addressed directly with behavioral procedures concern the localization of VOT mechanisms in the cortex and how such mechanisms change as the child develops into a sophisticated language user. Since VOT is known to be an important speech cue and speech processes have generally been thought to be controlled by the language dominant hemisphere—generally the left hemisphere—most scientists have concluded that VOT perception is controlled by mechanisms within the left hemisphere (LH). This question has never been systematically addressed, however. A final question concerns the nature of the VOT cue itself. Is VOT processed by specialized speech mechanisms or by more basic acoustically tuned cortical mechanisms (Pisoni, 1977; Stevens & Klatt, 1974)?

Cortical Mechanisms

To investigate these issues, our laboratory utilized electrophysiological recording procedures as well as behavioral techniques. The electrophysiological techniques involve the presentation of an auditory stimulus and the recording of the brain's auditory evoked response (AER), which is triggered by this event. Various parts of components of these AERs have been found to reflect different stimulus properties as well as the cognitive states and activities of study participants (Callaway, 1975).

In the earliest electrophysiology study on adult VOT perception, Molfese (1978a) recorded AERs from the left and right temporal regions of 16 adults during a phoneme identification task. Subjects were presented with randomly ordered series of synthesized bilabial stop consonants that varied in VOT with values of 0, +20, +40, and +60 msec. Subjects were asked to press one button after each stimulus presentation if they heard a /b/ and a second button if they heard a /p/. The percentage of times that the consonant–vowel (CV) syllables were identified by all participants as /ba/ and /pa/ during the key pressing task are presented in Figure 6.1.

As indicated in Figure 6.1, individuals identified the CV with VOT values of 0 and +20 msec as /ba/ approximately 97% and 93% respectively, whereas the CV with VOT times of +40 and +60 msec were identified respectively 94% and 98% of the time as /pa/. AERs to each stimulus were

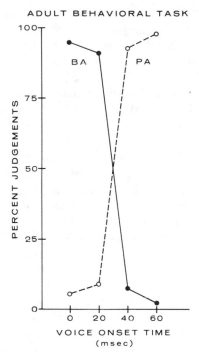

FIGURE 6.1. The percentage of identification response obtained in the behavioral task as a function of stop-consonant voice onset time.

recorded during the identification task and then later analyzed using standard averaging techniques. Subsequent analyses involving principal components analysis and analyses of variance indicated that two early AER components recorded from electrodes placed over the right hemisphere (RH) varied systematically as a function of the phoneme category of the evoking stimulus. Stimuli with VOT values of 0 and +20 msec elicited different AER waveforms from the RH sites than did the +40 and +60 msec stimuli. No differences in the AER waveforms were found between the VOT values within a phoneme category (i.e., no differences were found between the +40 and +60 msec responses). These AER patterns of responding were consistent with the behavioral responses given by these subjects during the testing session.

Similar effects have also been found with 4-year-old children in a study in which velar stop consonants (/k, g/) were presented (Molfese & Hess, 1978). In this study AERs were recorded from the left and right temporal regions of 12 nursery school age children (mean age = 4:5) in response to a series of synthesized consonant–vowel syllables that varied in VOT for the initial consonant (0, +20, +40, +60 msec). As with the adults, one AER component from the RH electrode site was found to vary systematically as a function of phoneme category, but it did not distinguish between VOT values within a phoneme category, $F(1, 30) = 21.57, p < .01$. A second and distinct (orthogonal) AER component also discriminated between VOT values along phoneme boundaries. Unlike that sound for adults, however, this component was common to recording sites over both hemispheres, $F(3, 30) = 11.82, p < .01$.

The group averaged AER recorded from all the children is presented in Figure 6.2 along with the four factors or components of the AER that were found to vary as a function of stimulus parameters and scalp recording sites. The centroid or grand mean AER characterized the information and wave-form characteristics common to all the AERs recorded from children in that study. It contained three major peaks, a N_{156} peak that reached its most negative point 156 msec after stimulus onset, a large positive wave (P_{312}) that peaked at 312 msec following stimulus onset and a final negative wave N_{444} with a peak latency of 444 msec. The four components or factors reflected variations in component or peak structure from the centroid. By means of an analysis of variance, several of the factors were found to vary systematically as a function of VOT. These included factor 1 (with peak latencies of 198 and 342 following stimulus onset) and factor 2 (peak latencies at 120, 312, and 444 msec).

When Figure 6.3 (which presents the group averaged AERs for the various stimulus conditions) is examined, it is possible to see the contribution of these two factors to the AER waveforms for the various conditions. For example, factor 1 affects the overall amplitude from 198 to 342 msec. This includes the centroid region from the first large negative peak (N_{156}) to the first large positive peak (P_{312}). If this area of the AERs from both hemi-spheres is examined, one can note that the overall amplitude from the N_{156} to the P_{312} components declines steadily from the 0 msec stimulus to the 60 msec stimulus. If the impact of factor 2 (which largely reflects the relative amplitude of the wave from P_{312} until N_{444}) is observed, however, it is clear that this region is considerably larger for the AERs recorded over the RH for the 0 msec and +20 msec stimuli than for the +40 msec and +60 msec stimuli. No such effect can be observed in the LH. Identical effects were found with 2- to 5-month-old infants (Molfese & Molfese, 1979b). One portion of the cortical AER that was detected at only the RH site discrim-inated between VOT values from different phoneme categories while a second portion of the AER that responded in a similar fashion was present over both hemispheres. No evidence of any phoneme categorical-like VOT effect was found with newborn infants (Molfese & Molfese, 1979b).

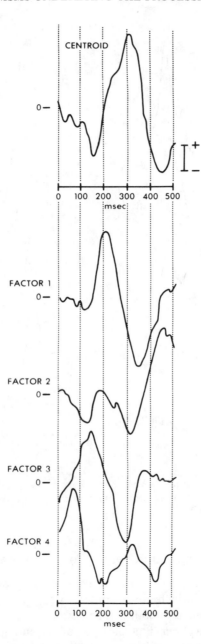

FIGURE 6.2. The centroid and the four factors extracted over all stimulus conditions by the varimaxed principal components analysis. The calibration marker is 1.5μV with positive up. The time course is 498 msec.

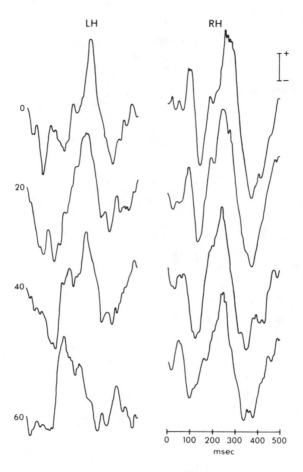

FIGURE 6.3. The group averaged AERs from 12 preschool aged children recorded from the left and right hemisphere temporal regions in response to four velar stop consonant-vowel syllables that varied in VOT.

Three general findings have emerged from this research:

1. Perception of the VOT cues is controlled by several cortical processes—some of which are restricted to only the RH site and some of which are common to both hemispheres.
2. There is a developmental pattern to the emergence of mechanisms related to VOT perception.
3. VOT perception at the cortical level occurs along phoneme boundaries.

An additional study (Molfese, 1980a) was conducted in order to determine whether VOT is controlled by mechanisms that are specific to language, or whether this cue, in turn, is based on more basic acoustic relationships which are not restricted solely to speech.

Acoustic Properties

Tone Onset Time

This study utilized a subset of stimuli that had been developed and tested in a series of behavioral tasks by D. David Pisoni (1977). Pisoni was one of the first to suggest that the ability to discriminate changes in VOT could depend on nonspeech auditory processing units that are sensitive to the temporal changes in the onset of different events. During an initial training period, Pisoni presented eight subjects with a series of two-tone stimulus sequences. The stimuli for this tone onset time (TOT) training session consisted of two tones: a 500 Hz (formant 1) and a 1500 (formant 2) tone. One training stimulus (-50 msec) was characterized by the first formant (F_1) beginning 50 msec prior to the second formant (F_2), whereas for the second training stimulus, F_1 began $+50$ msec after F_2. Both tones terminated together. Subjects were trained to press one button if they heard the -50 msec stimulus and a second button if a $+50$ msec stimulus had been presented. Visual feedback was provided to all subjects after each response.

After training, subjects were given identification tests (with no feedback) on the original training stimuli plus nine other TOT stimuli, which varied in 10 msec steps from -50 to $+50$ msec. In general, subjects identified the TOT stimuli from -50 to $+20$ msec as one stimulus whereas stimuli with temporal lags between $+30$ and $+50$ msec were identified as a different stimulus. Subsequent discrimination tests indicated that subjects could only discriminate between stimuli from different identification groups. Stimuli from the -50 to $+20$ msec category were discriminated from the $+30$ to $+50$ msec category. Discrimination scores within a temporal category were at chance levels, however.

In light of this finding, that the discrimination boundaries for the TOT stimuli closely resembled those for the speech VOT stimuli, Pisoni concluded that VOT perception may depend on properties of the sensory systems that are sensitive to the temporal order between two events. VOT perception, then, would rely on acoustic processing mechanisms that are sensitive to temporal lags between components of particular stimuli. Pisoni suggested that because of the salience of these differences, linguistic systems over time have incorporated this cue as a useful and important one for speech perception.

Temporal Differences: Speech and Nonspeech Sounds

Given previous findings regarding the involvement of the RH in the detection of phoneme boundary changes in VOT (Molfese, 1978a; Molfese & Hess, 1978; Molfese & Molfese, 1979b), a decision was made to test whether similar types of processes might subserve the detection of temporal differences for nonspeech stimuli such as those employed by Pisoni (1977). If similar cortical effects could be found for both speech and nonspeech materials, some conclusions could be reached regarding the similarities in mechanisms that might underlie perception for those different stimuli. Specifically, if an acoustic temporal distinction forms the basis for phoneme category distinctions, similar electrocortical responses should be elicited by both the VOT speech and TOT nonspeech materials. Since the 0 and +20 msec VOT stimuli have been found to be processed differently in the RH than the +40 and +60 msec VOT stimuli, similar patterns of responding should be elicited by the TOT stimuli. No differential left hemisphere (LH) responses should be noted. The stimuli employed in this study are presented in Figure 6.4.

Only four TOT stimuli from the Pisoni (1977) materials were selected for this study. These contained temporal relationships comparable to the voicing contrasts of the synthesized speech syllables previously employed in our laboratory (Molfese, 1978b; Molfese & Hess, 1978; Molfese & Molfese, 1978b). This was done to facilitate comparisons with the earlier electrophysiological research. Additionally, only with these stimuli (with temporal lags after the onset of formant 2) could overall stimulus length be controlled.

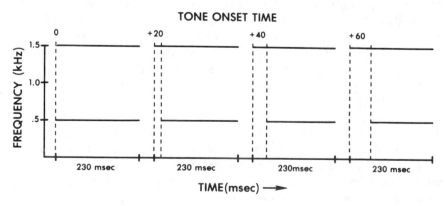

FIGURE 6.4. Schematic representation of the four TOT stimuli that differed in relative onset time of F_1 relative to F_2.

AER differences would not then reflect overall differences in stimulus duration (all stimuli would be 230 msec in duration). The four two-tone stimuli differed from each other in the onset time of the lower tone in relation to the higher tone. For the 0-msec stimulus, the lower tone began at the same time as the higher tone. The lower tone lagged 20 msec behind the higher tone for the +20 msec stimulus. For the +40 msec stimulus, the lower tone was delayed 40 msec after the onset of the higher tone while for the +60 msec stimulus this delay was increased to 60 msec. Both tones ended simultaneously.

Sixteen naive adults who had no prior experience with speech perception experiments or electrophysiology procedures were presented with a series of TOT stimuli. AERs from four scalp sites over each hemisphere were recorded in response to each stimulus and later analyzed using the principal components analysis of variance procedures noted earlier (Molfese, 1980a).

Nine factors accounting for approximately 81% of the total variance were isolated and identified in this manner (confidence levels were set at .01). One AER component (factor 8 with a peak latency of 355 msec and which influenced the AER waveform from 300 to 400 msec) that was common to all four electrode sites over the RH, discriminated the 0-msec-TOT and +20-msec-TOT stimuli from the +40-msec-TOT and +60-msec-TOT stimuli $F(3,45) = 5.68, p < .01$. The RH lateralized process is evident in the group averaged AERs of Figure 6.5. As noted previously the major component of factor 8 began 300 msec following stimulus onset and reached its peak 355 msec after onset. This factor contributed to the P_{330} and N_{405} components of the AERs depicted in this figure. This effect can readily be observed in the relationship between the final two negative components of the RH AERs for the four TOT latencies. These two late negative components reach equal levels of negativity (their lowest points) for the 0- and +20-msec-TOT stimuli whereas the final negative peak appears much larger than the preceding component for the +40 and +60 msec stimuli. No such effect can be observed for these two components for the left hemisphere. This right hemisphere effect was similar to that previously reported for 2-month-old infants (Molfese & Molfese, 1979b), 4-year-old children (Molfese & Hess, 1978) and adults (Molfese, 1978b). In addition, a bilateral process common to electrode sites over both hemispheres also discriminated the 0- and 20-msec-TOT stimuli from the 40 and 60 msec stimuli (factor 6), $F(3,135) = 27.56, p < .01$. Although the bilateral process noted here was not previously identified in adults (Molfese, 1978b), it should be noted that this bilateral response occurred in cortical regions (C_3, C_4, P_3, P_4) not previously tested by Molfese (1978b). Consequently, these more recent findings are not inconsistent with earlier reports.

DENNIS L. MOLFESE

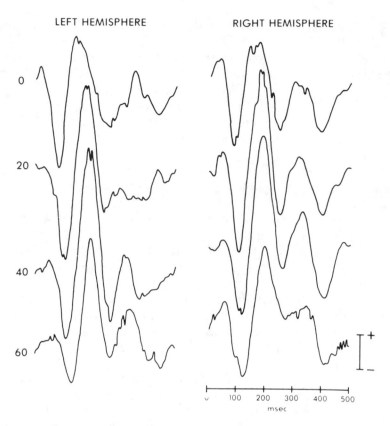

FIGURE 6.5. the group averaged AERs for each hemisphere but collapsed across electrode sites that were elicited in response to each TOT stimulus. The calibration make is 2 μV with positive up. Time course is 500 msec.

Implications for Language Development

The similarities in the findings outlined here for VOT perception and TOT perception as measured by scalp recorded AER techniques suggest that similar processes may underlie the perception of these two cues (Pisoni, 1977). VOT perception specifically (and language perception in general) may depend on the development and emergence of basic acoustic processes at the cortical level, which are involved in the basic perceptual activities that underlie language comprehension. Given that these processes appear to change with development, the role they play in language acquisition could change over time. Language development, then, might not depend simply on the presence or absence (or degree) of lateralization, but rather on the ability of basic acoustic processing mechanisms to detect, identify, and discriminate between certain cues such as voicing contrasts that are critical to speech perception.

Although the mechanisms responsible for the processing of voicing contrasts followed a clear developmental pattern in which the RH appeared to play an important role, independent bilaterally represented processes that appeared to carry on the same functions as the RH process were also present. This point suggests, perhaps, that there may be some degree of redundancy in the cortical mechanisms employed for this type of perception. Such redundancy could be of importance in cases of damage to one cortical region in terms of "recovery" or "reemergence" of functions.

Although the temporal contrasts described in the preceding series of studies appear important for language perception, there is data to suggest that different language-relevant cues are perceived and processed differently. More specifically, data have also been collected, which suggests that the developmental pattern and the neural substrate for speech-related perceptual mechanisms may differ depending on the specific type of information that is perceived.

PLACE OF ARTICULATION CONTRASTS

Several studies have been undertaken in an attempt to identify the electrocortical correlates of acoustic and phonemic cues that are important to the perception of consonant place of articulation information (Molfese, 1978b; Molfese, 1980b; Molfese & Molfese, 1979a). In general these studies have indicated that multiple processing mechanisms, which include LH and bilateral processes, are involved in the perception of such cues as second formant (F2) transition and formant bandwidth. These findings are in agreement with recent behavioral studies that have utilized dichotic temporal processing procedures (Cutting, 1974). Cutting found that both bandwidth and transition cues influenced discrimination scores. Stimuli with speech formant structure or which contained an initial transition element were better discriminated by the right ear (RE). Since the RE is thought to have the majority of its pathways projecting to the LH, Cutting reasoned that such findings reflected differences in the processing capabilities of the two cerebral hemispheres. Cutting further noted that the perception of transitions occurred in the LH independent of formant structure changes. He concluded on the basis of these findings that different cortical mechanisms may be responsible for processing the different cues.

Adults

   In an attempt to isolate the neuroelectrical correlates and to localize these correlates within specific cortical regions, Molfese (1978b) presented a series of computer-generated consonant–vowel syllables in which the stop consonants varied in place of articulation (/b, g/), formant structure (speech-like formants with bandwidths of 60, 90, and 120 Hz for formants 1, 2, and 3 respectively), and phonemic versus nonphonemic transitions (the direction of the frequency changes for formant 1 and formant 3 were either rising to produce a phonetic transition in the sense that it could characterize human speech patterns, or these transitions were falling and therefore occurred in a manner not found in an initial position in human speech patterns). An example of each stimulus type for the /bæ/ syllable is presented in Figure 6.6. *Formant* here refers to stimuli with speechlike formant structure whereas *sinewave* refers to nonspeech stimuli with formants 1 Hz in bandwidth.

   Using the principal components analysis to isolate major features of the AERs recorded from the LH and RH of 10 adults, Molfese found six major AER components that accounted for 97% of the total variance. Further analyses involving analysis of variance (confidence levels were set at .01) on the gain scores for these factors resulted in the identification of these components as sensitive to the various stimulus and subject variables under investigation. One AER component that characterized only the LH was

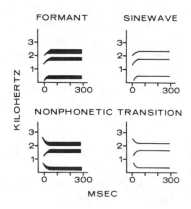

FIGURE 6.6. Schematic spectrogram of the speech (normal) formant structure and nonspeech (sinewave) formant structure stimuli for /bæ/ with phonetic and nonphonetic transitions (after Cutting, 1974).

found to vary systematically to changes in $F2$ transition, $F(1,8) = 27.72, p <$ .001. The LH was also found to discriminate consonant place of articulation information in a second study in which 16 adults were presented a series of consonant–vowel syllables that varied in the initial consonant, /b, g/, and the final vowel, /i, æ, ɔ/ while AERs were recorded from 3 scalp locations over each hemisphere (Molfese, 1980b).

Utilizing the analyses just outlined, one component of the brain's AER was found to reflect the ability of only the LH to differentiate between the consonants /b/ and /g/, independent of the following vowel, $F(1,19) =$ 19.12, $p < .001$. The group-averaged AERs elicited in response to the /b/ initial syllables (dashed line) and in response to the /g/ initial syllables (solid line) are presented in Figure 6.7 along with the two factors (1 and 3) that reflected a LH lateralized process (factor 1) and a bilateral process (factor 3). Factor 1, with peak latencies of 10, 290, and 460 msec contributed to the AER differences at those latencies whereas factor 3's contribution between 100 and 230 msec was restricted to the AER component surrounding P_{200}. These latter findings are important in terms of their implications for the problem of consonant invariance.

For the most part, acoustic scientists have been unable to isolate a set of acoustic properties that are invariant for a particular consonant place of articulation. Although such invariance exists for vowels, acoustic cues for consonants change as a function of subsequent sounds. Consequently, speech scientists have, until recently, assumed that consonant and vowel information is processed together as a unit (Blumstein & Stevens, 1978). This electrophysiological study by Molfese (1980b) represented the first indication that the brain may in fact respond to consonant sound configurations independent of vowel contexts.

Infants

Molfese & Molfese (1979a) investigated the point in development at which infants are able to respond differentially to place of articulation contrasts by recording AERs from 16 newborn infants in response to two stop consonants that differed only in $F2$ transition and formant bandwidth. As was found with adults, one AER component that was recorded only over the LH differentiated between consonants, $F(1,14) = 18.69, p < .001$. A second orthogonal AER component, which occurred earlier in time and which was recorded by electrodes over the LH and RH also distinguished between the stop consonants, $F(1,14) = 10.51, p < .01$.

The contribution of the bilateral (factor 3) and LH lateralized processes

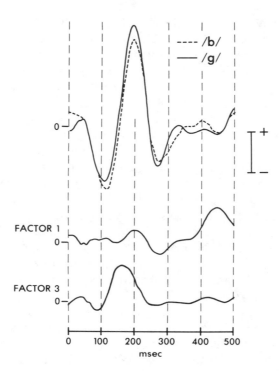

FIGURE 6.7. The group averaged AERs elicited in response to the /b/ and /g/ initial syllables (collapsed across vowels) with factor 1 and factor 3. Calibration marker is 2 μV with positive up. Time course is 500 msec.

(factor 4) can be seen in Figure 6.8 Here, the LH component of factor 4 influences the relative size and shape of the initial large negative wave (N_{230}). This portion of the waveform changed in response to a rising or falling F_2 transition with speech formant structure only over the LH recording site. The later AER components between 490 msec and 704 msec changed over both the LH and RH regions in response to changes in these same stimulus features.

There appears, then, to be some basic differences in the organization and localization of brain mechanisms that respond to the temporal information contained in VOT and TOT stimuli and to place of articulation contrasts. Although both contrasts involve both hemispheres (bilateral processes), they differ in important respects. Voicing contrasts involve an additional RH process whereas place of articulation contrasts involve a LH process.

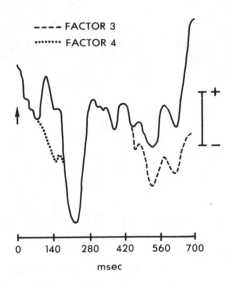

FIGURE 6.8. The reconstructed infant group AERS elicited in response to rising and falling F_2 transitions.

DEVELOPMENTAL ISSUES

The mechanisms that are sensitive to voicing and place of articulation contrasts appear to develop at different times. Although no evidence for VOT phoneme boundary perception was found for newborn infants, two distinct processing mechanisms sensitive to such differences were present by 2 months of age (Molfese & Molfese, 1979b). One mechanism, as reflected by a component in the initial portion of the AER that was common to both hemispheres, responded to the VOT cue along phoneme boundaries. A second process, restricted to the RH and reflected in later portions of the AER waveform, responded in a similar fashion. These different mechanisms persisted into the early childhood years with a bilateral process sensitive to phoneme boundaries reflected in early AER components whereas a RH lateralized process with similar capabilities occurred somewhat later in time (Molfese & Hess, 1978). It was only in the cortical responses of adults that substantially different responses were noted (Molfese, 1978b). Here, two distinct early occurring RH mechanisms were noted from the anterior temporal recording electrode. No bilateral VOT process was found at these temporal recording sites. Apparently sometime between 4 years and adulthood either the bilateral VOT process becomes lateralized to the RH or it is replaced by a different mechanism that is restricted to the RH. Alternately, the bilateral process may be displaced (the generators repositioned or their fields shrinking) to posterior cortical regions as suggested by Molfese (1980a).

In contrast, place of articulation contrasts were made within the LH of infants under 30 hours of age (Molfese & Molfese, 1979a), 2 months before the RH mechanisms could make VOT distinctions (Molfese & Molfese, 1979b). These place of articulation contrasts, then, do not appear to change to any great extent into adulthood (Molfese, 1978a, 1980b).

The different perceptually important cues for speech perception reviewed here appear to be subserved by different regions of the brain and to develop at different rates. Analyses of the electrophysiological responses indicate that each cue is processed by a number of distinct mechanisms, some of which are bilaterally represented and some of which are lateralized to one cortical region. How these bilateral and lateral processes interact or if they interact, we do not know at the present time. We can see, however, that these processes appear at different points in development and mature at different rates. Clearly, then, given the complexity of such findings to date, it would seem that language perception for even relatively simple discriminations must depend on multidimensional and complex processes. It is also clear that language perception can no longer be described solely as a "left" or "right" hemisphere task.

Perhaps, rather than continuing discussions concerning the presence or absence of hemispheric differences, it is time to turn our attention to the fundamental nature of the processes that at some point give us the impression of hemispheric differences. Although the use of electrophysiological techniques to study language and cognitive development is still very much in its infancy, such procedures may offer a useful means to increase our knowledge of this area.

ACKNOWLEDGMENT

The author gratefully acknowledges the assistance of Dr. James Cutting, Dr. Alvin Liberman, Dr. David Pisoni for providing stimulus materials and computer-synthesizer access, and to Dr. Ira Hirsch and Mr. Arnold Hiedbreeder for the use of the RAP computer system at the Central Institute for the Deaf in St. Louis, Mo., for stimulus modification and tape construction. The author also wishes to thank Drs. Victoria Molfese, Andrew Papanicolaou, and Thomas Hess and Mr. Albert Schmidt and Mr. Roland Erwin for their assistance on various aspects of the research reported here.

REFERENCES

Blumstein, S. E., & Stevens, K. N. Invariant cues for place of articulation in stop consonants. *Journal of the Acoustical Society of America*, 1978, *64*, 1358–1368.

Callaway, E. *Brain electrical potentials and individual psychological differences*. New York: Grune & Stratton, 1975.

Caplan, P. J., & Kinsbourne, M. Baby drops the rattle: Asymmetry of duration of grasp by infants. *Child Development*, 1976, *47*, 532–534.

Crowell, D. H., Jones, R. H., Kapuniai, L. E., & Nakagawa, J. K. Unilateral cortical activity in newborn humans: An early index of cerebral dominance? *Science*, 1973, *180*, 205–208.

Cutting, J. E. Two left hemisphere mechanisms in speech perception. *Perception & Psychophysics*, 1974, *16*, 601–612.

Davis, A. E., & Wada, J. A. Hemispheric asymmetries in human infants: Spectral analysis of flash and click evoked potentials. *Brain and Language*, 1977, *4*, 23–31.

Dennis, M., & Kohn, B. Comprehension of syntax in infantile hemiplegics after cerebral hemidecortication: Left hemisphere superiority. *Brain and Language*, 1975, *2*, 472–482.

Dennis, M., & Whitaker, H. A. Language acquisition following hemidecortication: Linguistic superiority of the left over the right hemisphere. *Brain and Language*, 1976, *3*, 404–433.

Donchin, E., Kutas, M., & McCarthy, G. Electrocortical indices of hemispheric utilization. In S. Harnad, R. W. Doty, L. Goldstein, J. Jaynes, & G. Krauthamer (Eds.), *Lateralization in the nervous system*. New York: Academic Press, 1977. Pp. 339–384.

Eimas, P. D., Siqueland, E., Jusczyk, P., & Vigorito, J. Speech perception in infants. *Science*, 1971, *171*, 303–306.

Gardiner, M. F., & Walter, D. O. Evidence of hemispheric specialization from infant DDG. In S. Harnad, R. Doty, L. Goldstein, J. Jaynes, & G. Krauthamer (Eds.), *Lateralization in the nervous system*. New York: Academic Press, 1977. Pp. 481–500.

Gazzaniga, M. S. *The bisected brain*. New York: Appleton, 1970.

Geschwind, N. Disconnection syndromes in animals and man. *Brain*, 1965, *88*, 585–644.

Geschwind, N., & Levitsky, W. Human brain: Left–right asymmetries in temporal speech regions. *Science*, 1968, *161*, 186–187.

Glanville, B., Best, C., & Levenson, R. A cardiac measure of cerebral asymmetries in infant auditory perception. *Developmental Psychology*, 1977, *13*, 54–59.

Kimura, D. Functional asymmetry of the brain in dichotic listening. *Cortex*, 1967, *3*, 163–178.

Lenneberg, E. *Biological foundations of language*. New York: Wiley, 1967.

Liberman, A. M., Cooper, F. S., Shankweiler, D., & Studdert-Kennedy, M. Perception of the speech code. *Psychological Review*, 1967, *74*, 431–461.

Liberman, A. M., Delattre, P. C., & Cooper, F. S. Some cues for the distinction between voiced and voiceless stops in initial position. *Language and speech*, 1958, *1*, 153–167.

Lisker, L., & Abramson, A. S. A cross language study of voicing in initial stops: Acoustical measurements. *Word*, 1964, *20*, 384–422.

Lisker, L., & Abramson, A. S. The voicing dimension: Some experiments in comparative phonetics. In *Proceedings of the 6th International Congress of Phonetic Sciences*. Prague: Academia, 1970.

Luria, A. R. *The higher cortical function in man*. New York: Basic Books, 1966.

Molfese, D. L. Cerebral asymmetry in infants, children and adults: Auditory evoked responses to speech and music stimuli (Doctoral dissertation, Pennsylvania State University, 1972). *Dissertation Abstracts International*, 1972, *33*. (University Microfilms No. 72–48, 394)

Molfese, D. L. Left and right hemisphere involvement in speech perception: Electrophysiological correlates. *Perception and Psychophysics*, 1978, *23*, 237–0243. (a)

Molfese, D. L. Electrophysiological correlates of categorical speech perception in adults. *Brain and Language*, 1978, *5*, 25–35. (b)

Molfese, D. L. Cortical involvement in the semantic processing of coarticulated speech cues. *Brain and Language*, 1979, *7*, 86–100.

Molfese, D. L. Hemispheric specialization for temporal information: Implications for the perception of voicing cues during speech perception. *Brain and Language*, 1980, *11*, 285–299. (a)

Molfese, D. L. The phoneme and the engram: Electrophysiological evidence for the acoustic invariant in stop consonants. *Brain and Language*, 1980, *9*, 372–376. (b)

Molfese, D. L., Freeman, R. B., & Palermo, D. S. The ontogeny of brain lateralization for speech and nonspeech stimuli. *Brain and Language*, 1975, *2*, 356–368.

Molfese, D. L., & Hess, T. Hemispheric specialization for VOT perception in the preschool child. *Journal of Experimental Child Psychology*, 1978, *26*, 71–84.

Molfese, D. L., & Molfese, V. J. Hemisphere and stimulus differences as reflected in the cortical responses of newborn infants to speech stimuli. *Developmental Psychology*, 1979, *15*, 505–511. (a)

Molfese, D. L., & Molfese, V. J. VOT distinctions in infants: Learned or innate? In H. A. Whitaker & H. Whitaker (Eds.), *Studies in neurolinguistics* (Vol. 4). New York: Academic Press, 1979. (b)

Molfese, D. L., Nunez, V., Seibert, S. M., & Ramanaiah, N. V. Cerebral asymmetry: Changes in factors affecting its development. *Annals of the New York Academy of Sciences*, 1976, *280*, 821–833.

Morrell, L. K., & Salamy, J. G. Hemispheric asymmetry of electrocortical responses to speech stimuli. *Science*, 1971, *174*, 164–166.

Pisoni, D. B. Identification and discrimination of the relative onset time of two component tones: Implications for voicing perception in stops. *Journal of the Acoustical Society of America*, 1977, *61*, 1352–1361.

Regan, D. *Evoked potentials in psychology, sensory physiology, and clinical medicine*. New York: Wiley, 1972.

Shankweiler, D., & Studdert-Kennedy, M. Identification of consonants and vowels presented to left and right ears. *Quarterly Journal of Experimental Psychology*, 1967, *19*, 59–63.

Stevens, K. N., & Klatt, D. H. Role for formant transition in the voiced-voiceless distinction for stops. *Journal of the Acoustical Society of America*, 1974, *55*, 653–659.

Teszner, D., Tzavaras, A., Gruner, J., & Hecaen, H. L'asymetrie droite–gauche du planum temporale: A propos de l'etude anatomique de 100 cerveaux. *Revue Neurologique*, 1972, *126*, 444–449.

Treub, S., & Rabinovitch, M. Auditory–linguistic sensitivity in early infancy. *Developmental Psychology*, 1972, *6*, 74–77.

Turkewitz, G., & Creighton, S. Changes in lateral differentiation of head posture in the human neonate. *Developmental Psychobiology*, 1974, *8*, 85–89.

Wada, J. A., Clarke, R., & Hamm, A. Cerebral hemispheric asymmetry in humans. *Archives of Neurology*, 1975, *32*, 239–246.

Witelson, S. F., & Pallie, W. Left hemisphere specialization for language in the newborn: Neuroanatomical evidence of asymmetry. *Brain*, 1973, *96*, 641–647.

7
Interrelationships in the Brain Organization of Language-Related Behaviors: Evidence from Electrical Stimulation Mapping

GEORGE A. OJEMANN

Modern neuropsychology includes widely accepted concepts of the way the brain is organized for language. According to these views, language is considered to be lateralized to the left cerebral hemisphere. There are anatomic asymmetries in the region of the posterior Sylvian fissure, specifically an area called the planum temporale, that may subserve this lateralized capacity (Witelson, 1977).[1] These asymmetries are present in the fetal brain (Wada, 1977). Within the left cerebral hemisphere, language is localized in two areas. One, in the region of the posterior portion of the third frontal convolution, is important for language output. This is referred to as *Broca's area*. Damage to it leads to nonfluent, motor, expressive aphasia. The second area is important to language understanding and lies in the posterior-superior temporal gyrus and in the adjacent angular gyrus. The temporal region is

---

[1]What, if any, role this area has in language is unknown, however. It is in the right place, between auditory cortex and Wernicke's area, but there is no data, lesion, or otherwise, on its language role.

129

commonly known as *Wernicke's area*. Damage to this region leads to fluent, sensory, receptive aphasia.

LESION STUDIES: A CRITIQUE

In view of the general acceptance of these concepts, it comes as something of a surprise that the actual data on which they are based are not overwhelmingly convincing. For example, the lesion in the patient Leborgne, that led Broca to locate the frontal language area in the left hemisphere, is not confined to Broca's area at all (Mohr, 1976). Rather it has the distribution of an infarct in the upper division of the middle cerebral artery involving portions of posterior frontal, temporal, and parietal lobes. Further, Mohr has recently demonstrated that infarcts confined to the classical Broca's area often do not produce a persisting language deficit in adults. The classical expressive or Broca's language deficit is rather the end stage of a large middle cerebral upper division artery infarct destroying most of the peri-Sylvian cortex.

Indeed, the concept that language disorders can be divided into exclusively receptive or expressive categories has been questioned recently. Using a relatively sensitive measure of language understanding, the token test, DeRenzi and Vignolo (1962) demonstrated the presence of receptive disturbances in patients with classical nonfluent motor expressive aphasia. Conversely, Kimura and her associates have found major deficits on tasks involving mimicry of both oral and manual motor sequences in patients with fluent as well as nonfluent language disturances (Mateer & Kimura, 1977). Even the exclusive lateralization of language functions to the left brain has been called into question by observations of patients with division of the corpus callosum that suggest that the right cerebral hemisphere retains at least some capacity for language understanding (Zaidel, 1979). At the very least, a critical attitude toward the contemporary concepts of brain localization of language seems warranted, with particular emphasis on how well the actual data support those conclusions.

These concepts have been derived largely from studies of the effects of brain lesions on behavior. These studies have been refined in recent years by the use of careful measures of behavior and by the availability of new techniques that allow more precise assessment of the area of brain damage, such as the computerized tomographic (CT) scanner. The data derived from brain lesions have also been extended by careful study of the behavioral changes that follow a variety of surgically induced lesions, such as division of the corpus callosum for the treatment of intractible seizures, and the temporary inactivation of one cerebral hemisphere by intracarotid injection of short-acting barbiturates.

NEW TECHNIQUES

The development and utilization of a variety of additional techniques to relate function of a particular brain area to behavior has expanded the database for neuropsychological models beyond that derived from lesions. Behavioral measures allowing assessment of lateralization in the intact brain such as dichotic and dichaptic techniques of simultaneous presentation of competing information to opposite ears or visual half fields are among these new techniques. Other approaches involve the establishment of relationships between various electroencephalographic changes, particularly changes in event-related potentials, and specific types of behavior (Molfese reviews some of these relationships in Chapter 6, this volume). Techniques are now available to identify increased metabolic activity of neurons in the intact brain. When related to a specific behavioral task, it is possible to determine, where, in the brain, neurons are working during the task (though, of course, not indicating what they are doing). At present, behaviorally induced alterations in metabolic activity are detected by isotopic cerebral blood-flow measures as working neurons increase the blood flow locally. Some of these relations between blood flow and behavior have recently been reviewed (Woods, 1979). On the immediate horizon is position emission tomography (PET scan) that will allow measurement of other more specific metabolic changes such as glucose utilization during specific behavioral tasks.

Each of these new techniques requires sophisticated behavioral test designs to determine accurately the behavioral change that is related to sites of altered brain function. Each technique has a variety of limitations that color the interpretation of the data that are generated. Development of accurate concepts of brain organization for language, then, require evaluation of data derived from all of the available sources, with particular weight given to data that can be cross validated by a number of techniques.

ELECTRICAL STIMULATION MAPPING

Electrical stimulation mapping during neurosurgical operations under local anesthesia is another technique for relating alterations in function of particular brain sites to behavior. The technique has been available for over a quarter of a century, but it has been only utilized sporadically in neuro-psychological research. Penfield and his associates used it extensively to study the cortical organization for motor and sensory mechanisms (Penfield & Jasper, 1954), language as measured by naming (Penfield & Roberts, 1959), and retrieval of memories (Penfield & Perot, 1963). There has been renewed interest in the technique during the last decade. Factors contributing to this are the capacity to apply more standardized and precise tests of a wide

range of specific behaviors with multiple sampling of stimulation effects, the
availability of statistical procedures to evaluate the findings, and the appearance of several additional neurosurgical procedures that can be done under
local anesthesia. This allows for the assessment of not only cortical but also
some subcortical areas, in particular, thalamus. This chapter reviews some
recent studies of the author and his associates[2] utilizing the stimulation
mapping technique to study brain organization of a number of language
related behaviors.

Critique

The effect of electrical stimulation on complex behaviors such as language
is largely disruptive. The application of electrical currents to nervous tissue
produces both local excitatory and surrounding inhibitory effects. Whether
this disruptive effect of electrical stimulation on complex behaviors represents a predominance of local inhibitory effects, or whether the 60 Hz pulses
represent noise to the nervous system, thus acting like a temporary lesion, is
unknown. Neverthless, the empirical observation is that activating effects,
such as evoked speech, are rarely seen; most of the effects are disruptive.
Examples of such disruptive effects when electrical currents are applied
during an object naming task are an "arrest" of language, or the phenomenon
called *anomia*, that is, the inability to correctly name with retained ability to
speak. This predominance of disruptive effects with stimulation influences
the design of the behavioral measures used with stimulation mapping. Tasks
used must have low control error rates so that disruptive effects can be
clearly demonstrated.

Behaviorally, the effects of stimulating a particular site are frequently quite
reproducible, at least during the time frame of stimulation mapping at
operation, a period of an hour or so. Estimates of the area of tissue altered by
the stimulating current, obtained by measuring the area of evoked metabolic
alterations, suggests that this area changes somewhat with recurrent stimulation of the same site (Van Buren, Lewis, Schutte, Whithouse, & Ajmone
Marsan, 1978). Nevertheless, behavioral alterations are often consistent
whenever the same site is stimulated. Whether stimulation effects are
reproducible months or years later is unknown. The few occasions when the
opportunity for remapping has occurred are generally confounded with
effects of brain resection that followed the first mapping (Ojemann, 1980).

[2]Drs. Harry Whitaker, Catherine Mateer, Samuel Polen, and Itzhak Fried.

Bipolar electrical stimulation between contacts separated by 5 mm, as used in the studies reported here, is quite gross on the scale of individual nerve cells, but it provides more discrete functional localization than any other technique presently used to relate brain function to behavior. This is a major advantage of the technique. Functional changes at a cortical level have been demonstrated with movement of electrodes over distances as small as 2–3 mm. Stimulation mapping also allows sampling of functional changes in multiple areas of the brain in the same patient, so that differential patterns of localization of various functions can be determined. The effects of stimulation are so brief that the question of recovery of function, a problem that confounds almost all data on the effects of brain lesions on behavior, does not arise. The stimulation mapping technique is particularly valuable for looking at intrahemispheric localization of functions; it is of relatively limited value for studying lateralization, since it is not often possible to obtain samples of stimulation effects on both sides of the brain under similar conditions in the same patient.

The major limitation of the stimulation mapping technique is that it is applicable only to selected populations, those who have the indications that warrant neurosurgical intervention under local anesthesia. Thus there is uncertainty as to the degree to which the findings with stimulation mapping can be generalized to other populations including "normals." This is a particular problem when the patients have medically intractible epilepsy. These patients provide most of the opportunities for determining stimulation effects on cortex. Patients who have had seizure onset in early life, and whose epileptic focus is in frontal or parietal lobes, have an increased probability of unusual lateralization of language (Rasmussen & Milner, 1977). Preoperative intracarotid amytal assessment of lateralization, as is available for our patients who come to craniotomy for epilepsy, allows the exclusion of cases with unusual language lateralization. All data reported in this chapter are from patients with left lateralization.

It is not known whether seizure foci present in infancy also produce unusual patterns of intrahemispheric localization. Major brain damage in infancy can sometimes produce dramatic intrahemispheric reorganization of cortical localization of the motor system. Case 9, in Ojemann and Whitaker (1978a), illustrates such a distortion of motor cortex following birth injury. In this patient, leg representation is located in the middle of lateral parietal lobe. Before generalizing the findings from stimulation mapping to other populations, including "normals," corroborative data from other techniques should be sought. Unfortunately, the particular advantage of stimulation mapping, the discreteness of effects, occasionally produces a situation where other data are simply not available. (Note that this same difficulty applies to some other types of neuropsychological data [Whitaker & Ojemann, 1977b.] It is common for "split brain" patients to have seizure disorders that began in early life and to show other evidence of damage to one hemisphere, with unknown effects on "normal" lateralization).

The areas of brain that are accessible to stimulation mapping are, of course, limited by the clinical indications for neurosurgical operations under local anesthesia. Presently these include various areas of cortex in patients with medically intractible epilepsy, lateral thalamus in patients with dyskinesias, and medial thalamus in patients with certain types of chronic pain. Thus, there is confounding between the type of patient population and areas of brain accessible to stimulation. Neverthless, this does not affect differential findings at cortical or thalamic levels.

Techniques

The language-related behaviors whose localization in dominant hemisphere are reviewed here are naming of simple objects, reading of simple phrases, identification of phonemes, the ability to mimic single and sequential orofacial movements, and short-term verbal memory. The standardized tests used to assess these behaviors, and techniques for stimulation mapping have been published in detail elsewhere (Ojemann & Mateer, 1979a, b; Ojemann & Whitaker, 1978a). Techniques for mapping cortical and thalamic sites differ in some details; the technique for the cortical mapping studies will be briefly reviewed.

Naming, reading, and short-term verbal memory are measured together in a test that consists of a series of consecutive trials. Each trial consists of a sequence of three slides. Each slide has a uniform exposure for a given patient, usually 4–5 sec for the first and third slildes and 6–8 sec for the second slide. The first slide is a picture of a common object; the patient names this aloud. The second slide contains a short phrase with a portion omitted; the patient reads this aloud and completes the omitted portion. The third slide has the word "recall" on it; this acts as a retrieval cue for a single item short-term verbal memory task. The object name on this trial must be held in memory during the distraction provided by the reading of a phrase.

Stimulation is applied during the total time of exposure of the object-naming slide on some trials, during the reading slide on other trials, and during the recall slide on still other trials. Control trials without stimulation are interspersed. Stimulation is applied during these different test conditions in a predetermined pseudorandom order at 6 to 10 arbitrarily selected cortical sites. Three samples of stimulation effects on each test condition are obtained at each site. Data are analyzed using single-sample binomial methods. The location of the cortical sites is reconstructed by comparing the relationship of superficial cortical veins on photographs taken during the operation to those previously visualized on venous phase arteriography. Stimulation uses 60-Hz 2½-msec total duration biphasic square wave pulses in trains. The current is constant for all sites and test conditions in a particular patient. This level of current is just under the threshold for electrocorticographic afterdischarge in the region of the exposed cortex. This is commonly in the range of 4–8 mA, as measured between peaks of the biphasic pulses. The threshold for responses from motor cortex using the same stimulation parameters is on the order of 2–4 mA.

Identification of phonemes is measured in a separate test, a modification of the Stitt consonant identification task. The stop consonants /p/, /b/, /d/, /g/, /k/, and /t/ are imbedded in the carrier phrase /æ____ ma/. In that task, stimulation is applied only during the 2 sec in which the consonant is presented. A 2-sec response period without stimulation is allowed so that ability to detect the imbedded consonant is not confounded with effects on motor output mechanisms. Motor mimicry is measured in a third task. The patient is instructed to mimic postures displayed on a slide. In one series of slides, the same orofacial posture is repeated three times; in another, three different postures are shown, which the patient is to follow in sequence. There is no memory component to this task. The slide model is displayed during the entire time that the mimicry occurs. Stimulation occurs at each site during randomly selected items of each type. Responses are recorded on videotape for offline analysis that is blind to whether stimulation has occurred.

ELECTRICAL STIMULATION MAPPING: RESULTS

Findings related to intrahemispheric organization of language functions will be considered first for cortex and then for thalamus. The discussion will close with some preliminary cortical electrophysiologic observations that seem to tie together thalamic and cortical language mechanisms.

Cortex

Stimulation mapping suggests several major features of the organization of language-related functions in the dominant hemisphere. There appears to be discrete localization of many functions. The different sites appear to demonstrate the property of graded responsiveness (Whitaker & Ojemann, 1977a) suggesting that there may be primary and secondary areas for a given language function. In general, diffferent functions are localized to different cortical sites. The few exceptions to this differential localization pattern indicate the presence of particular sites of cortex at which a common mechanism subserves several language-related functions. Two have been identified: a final motor pathway in posterior-inferior frontal lobe, where all processes requiring some type of speech output are altered; and areas of peri-Sylvian cortex where both the ability to sequence orofacial motor movements and to discriminate speech sounds are altered. This area of cortex common to both language production and understanding, is a likely candidate for the anatomic substrate for the pattern of speech decoding described by the motor theory of speech perception (Liberman, Cooper, Shankweiler, & Studdert-Kennedy, 1967). The evidence for these general findings follows.

Naming

Stimulation at one cortical site will alter a particular language behavior, whereas stimulation at adjacent surrounding sites with the same parameters frequently will not. This occurs even along a continuous gyrus. An example is illustrated in Ojemann and Whitaker (1978a) where stimulation at sites separated by 2 cm along a continuous inferior parietal gyrus altered naming on each of three samples at one site, and not at all adjacent sites on each side. An additional example is illustrated by the patient in Figure 7.1. Naming in English is altered at a posterior-superior temporal gyrus site but not at immediately anterior sites (including some that should be on the lateral surface of the planum temporale). When a response has been reliably evoked, the transition from the site where that response occurs to one where it does not occur is often quite abrupt, appearing over a distance of a few millimeters. This suggests that the cortical organization for some language related function has a mozaic or "macrocolumnar" pattern, perhaps analogous on a gross scale to the columnar organization described for sensory or visual cortex.

Within the areas where a particular language function is altered, one frequently encounters the phenomenon of graded responsiveness. When a constant stimulating current is used, there are some sites where the language function is altered on every trial, other sites where it is altered only occasionally, and of course, still other sites where there are no alterations at all. This has been studied particularly for naming (Whitaker & Ojemann, 1977a). One of the practical goals of stimulation mapping during craniotomies under local anesthesia is to identify cortex that is essential for a language function, so that the surgeon may avoid this area. If surgical excision encroaches on sites where stimulation alters language function on every trial, a persisting language disturbance has often followed. On the other hand, at least in the temporal lobe, some of the sites where stimulation evoked errors occurs only occasionally have been removed without any language disturbance (Ojemann, 1979a). This suggests that the sites where errors are evoked on every trial are particularly important to that language function and may represent primary or essential areas, whereas the sites where only occasional errors occur are of secondary importance. Perhaps these sites are involved in the recovery of function when primary areas are damaged.

Naming in Two Languages

Not only are individual language functions discretely localized, but also the same functions expressed in different languages are often localized at least in part in different cortical areas. The study of effects of stimulation on naming in bilingual patients provide particularly good examples of this. Figure 7.1 illustrates stimulation mapping in a patient who had grown up in a bilingual family, with English as the primary language. Greek, a secondary language, was used largely in conversations with grandparents who did not know English. This 30-year-old female was much more competent in English than in Greek. Stimulation mapping during naming was carried out using object pictures that could be readily named in either language. As indicated in Figure 7.1, naming in English was altered by stimulation of a single site in posterior-superior temporal gyrus, whereas naming in Greek was altered at two more anterior sites in superior temporal gyrus. In the 9 cortical sites sampled, no sites were found where naming in both languages was altered. Two additional cases of stimulation mapping in bilingual patients have been published by Ojemann and Whitaker (1978b). In both these cases, some sites common to both languages were demonstrated, but in addition, each case showed sites where only a single language was altered. Thus, even naming in two different languages can be altered by stimulation of different cortical sites.

There is a suggestion in these data that the areas of the brain where the less competent language can be altered are larger than the areas where stimulation alters naming in the more competent language. It may be that relatively large areas of cortex are used when a language is first acquired. With increased competency, the day to day manipulation of simple language tasks may require only more focal areas of cortex. Again, the larger areas involved in language acquisition may provide a compensatory reserve that is available if the primary areas involved in day to day processing are damaged.

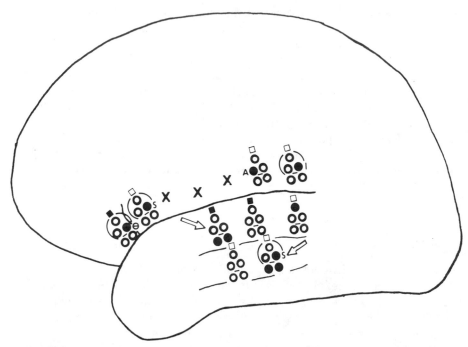

FIGURE 7.1. Patterns of localization as determined by stimulation for six language-related behaviors in peri-Sylvian cortex of the dominant (left) hemisphere of a 30-year-old female. Stimulation mapping at nine cortical sites used trains of 60 Hz, biphasic square wave pulses at 2.5 msec total duration at a current of 3 mA between peaks of the pulses. The symbols at each cortical site indicate performance on the different language-related behaviors. When performance during stimulation differed from control performance at the 5% level of statistical significance, the symbol is filled in at that site for that behavior. The small square at the top of each site represents naming in Greek, this patient's second language. The circle immediately below the square is naming in English, the patient's first language. The circles in the next row just above the small line represent performance in reading simple sentences on the left and performance on the short-term memory task on the right. Circles in the bottom row represent performance on phonemic identification (left) and mimicry of orofacial movement (right). Types of errors were as follows: All naming errors were anomia; reading errors were arrests; short-term memory errors varied at different sites as indicated by the letters: "I" errors with stimulation during input to memory; "S" memory errors with stimulation during the distraction (reading task); "θ" errors with stimulation at the time of retrieval. The open arrows indicate two sites where the ability to mimic sequential orofacial movements was altered. At each of these sites the ability to identify phonemes was also disturbed, the association that identifies the common cortex for motor sequencing and phoneme identification discussed in the text. Repetitive orofacial movements were not altered at any of the sites formally tested,but the Xs represent sites where face movement were evoked, as part of the initial identification of Rolandic cortex. The large broken circles identify four sites where short-term verbal memory changes occured, two of them independent of any other changes in language-related behaviors. The separation of sites where naming is altered in the two languages is also evident.

This patient's verbal IQ was 103. Her temporal lobe seizures began at age 8 after several grand mal seizures of age 4 and were being treated with phenytoin at the time of craniotomy. The epileptic focus was in the temporal tip, and did not extend to any of the sites of stimulation mapping. Her control trial error rates were: 0% for naming in English; 3.6% for naming in Greek; 0% for reading; 0% for short-term memory; 3.7% for phoneme identification; and 0% for mimicry of orofacial movements.

Reading

Differential localization of language-related functions is also evident for cortical sites where reading tasks are altered by stimulation. Figure 7.1 illustrates a site of isolated reading changes in inferior parietal lobe. Reading sites are usually separate from sites where stimulation alters naming or memory, outside of the final motor pathway in inferior frontal lobe where all speech output and all types of facial mimicry are altered. In a series of 7 consecutive patients, with stimulation of 80 sites[3], either naming and/or reading were altered at 35 sites outside of the final motor pathways, but both only at 9 sites, reading alone at 17, naming alone at 9; only 20% of sites with any reading changes showed any type of evoked alteration in memory.

Half of these sites with reading changes, however, showed alteration in mimicry of sequential orofacial movements and phoneme discrimination as part of the common cortex for these functions discussed in the following and illustrated in Figure 7.2. The changes in reading evoked at sites shared with other language-related functions are arrest or truncation of reading, or productive of jargon, particularly for noun and verb stems. Another type of reading error, however, seems to occur in isolation from all other language related behaviors measured. At these sites, ("G" in Figure 7.2) the evoked errors are confined to verb endings, prepositions, pronouns, and conjunctions. This type of error was not seen on control trials. It suggests that these sites are important in the generation of syntax.

Short-Term Verbal Memory

Short-term memory verbal memory (STVM) was altered at sites that are largely separate from, although adjacent to, the sites where naming or reading are altered (Ojemann, 1978; Ojemann & Mateer, 1979a). In the 7 cases, 16 of the 24 sites outside of the final motor pathway where STVM was altered by stimulation showed no change in any other language functions (Figure 7.2). Indeed, the separation between naming and STVM is such that at sites

---

[3]Findings in these 7 adult patients have been published elsewhere (Ojemann, 1980, 1982; Ojemann & Mateer, 1979a, b). They represent an average population of patients with medically intractible epilepsy; 4 are female; the mean verbal IQ is 99 (90–111). Six had peri-Sylvian cortical exposure; 1 frontal. Range in number of sites sampled is 9–15; mean stimulation current was 5.1 mA (3–8), between peaks of biphasic pulses. Sites of stimulation are generally not in the epileptic foci, though some are on the edges of the focus. Local anesthesia in these patients used Lidocaine or Bupivacaine, supplemented by Fentanyl and Droperidol 3–4 hours before testing. All patients are also on chronic anticonvulsant therapy. Localication of sites where stimulation altered naming and/or reading, mimicry of single or sequential facial movements, and short-term verbal memory in these patients is shown in Figure 7.2. A function was considered to be altered by stimulation of a particular site when the error rate on the multiple samples of that function obtained during stimulation of that site exceeded the 5% level of the chance probability, based on performance on interspersed control trials without stimulation.

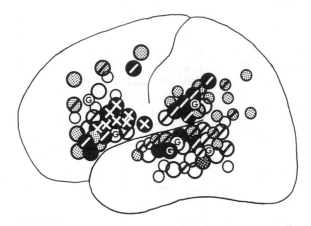

FIGURE 7.2. Location of the sites where stimulation altered language, as measured by naming or reading, the ability to mimic orofacial movements, and short-term verbal memory in the seven patient series described in the text. Each large circle represents a site from one of those patients where five language-related behaviors were measured: naming, reading of simple sentences, short-term verbal memory, mimicry of orofacial movements, and phoneme identification. The smaller circles represent sites where only the first three of these behaviors were measured. Filled circles are the sites where stimulation altered mimicry of orofacial movements. Stippled sites are those where stimulation altered short-term verbal memory, outside of the final motor pathway. Slashes across the circles, either white or black, represent sites where language was altered by stimulation as indicated by evoked changes in naming and/or reading. White crosses identify sites that are part of the final motor pathway for speech as indicated by arrest of naming, arrest of reading, omitted responses with stimulation during retrieval from memory and the impairment of mimicry of single facial movements. At the remaining sites where motor mimicry was altered, only the ability to sequence movements was impaired. There is considerable overlap between these sites and the sites where the ability to identify phonemes was altered, as discussed in the text. The letter G identifies sites where the evoked alterations in reading involve only syntax. The final motor pathway, identified by the filled circles with crosses, is surrounded by the peri-Sylvian motor-sequencing–phoneme identification system, indicated by the remaining filled circles. The short-term verbal memory system that surrounds the motor-sequencing–phoneme-identification system is identified by the stippled sites. Note that there is only a single site where there is any overlap between these systems. Sites where more complex language functions such as syntax were altered (G) are located at the interface between the motor-sequencing–phoneme-identification and short-term verbal memory system. The individual pattern of localization of these language-related behaviors for four of the patients in this series have been published in Ojemann and Mateer (1979a) a fifth patient is illustrated in Figure 7.1.

where anomia is reliably produced by stimulation, the same currents produced no memory errors at all, regardless of where during the task the current was applied (Ojemann, 1978). Of particular interest are sites where stimulation during the distractor task altered STVM. During this period, information must be held in short-term memory. Application of currents at these sites had no effect on the distractor task itself, but apparently altered the stored material so it could not be retrieved later. These sites may be involved in the actual storage of short-term verbal memories, which is generally thought to be an active neuronal process. They are most common in posterior temporal and parietal lobes, and relatively infrequent in the frontal lobe. By contrast, memory errors at frontal lobe sites are evoked most often when the current is applied at the time of cued recall. When this occurs in the absence of any other evidence of an evoked disturbance of speech output, it suggests that these sites may be important in retrieval processes of short-term verbal memory.

Final Motor Pathway

On the other hand, at some sites stimulation regularly altered several language-related functions. The pattern of these alterations provides insight into the underlying mechanism. In posterior-inferior frontal lobe, in an area of cortex just in front of face motor area, all tasks requiring speech output are altered. Frequently during naming, there was an arrest of all speech, including an inability to read the phrase "This is a." Similarly, during reading there was an arrest of output, though this was seen slightly less often than was an arrest of naming.

In the short-term verbal memory task, the patients made no response when the current was applied at the time of output. Application of the current at the time of input or during the time that the memory must be stored produced no effects, however. Stimulation at these sites during the motor mimicry task altered the ability to produce even single oral facial movements (Figure 7.2). Thus, these sites appear to be part of the final motor pathway for oral facial movements, a pathway that extends forward from face motor area into posterior-inferior frontal cortex. This area is distinguished from face motor cortex by the absence of evoked movements. Stimulation in the homologous area of the nondominant hemisphere did not produce any language disturbance or changes in motor mimicry, although stimulation of motor cortex in the nondominant hemisphere does alter the ability to produce single facial movements and evokes an arrest of speech (Ojemann & Whitaker, 1978a; Penfield & Roberts, 1959). Thus, the area involved in direct control of face movements appears to be appreciably larger in dominant than nondominant hemisphere, extending forward into inferior frontal cortex.

There is an intriguing association between the ability to mimic orofacial movements and to discriminate phonemes. Half of the final motor pathway sites showed evoked disturbance in identification of phonemes, even though current was not applied at the time of output during the phoneme identification task. Defects in phoneme identification have also been reported after resection of dominant hemisphere face motor cortex (Darwin, Taylor, & Milner, 1975), though without any detectable aphasia.

Sequential Motor-
Phoneme Identification System

An even more striking association is present between sites where stimulation altered only the ability to mimic a sequence of orofacial movements and those where phoneme identification was altered. At these sites single repeated movements were performed correctly, but errors were made in the sequence of movements. In the 7 patient series previously described, sequential movements were altered at 14 sites in peri-Sylvian cortex of the dominant hemisphere, in portions of inferior frontal, superior temporal, and parietal lobes. This may well identify the cortex that underlies lateralized control of sequential facial and arm movements, described by Kimura (1976). Of the sites showing sequential motor changes, 77% also showed changes in phoneme identification; this accounts for 85% of the sites where phoneme identification was affected. Thus, there appears to be an area of cortex common to the decoding of speech sounds and to the sequencing of motor movements (Figure 7.2). Liberman and associates (1967) suggested that such a common mechanism was involved in speech perception. Their "motor theory of speech perception" is based on the observation that separation of phonemes does not follow continuously varying acoustical cues, but rather shows the quality of categorical perception. They suggest that this occurs because the brain generates a motor model of speech as part of the decoding process. The peri-Sylvian cortex where stimulation mapping shows changes in both motor sequencing and phoneme discrimination could be an appropriate anatomic substrate for this process.

That such cortex also plays a significant role in language is evident from the alterations that occurred in naming or reading. In the 7 patient series, 71% of the sites with sequential motor change showed changes in naming or reading. This accounts for 56% of the sites where stimulation altered naming and/or reading. The sites of brain lesions that produce persisting motor aphasias, as described by Mohr (1976), encompass this same peri-Sylvian cortex. This cortex is likely to be one of the crucial substrates for the generation of language and is probably damaged in most patients with persisting aphasias. Because of its association with motor sequencing and speech decoding, damage to this area may account for the presence of both motor and receptive deficits that characterize most aphasic patients.

The primary role of the peri-Sylvian cortex that is common to motor sequencing and phoneme identification remains unclear. It may subserve oral and manual motor sequencing, as suggested by Kimura (1976). Other data suggest that some aspects of temporal processing, which is important to both motor and perceptual mechanisms, may be the special function of this cortex. Efron (1963) has presented evidence that the dominant hemisphere has special mechanisms for the ordering of temporal events. Tallal and Newcombe (1978) and Tallal and Stark (Chapter 5, this volume) suggest that fine timing discriminations are a dominant hemisphere function. Perhaps this cortex functions first in the identification of sounds and then, as meaningful sounds are identified in the course of language acquisition, the same cortex patterns sequential motor activity to produce similar sounds.

New Hypotheses for Brain Organization of Language

Several new hypotheses of brain organization for language are suggested by these stimulation mapping studies. The brain areas that subserve language also have a motor role, an hypothesis previously put forth by Kimura (1976). One of the major components of the cortical language system is the peri-Sylvian common cortex for motor sequencing and phoneme identification. This is surrounded by cortex subserving short-term verbal memory. At the interface between these two cortical areas are sites where some of the more specialized aspects of language can be altered, particularly the sites at which isolated naming or reading changes occur, especially those of the grammatical type (Figure 7.2). Perhaps phylogenetically, language arises with the development of two systems: a motor sequencing system and a memory system, with specialized language functions arising at the interface between them. If this were so, one might expect to find evidence of either or both of these systems lateralized in higher primates. And indeed, Dewson (1977), has demonstrated evidence for a lateralized memory system in temporal cortex of monkey.

Individual Variability

Although the discreteness of localization, the presence of some isolated naming, reading and memory functions, and the presence of sites capable of subserving more than one function—such as motor sequencing and phoneme identification—are quite uniform from one patient to another, the exact location of the sites shows considerable individual variability across patients. This has been quantified for naming (Ojemann, 1979a; Ojemann & Whitaker, 1978a). In a series of 10 patients, all left-hemisphere dominant for language, the only area at which naming changes were evoked in all patients was posterior-inferior frontal cortex immediately in front of the face motor area. This may well represent part of the final motor-speech output pathway. From 20–70% of the patients showed no naming changes at all in the other traditional language areas.

In a second study involving a series of 18 patients (Polen & Ojemann, unpublished observations), the proportion of patients showing naming changes in the posterior language areas does not differ from the earlier study. The reason why there should be a high degree of variability in the precise cortical localization of language is not certain. It may be a function of the unusual patient population in which these functions are studied. There may be a subtle and variable effect of epileptic foci on intrahemispheric language localization.

Morphological Variability

On the other hand, indications that a high degree of cortical variability may be a general property comes from studies of cortical gyral morphology in presumably normal brains. Rubens and associates (Rubens, Mahowald, & Hutton, 1976) found the gyral morphology at the end of the Sylvian fissure in the dominant hemisphere to be highly variable. Stenssas, Eddington, and Dobelle (1974), in a study carried out in conjunction with the visual prosthesis project, evaluated the total area and the surface area of visual cortex in 25 normal brains. They found that, even in this system that one would expect to be relatively uniform, there was a variance of 300% in the estimated total area and 400% in surface area. These morphologic studies then, suggest that there is a high degree of individual variability in the detailed anatomy of cortex. Mapping studies suggest that this is paralleled by a high degree of variability in exact functional localization. There may be as much individual variability in the morphology and functional anatomy of cortex as there is in our faces.

Verbal IQ and Pattern of Localization

There is some suggestion that a relationship exists between some individual patterns of language localization and overall level of language performance. Of the 18 patients studied by Polen and Ojemann, 8 had a verbal IQ (VIQ) of less than 95, and 10 had a verbal IQ above 95 (range of VIQ for these patients was 69–115). The pattern of localization in posterior language areas where naming changes were evoked differed in the patients along the dimension of verbal IQ. Six of the 8 patients with a verbal IQ below 95 demonstrated naming changes when the parietal operculum was stimulated; only 2 of the 9 patients with an IQ above 95 demonstrated similar changes in naming when that area was stimulated. There is less than a 5% probability that this association occurred on a chance basis. Although patients with a VIQ above 95 were more likely to show naming changes when superior temporal gyrus was stimulation than those with a lower verbal IQ (7 of 10 versus 4 of 8), this difference did not achieve a 5% level of statistical significance. There was only a slight, and not statistically significant, suggestion that naming changes were evoked at a larger number of the posterior naming sites sampled in patients with a low VIQ (44%) compared to those with a higher VIQ (35%). Thus the presence of parietal representation for naming in patients with a lower VIQ is not a result of a larger posterior language area. Rather, it may be that the parietal lobe is less than an optimal substrate for language. This suggests that there may be a structural basis for poor language functions.

In addition, the findings suggest that the biological substrate of human language may be a process undergoing relatively rapid evolution. Substantial individual variability characterizes traits selected by environmental pressure for development. Brain organization for language seems to have these properties of substantial individual variability. Cultural selection for verbal processes is of course well known.

Thalamus

Language is generally considered to be a cortical function despite observations, going back at least to Pierre Marie, in the early 1900s, that lesions producing aphasia sometimes involve subcortical areas. With the advent of subcortical surgical procedures, such as stereotactic operations for the treatment of Parkinsonism and other dyskinesias, and the development of diagnostic techniques, such as CT scanning that can show small lesions in subcortical structures, it has become apparent that isolated subcortical lesions are sometimes associated with specific language deficits.

Modern neuropsychological assessments of patients with discrete left-thalamic lesions have demonstrated specific language disturbances. Typically, the patient's speech is fluent and comprehension is relatively intact. The patient has considerable difficulty with naming, however, and frequently perseverates on words or phrases that are wildly extraneous to the topic at hand. The level of performance tends to fluctuate greatly from one moment to the next (Luria, 1977; Mohr, Watters, & Duncan, 1975; Ojemann, 1976; Reynolds, Harris, Ojemann, & Turner, 1978).

Electrical stimulation mapping carried out during the course of stereotactic thalamotomy, using measures of naming and short-term verbal memory similar to those described previously, has demonstrated discrete localization within areas in thalamus where naming changes can be evoked: left medial-central portions of ventral lateral nucleus extending into anterior-superior pulvinar (Ojemann, 1977). The kind of naming error produced in the posterior portions of this thalamic area is the same as that evoked from cortex, that is, a mixture of omissions and misnamings. More anteriorly in lateral thalamus, unique types of naming changes have been evoked. These include perseverations on portions of the correct name and the incorrect production of a particular name each time it must be produced during stimulation (Ojemann, 1975, 1976, 1977). On several occasions, this has been the name of the last object correctly named at a subthreshold current.

In further contrast to cortex, the areas where naming changes and memory changes are evoked overlap in left-lateral thalamus. There appears to be a substantial interrelationship between naming and memory. The magnitude of memory errors evoked at the time of operation shows a high correlation with the postoperative appearance of a language disturbance, suggesting that a common mechanism underlies both. The nature of the memory errors with left-thalamic stimulation give some insight into that underlying mechanism. Left-thalamic stimulation, at the time of retrieval from short-term memory, produces an increase in the error rate that is about double the nonstimulation-control error rate (Ojemann, 1975, 1976, 1977; Ojemann, Blick, & Ward, 1971). Stimulation shortens the latency for correct responses (Ojemann, 1974). Stimulation of the same sites at the same currents, but at the time of input of information into short-term memory, results in a decrease in errors to about half the control level. Application of the current during the storage phase of the task or at the time of both input and output on the same trial produces changes that are indistinguishable from control performances.

This thalamic stimulation effect on short-term memory has been described as the activation of a "specific alerting" circuit that directs attention to verbal material in the external environment, while simultaneously blocking retrieval of already internalized material from either short-term or long-term memory (Ojemann, 1975, 1977, 1979b; Ojemann, Blick, & Ward, 1971). A similar mechanism for visuospatial memory is present in right thalamus (Ojemann, 1977; 1979b). True dominance of the verbal "specific alerting" mechanism can be demonstrated. When the left-thalamic-specific alerting mechanism is activated in a setting where there is only spatial information in the external environment, that information is effectively ignored; when the right-thalamic alerting mechanism is activated in the presence of external verbal information, that information is handled in the same way as control information.

This thalamic-specific alerting mechanism may well play a major role in learning. It acts as a gate controlling access to or from short- and probably long-term memory for the appropriate type of material. When the mechanism is active, the type of material present in the external environment will be more readily retained, but material of the same type already in memory is less readily available. Thus, the level of activity of this mechanism in the right or left thalamus may determine both the degree to which spatial or verbal features of incoming information will be retained and the degree to which previously internalized spatial or verbal material will be available to develop associations to incoming information.

The major area of lateral thalamus in which these effects are evoked, the ventral lateral nucleus, is generally thought to play a role in motor functions. Indeed, the operations in which these studies are carried out are designed to modify motor disabilities by the placement of ventral-lateral thalamic lesions. Thus, this is another area of brain where mechanisms of motor control and those of language overlap. Perhaps, in the development of lateralized language processes, some of the mechanisms phylogenetically develope for motor learning have been taken over for language, in this case, a specific alerting circuitry.

INTERRELATIONSHIP BETWEEN CORTICAL
AND THALAMIC LANGUAGE MECHANISMS

Further evidence of the importance of the thalamic alerting mechanisms in language has come from the study of physiologic changes in language cortex that are specific to language tasks. During silent naming, Fried, Ojemann, and Fetz (1981) recorded event-related potentials directly from sites in dominant cortex whose relation to language was subsequently determined by stimulation mapping during naming. The event-related potentials followed 100 msec exposures of a series of visual inputs containing both a picture of an object and a spatial feature. The task required silent naming of the pictured object on some blocks of trials and matching the spatial feature on others; the same visual inputs were used for both tasks. These tasks also included a cued delayed-speech output to check that the tasks were performed without confounding event-related potential changes to those related to motor speech output.

Two changes in the event-related potentials following silent naming were identified at the cortical sites that subsequent stimulation mapping related to naming. The changes at those sites were observed only with silent naming and not with the spatial matching task. One of those changes was a local desynchronization in the event-related potential at sites in the posterior temporal-parietal cortex related to naming. This desynchronization involved a decrease in activity in the 8–12 Hz range. It appeared about 180 msec after the onset of the flash and lasted for about one sec. The second change was a slow potential shift during silent naming at posterior frontal sites identified by stimulation mapping as being related to naming. This potential had a time course similar to the desynchronization seen at posterior sites, peaking at about 700 msec.

Spontaneous or cued speech output is preceded by slow potential shifts that are largest at the same frontal sites that show the slow potential shifts with silent naming. Slow potential shifts with silent naming, then, likely reflect processing to a stage of subvocalization, inner speech, or effector readiness. These potential shifts preceding overt speech seem to differ from those associated with silent naming by being more widespread, more prominent in motor cortex, and also apparently present in nondominant motor and premotor cortex. No slow potential shift was recorded from nondominant hemisphere with silent naming.

Both of these patterns of EEG change with silent naming, slow potential shifts in premotor cortex, and local desynchronization have been described with stimulation of thalamocortical activating circuits in experimental animals (Jasper, 1960; Skinner & Yingling, 1977). This suggests that electrophysiological changes that are specific for a language task in human language cortex reflect activation of thalamic circuits. Thalamic activating circuitry, then, may have a major role in the generation of language processes in cortex.

LANGUAGE PROCESSES IN THE NONDOMINANT HEMISPHERE

Electrical stimulation of the nondominant hemisphere, at either cortical or thalamic levels, during the language-related tasks described previously has very little effect. Although stimulation of nondominant face motor cortex disrupts all types of orofacial movement and blocks speech output, the disruption does not extend into premotor cortex, as it does in dominant hemisphere. Aside from this, no statistically significant alterations in any language task have been evoked from the nondominant hemisphere at either cortical or subcortical levels. These observations correlate with the absence of language deficits subsequent to spontaneous lesions in the nondominant hemisphere and with the observations obtained during intracarotid amytal testing. Perfusion of the nondominant hemisphere has little or no effect on language tasks, including naming, any aspect of reading, and short-term memory. These observations are somewhat at variance with observations obtained by using dichotic techniques with "normals," or from the study of "split-brain" patients, with division of corpus callosum (Zaidel, 1979). A variety of language-related functions have been ascribed to the nondominant hemisphere with these techniques, particularly varying degrees of language understanding. Some studies even suggest that the nondominant hemisphere has some capacity for language expression (Gazzaniga, 1970). The discrepancies regarding the role of the nondominant hemisphere in language that derive from the use of different techniques and different clinical populations await resolution. At the very least, it appears that the dominant hemisphere can handle many language functions by itself, independent of even major changes in the nondominant hemisphere.

CONCLUSIONS

Electrical stimulation mapping studies of language-related functions in the dominant hemisphere suggest that some revisions in the present concepts of the brain organization of language be made. Language processes appear to be discretely localized in dominant hemisphere at both cortical and thalamic levels. Peri-Sylvian language cortex contains a common mechanism for sequencing movements and discrimination of phonemes; this mechanism could be the substrate for the motor theory of speech perception. This area is surrounded by cortex that is related to short-term verbal memory. Cortical sites related to complex language functions, such as syntax, are located at the interface between these systems. There is considerable individual variability in the exact cortical anatomic localization of language processes. It is possible that anatomic variability may account for some individual differences in overall verbal behavior. Lateralized thalamic activating circuits seem to be important in both cortical language mechanisms and in attentional mechanisms essential to verbal learning. At both cortical and thalamic levels, language processes utilize mechanisms that are also part of the motor system.

Concepts of brain organization for language will continue to evolve as new data become available. This should be a major thrust of contemporary neuropsychology. A greater understanding of disabilities in verbal processes is likely to follow identification of the specific mechanisms in particular brain areas that are important to language.

ACKNOWLEDGMENTS

The research reported here is supported by Grant NS 04053 NIH/DHHS. I am an affiliate of the Child Development and Mental Retardation Center, University of Washington. Some of the patients included in these studies were under the care of Drs. A. A. Ward, Jr. and A. R. Wyler. Dr. C. Dodrill provided preoperative IQ and intracarotid amytal data. The procedure for obtaining informed consent for my research studies included here are annually reviewed and approved by the University of Washington Committee for the Protection of Human Subjects.

REFERENCES

DeRenzi, E., & Vignolo, L. The token test: A sensitive test to detect receptive disturbances in aphasics. *Brain*, 1962, *85*, 665–678.

Dewson, J. H., III Preliminary evidence of hemispheric asymemtry of auditory function in monkeys. In S. Harnard, R. Doty, L. Goldstein, J. Saynes, & G. Krauthamer (Eds.), *Lateralization in the nervous system*. New York: Academic Press, 1977. Pp. 63–71.

Darwin, C., Taylor, L., & Milner, B. Proceedings of the Seventeenth International Symposium of Neuropsychology. *Neuropsychologia*, 1975, *13*, 132.

Efron, R. Temporal perception, aphasia and *deja vu*. *Brain*, 1963, *86*, 403–424.

Fried, I., Ojemann, G., & Fetz, Language related potentials specific to human language cortex. *Science*, 1981, *212*, 353–355.

Gazzaniga, M. *The bisected brain*. New York: Appleton, 1970.

Jasper, H. Unspecific thalamocortical relations. In J. Fields, H. Magoun and V. Hall (Eds.), *Handbook of Physiology*, Section 1, Neurophysiology, V: 2. Washington, DC: American Physiological Society, 1960. Pp. 1553–1593.

Kimura, D. The neural basis of language qua gesture. *Studies in neurolinguistics*. New York: Academic Press, 1976. Pp. 145–156.

Liberman, A., Cooper, F., Shankweiler, D., & Studdert-Kennedy, M. Perception of the speech code. *Psychological Review*, 1967, *74*, 431–461.

Luria, A. On quasi-aphasic speech disturbance in lesions of the deep structures in the brain. *Brain and Language*, 1977, *4*, 432–359.

Mateer, C., & Kimura, D. Impairment of non-verbal oral movements in aphasia. *Brain and Language*, 1977, *4*, 262–276.

Mohr, J. Broca's area and Broca's aphasia. *Studies in Neurolinguistics*, 1976, *1*, 201–236.

Mohr, J., Watters, W., & Duncan, G. Thalamic hemorrhage and aphasia. *Brain and Language*, 1975, *2*, 3–17.

Ojemann, G. Mental arithmetic during human thalamic stimulation. *Neuropsychologia*, 1974, *12*, 1–10.

Ojemann, G. Language and the thalamus: Object naming and recall during and after thalamic stimulation. *Brain and Language*, 1975, *2*, 101–120.

Ojemann, G. Subcortical language mechanisms. *Studies in Neurolinguistics*. 1976, *1*, 103–138.

Ojemann, G. Asymmetric function of the thalamus in man. *Annals of the New York Academy of Sciences*, 1977, *299*, 380–396.

Ojemann, G. Organization of short-term verbal memory in language area of human cortex: Evidence from electrical stimulation. *Brain and Language*, 1978, 5, 331–348.

Ojemann, G. Individual variability in cortical localization of language. *Journal of Neurosurgery*, 1979, *50*, 164–169. (a)

Ojemann, G. Altering memory with human ventrolateral thalamic stimulation. In E. Hitchcock, H. Ballantine, & B. Myerson (Eds.), *Modern concepts in psychiatric surgery.* Amsterdam: Elsevier, 1979. Pp. 103–109. (b)

Ojemann, G. Brain mechanisms for language: Observations during neurosurgery. In J. Lockard & A. A. Ward, Jr. (Eds.), *Epilepsy: A window to brain mechanisms.* New York: Raven, 1980. Pp. 243–261.

Ojemann, G. Interrelationships in the localization of language, memory and motor mechanisms in human cortex and thalamus. In R. Thompson & J. Green (Eds.), *Modern perspectives on cerebral localization.* New York: Raven, 1982. Pp. 157–176.

Ojemann, G., Blick, K., & Ward, A. A., Jr. Improvement and disturbance of short-term verbal memory with human ventrolateral thalamic stimulation. *Brain,* 1971, *94*, 225–240.

Ojemann, G., & Mateer, C. Human language cortex: Localization of memory, syntax and sequential motor–phoneme identification systems. *Science,* 1979, *205*, 1401–1403. (a)

Ojemann, G., & Mateer, C. Cortical and subcortical organization of human communication: Evidence from stimulation studies. In H. Steklis & M. Raleight (Eds.), *Neurobiology of social communication in primates.* New York: Academic Press, 1979. Pp. 111–131. (b)

Ojemann, G., & Whitaker, H. Language localization and variability. *Brain and Language,* 1978, *6,* 239–260. (a)

Ojemann, G., & Whitaker, H. The bilingual brain. *Archives of Neurology,* 1978, *35,* 409–412. (b)

Penfield, W., & Jasper, H. *Epilepsy and the functional anatomy of the human brain.* Boston: Little, Brown, 1954.

Penfield, W., & Perot, P. The brain's record of auditory and visual experience—A final summary and discussion. *Brain,* 1963, 86, 595–696.

Penfield, W., & Roberts, L. *Speech and brain mechanisms.* Princeton: Princeton Unviersity Press, 1959.

Rasmussen, T., & Milner, B. The role of early left brain injury in determining lateralization of cerebral speech functions. *Annals of the New York Academy of Sciences,* 1977, *299,* 355–369.

Reynolds, A., Jr., Harris, A., Ojemann, G., & Turner, P. Aphasia and the left thalamic hemorrhage. *Journal of Neurosurgery,* 1978, *48,* 570–574.

Rubens, A., Mahowald, M., & Hutton, J. Asymmetry of the lateral (Sylvian) fissures in man. *Neurology,* 1976, *26,* 620–624.

Skinner, J., & Yingling, C. Central gating mechanisms that regulate event related potentials and behavior: A neural model for attention. *Progress in Clinical Neurophysiology,* 1977, *1,* 30–69.

Stensass, S., Eddington, D., & Dobelle, W. The topography and variability of the primary visual cortex in man. *Journal of Neurosurgery,* 1974, *40,* 747–755.

Tallal, P., & Newcombe, F. Impairment of auditory perception and language comprehension in dysphasia. *Brain and Language,* 1978, *5,* 13–24.

Van Buren, J., Lewis, D., Schutte, W., Whithouse, W., & Ajmone Marsan, C. Flurometric monitoring of NADH levels in cerebral cortex: Preliminary observations in human epilepsy. *Neurosurgery,* 1978, *2,* 114–121.

Wada, J. Prelanguage and fundamental asymmetry of the infant brain. *Annals of the New York Academy of Science,* 1977, *299,* 328–354.

Whitaker, H., & Ojemann, G. Graded localization of naming from electrical stimulation mapping of left cerebral cortex. *Nature,* 1977, *270,* (5632), 50–51. (a)

Whitaker, H., & Ojemann, G. Lateralization of higher cortical functions: A critique. *Annals of the New York Academy of Sciences,* 1977, *299,* 459–452. (b)

Witelson, S. Anatomic asymmetry in temporal lobes. *Annals of the New York Academy of Sciences,* 1977, *299,* 328–354.

Woods, F. Noninvasive blood flow studies. *Brain and Language*, 1979, *9*, 1–148.
Zaidel, E. The Split and half brain as models of congenital language disability. In C. L. Ludlow
     & M. C. Doran-Quine (Eds.), *The neurological basis of language disorders in children:
     Methods and directions for future research*. Washington D. C.: NINCDS Monograph
     No. 22. U. S. Government Printing Office, 1979. Pp. 55–86.

IV DEVELOPMENTAL DISORDERS

8 Developmental Language Disorders: Nosologic Considerations

ISABELLE RAPIN
DORIS A. ALLEN

Preschool children who fail to develop effective speech at the expected age and whose behavior is often aberrant present a serious challenge to parents, educators, speech and language pathologists, and physicians. In fact, their problem is so poorly understood, even today, that there is no general agreement on a classification of disorders presenting with these symptoms. We have no firm evidence of their cause, we cannot predict a likely outcome with assurance, and we have few hard data on the effectiveness of our intervention programs.

This chapter is a preliminary attempt by a child neurologist and a developmental psycholinguist to bring some conceptual order to the problem of children with *developmental language disability* (DLD). This attempt is clinically based and does not have the rigor of systematically collected experimental data. It also lacks the underpinnings that could have been provided if neuropsychologic tests, EEGs, and computerized transaxial tomography (CT) scans had been available for all the children. But, as pointed out by Benton (1978), clinical and experimental methods are complementary, and clinical observation is often a necessary first step to later, more focused experimental studies.

NEUROPSYCHOLOGY OF
LANGUAGE, READING, AND SPELLING

WHY A NOSOLOGY OF DLD?

Nosology is a medical term referring to the process of delineating a disease entity. When physicians are confronted with a patient they attempt: (*a*) to isolate clusters of symptoms that enable them to *diagnose*, that is recognize, a particular condition; (*b*) to discover what causes the symptoms by gaining an understanding of the anatomic, physiologic, and metabolic derangements that gave rise to them (*pathogenesis*); (*c*) to determine the cause or *etiology* of these derangements as, for example, whether they were due to an infectious agent, a tumor, an allergic reaction, or a genetic defect; and (*d*) to provide an efficacious *therapy* for the patient. Physicians' choices of therapies depend on their level of understanding of the illness. For example, many therapies are discovered empirically and have a purely symptomatic effect. Understanding of pathogenesis, but not necessarily of etiology, is almost always required in order to devise new therapies that are specific and efficacious, such as insulin for diabetes and aspirin for fever.

Nosology can be viewed as a branch of taxonomy or classification. It refers to the descriptive, data-gathering step of inquiry, in which an attempt is made to identify clusters of symptoms and signs that will provide a basis for separating one condition from another. The strategy involves grouping patients with reasonably homogeneous symptoms on the premise—not alway correct—that patients within these groups are likely to be suffering from the same "disease" and patients in different groups from different "diseases." One must keep in mind that pathogenesis refers to the cause of particular symptoms, rather than to the cause of disease entities, and that in many cases therapy is based on pathogenetic rather than etiologic considerations. There is room, therefore, for an investigation of pathogenetic mechanisms that is independent of etiologic and taxonomic considerations.

This chapter attempts to provide a framework for developing a nosology of children with DLD by grouping them into tentative syndromes on the basis of their linguistic deficits. Our ultimate goal is to understand the pathogenesis of the symptoms particular to these syndromes, both in terms of underlying brain dysfunction and in terms of underlying linguistic processes. We see nosology as a heuristic first step toward this ultimate goal.

PREVIOUS ATTEMPTS AT CLASSIFICATION

Other professionals have endeavored to develop a nosology of DLD. Clinicians have viewed the children through the optics of their particular field, for example pediatrics (Ingram, 1975), neurology (Denckla, 1974), speech pathology (Eisenson, 1972; Morley, 1972; Myklebust, 1971), and psychology (Weiner, 1969). Multidisciplinary teams have studied children with DLD (Ajuriaguerra, Jaeggi, Guignard, Kocher, Maquard, Roth, &

Schmid, 1976), and several monographs present the points of view of professionals in these disciplines, as well as those of psycholinguists who have started to take an interest in children with deviant, as well as normal, language development (Morehead & Morehead, 1976; Rutter & Martin, 1972; Wyke, 1978).

Because of lack of data, nosologic studies attempting to classify DLD children according to neurologic criteria are almost nonexistent. Plasticity in the organization of the developing brain is such that investigators have, until recently, been reluctant to make inferences about underlying brain dysfunction in children with disorders of higher cortical function. Zaidel (1979) suggests that DLD may reflect the inadequate linguistic skills of the minor hemisphere called on to sustain language because of malfunction of the dominant hemisphere, but he has no direct evidence to support this view. Speculations about the neurologic basis of autistic behavior are more numerous than those concerning DLD (Damasio & Maurer, 1978; DeLong, 1978; Lockman, Swaiman, Drage, Nelson, & Marsden, 1979). They have centered about the possibility that subcortical (limbic?) as well as cortical (left more than right?) dysfunction gives rise to this syndrome.

In attempting to classify children with DLD, some investigators group them according to whether the deficits are in auditory processing or in linguistic decoding. Others divide them into those whose predominantly receptive deficits seem to explain the expressive deficits and those with expressive deficits alone or with receptive deficits that are too mild to account for grossly deficient expression. Most workers consider articulation deficits—with or without oromotor dysfunction—as speech disorders as opposed to language disorders although misarticulations are acknowledged to be frequent in children with language disorders.

A number of investigators seem to make the tacit assumption tht DLD children who hear normally and do not show evidence of "brain damage," global retardation, or serious emotional problems belong to a fairly homogeneous population. They group these children together in the hope of defining statistically significant differences in some aspect of behavior between DLD and normal children. Clearly, this type of study is not concerned with nosology but with pathogenesis. Many studies of this type have focused on possible disorders of auditory processing (Rees, 1973). Tallal and Piercy (1978), for example, found that 12 children with "dysphasia" had difficulty perceiving brief rapidly changing acoustic stimuli. Others focused on other single deficits such as impairments of speech discrimination (McReynolds, 1966), short-term verbal memory (Bliss & Peterson, 1975; Saxman & Miller, 1973), or syntactic skills (Menyuk & Looney, 1972a, b; Morehead & Ingram, 1973). Studies that start with the hypothesis that all children with DLD—"*the* dysphasic child"—suffer from the same disorder or that concentrate on a single aspect of language are likely to generate hypotheses that are oversimplistic, considering the complexity of connected discourse (Rees, 1973). We would go even further and suggest that one needs to consider not only the language produced by the child but also the entire communicative interaction.

This statement does *not* preclude the probability that some children among those with DLD may be suffering from a single specific deficit that is the necessary and sufficient cause for their language disorder. We have proposed, for example, that a deficit in phonologic decoding, possibly due to an auditory processing disorder of the type reported by Tallal and Piercy (1978), may be responsible for verbal auditory agnosia (Frumkin & Rapin, 1980; Rapin, Mattis, Rowan, & Golden, 1977). Since the processes that underlie language are so complex and so numerous, language must be vulnerable to many different deficits. Thus we, and others, fully expect to find many different syndromes among children with DLD (Denckla, 1974; Ingram, 1975; Rapin & Wilson, 1978).

Aram and Nation (1975), for example, were able to delineate 6 different patterns of deficit among 47 children with DLD aged 3 to 7 years. The children were clustered into syndromes using factor analysis of their scores on 14 language tasks thought to tap comprehension, "formulation," and repetition at the level of phonology, syntax, and semantics. The characteristics of these patterns or syndromes can be summarized as follows:

1. Ability to repeat better than the ability to comprehend or generate language
2. Generalized expressive deficiency
3. Relatively uniform deficiency for all language tasks
4. Deficit specific for the phonologic level affecting comprehension, formulation, and repetition
5. Comparable or higher level of performance on formulation–repetition tasks than on comprehension tasks
6. Formulation–repetition deficit with adequate comprehension

Although the Aram and Nation study was limited to standardized tasks, it is interesting to note resemblances with some of the syndromes we have derived independently from our study of children's linguistic performance under naturalistic conditions.

BRAIN–BEHAVIOR RELATIONSHIPS

Localization of Brain Function

That focal motor and sensory deficits arise as a result of focal brain pathology has been appreciated for centuries. The idea that complex behaviors such as language, the ability to calculate or to appreciate spatial relations or melodies might depend on activity in localizable systems within the brain is more recent. Serious investigation of this possibility goes back to Broca's report in 1861. He noted that aphasia is almost always the result of *left* brain damage.

Current views on the localization of higher cortical functions, including language, rest on five main lines of evidence. One source of data derives from an analysis of behavioral deficits, in particular acquired aphasia and other linguistic deficits, with reference to defined focal brain lesions. Patients in whom surgical section of the corpus callosum and other interhemispheric commissures results in the virtual isolation of each of the hemispheres have provided particularly rich data for the study of brain–behavior relationships (Gazzaniga & LeDoux, 1978; Sperry, 1974; Zaidel, 1979). A second line comes from cerebral stimulation studies of patients who are to undergo neurosurgical procedures for the treatment of epilepsy (Ojemann & Mateer, 1979; Penfield & Roberts, 1959). Coupled with these are the results of anesthetizing one hemisphere with short-acting barbiturates (Wada test) (Wada & Rasmussen, 1960). Third, gross anatomic differences between the two hemispheres, by autopsy or CT scan (Galaburda, LeMay, Kemper, & Geschwind, 1978), and microscopic inhomogeneity in the structure of the cortex within brain regions have been examined (Brodmann, 1909).

More recent physiologic techniques permit the investigation of brain function in normal persons while they are performing complex tasks. Some of these in current use include (*a*) behavioral methods such as reaction time coupled with dichotic auditory stimulation or tachistoscopic presentation of linguistic and nonlinguistic stimuli to half of the visual field (Dimond & Beaumont, 1974); (*b*) new computer techniques for processing of EEG and sensory-evoked responses during the performance of complex linguistic and nonlinguistic tasks (Duffy, Burchfiel, & Lombroso, 1979); (*c*) computerized tomography (CT) scans after the administration of stable isotopes (Phelps, Huang, Hoffman, Selin, Sokoloff, & Kuhl, 1979); and (*d*) cerebral blood-flow studies with isotopes to determine local metabolic rates (Lassen, Ingvar, & Skinhøj, 1978). Finally, information has been drawn from classical animal experiments, in which the behavioral effects of focal ablation, focal stimulation, and pharmacologic manipulation are analyzed. Unfortunately animal experiments have very limited value for the investigation of linguistic function.

Most of what we know concerning lateralization of linguistic function and localization of particular linguistic skills in the dominant hemisphere is based on careful study of adult patients with acquired focal brain lesions. Although lesion studies have been criticized because they tell us more about the altered function of remaining brain tissue than about the normal function of ablated tissue, cerebral blood-flow studies in normal persons have provided stunning confirmation of inferences about localization made on the basis of studies in aphasic patients. They have for the first time illuminated the function of areas in the mesial aspect of the frontal lobe that had been shown by electrical stimulation to affect speech (Penfield & Roberts, 1959). It now seems that they are concerned with programming of motor sequences, including speech. They are selectively activated during "internal speech," such as counting silently, when areas concerned with reception (*Wernicke's area*) and expression of speech (*Broca's area*) show no increased blood flow (Lassen *et al.*, 1978).

Plasticity in Cerebral Organization

Many investigators have been discouraged from making inferences about localization of pathology in children with language disorders by their awareness that some brain lesions incurred in early life result in less devastating deficits or in better recovery than the same lesions incurred in adult life. It was felt that *plasticity*, or the degrees of freedom in brain organization, was so great in children as to preclude the making of valid inferences about localization of dysfunction from an analysis of their symptoms. Recent studies indicate that plasticity is relative and that recovery of function is the end result of a variety of different, possibly synergistic, mechanisms (Finger, 1978; Goldberger, 1974).

Among the most frequently cited evidence for plasticity of brain function in early life is the lack of aphasia in children with hemiplegia incurred before one year, whether it reflects right or left brain pathology (Annett, 1973). Evidence from carotid amytal tests and from ablation studies in patients with lateralized brain lesions and epilepsy clearly shows that language depends on activity of the right hemisphere when the pathology involves the main peri-Sylvian langue area on the left (Milner, 1974). Indeed, hemispherectomy does not produce aphasia in such patients, indicating unambiguously that language can be contralaterally mediated (Basser, 1962). Early papers reported that in very young children aphasia was seen more often after right-sided lesions than in older children and adults, but more recent work (Woods & Teuber, 1978) explains away this finding by pointing out that many of the children described in preantibiotic days probably had sustained bilateral rather than strictly unilateral pathology. Functional linguistic recovery may be good in children with acquired aphasia but careful testing reveals persistent verbal deficits (Alajouanine & Lhermitte, 1965; Woods & Carey, 1979). If the lesion involves an entire hemisphere, deficits may be apparent even if the lesion is sustained before age one year: Children with normal intelligence with *only* a right hemisphere have poor word analysis and spelling skills compared to children with only a left hemisphere who in turn are inferior for visual spatial tasks (Dennis & Whitaker, 1976).

Having stressed recovery of speech and the preservation of many verbal skills in children with acquired unilateral brain lesions, one is led to inquire whether DLD necessarily implies bilateral damage. The answer to this question is not known. There are situations where a unilateral brain lesion may alter the function of the contralateral normal side. This situation is well recognized in patients with seizures in whom removal of epileptogenic cortex may produce a rise in IQ and overall functional improvement (Krynauw, 1950; Penfield & Jasper, 1954).

Cerebral Dysfunction in Children

Overt DLD and pathologically delayed language acquisition are assumed always to reflect cerebral dysfunction except in some cases of extreme social deprivation, when a peripheral hearing loss impedes language learning, or when muscle weakness precludes verbal expression without interfering with linguistic reception and inner language (Lenneberg, 1962). We will not discuss these disorders or those, such as elective mutism, which are assumed to reflect severe emotional stress (Rutter & Martin, 1972). We acknowledge that if the richness of the environment has important implications for linguistic development in normal children (Walsh & Greenough, 1976), it is probably even more critical for language-impaired children.

It is important to point out that cerebral dysfunction may be present and may not be detectable by neurologic examination and with such tests as a CT scan or EEG. The language deficit itself (and other deficits in higher cortical function that will almost always be detected by careful neuropsychologic testing) may be the sole sign of the brain dysfunction. We stress this point because many investigators divide children with, for example, learning disabilities into (a) those who have *organic brain damage* ("hard" motor signs, hydrocephalus, seizures, or EEG abnormalities); (b) those with *minimal brain dysfunction* (MBD) ("soft" signs of motor deficit); and (c) those with a *learning diability* "without neurologic evidence of brain dysfunction." Further confusion arises because the probably largely subcortical *attention deficit disorder* (ADD) with or without hyperkinesis is often confused with MBD since ADD and MBD often, but not necessarily, coexist in a given child. It seems clear to us that these distinctions have more to do with the severity and location of cerebral dysfunction than with its presence or absence.

One of the tacit assumptions of those who make such distinctions concerns etiology: Learning disability without other evidence of neurologic dysfunction is assumed to reflect a developmental lag (Kinsbourne, 1973) or genetically determined inefficiency in brain organization (Witelson, 1977) as contrasted with learning disability with overt brain damage, whereas MBD is an ambiguous "diagnosis," with some children suffering from organic dysfunction and others from a "developmental lag," We question this assumption and, furthermore, we wish to stress again that etiology and pathogenesis are questions of a different order that frequently have no bearing on one another: There are many severe aberrations of brain development and equally many mild acquired brain lesions.

Many writers speak of children with "pure" language disorders, that is, children who have no other intellectual, neurologic, or perceptual deficit. Our own experience is clearly biased by the fact that children referred to a neurologist for consultation are those with more severe linguistic deficits or with other evidence for brain dysfunction. In any case we find that most, if not all, of the children with DLD whom we see have other symptoms of brain dysfunction in addition to their language deficit. There is an important point to be made in this context. We need to make a clear distinction between (a) signs of organic dysfunction that bear witness to the underlying pathology but have no direct bearing on the language disability (concomitant signs): toe walking, seizures, or a visual field deficit; (b) signs of organic dysfunction that may explain some of the linguistic symptoms (pathogenetic signs): a deficit in short-term sequential auditory–verbal memory; and (c) signs of organic dysfunction that interact with but are not sufficient to account for the language disability (associated signs): dysarthria. All signs of organic brain dysfunction provide useful data for judging the location and severity of underlying pathology, but only pathogenetic signs have an explanatory value, provided we are smart enough to understand their relevance to the linguistic disability.

We wish to make a final comment concerning cognitive competence. Again and again investigators of children with DLD make the point that in order to have a "pure language disorder" the child must have normal or near normal intelligence, usually expressed as an IQ figure above a given level. The IQ is the summary score derived from performance on a psychological test battery that samples a broad range of behaviors. It enables one to compare a particular child to the norms established by testing a population of presumably normal children of the same age. The IQ is useful for making distinctions among normal children and for predicting academic performance. It is much less meaningful when tests are administered to handicapped children whose performance across tests is uneven: A summary score represents neither their areas of real deficit nor their strengths.

Typically, language-disordered children will do better on nonverbal tests of intelligence than on verbal tests, although performance on certain nonverbal subtests, for which a verbal strategy facilitates solution, may also be lowered (Wilson, Rapin, Wilson, & Van Denburg, 1975). An investigator may choose to study a particular subsample of children with "pure language disorders" because their deficits will be understood more readily. In our experience, the majority of children seen by clinicians do not have such "pure" syndromes. Yet, since their linguistic skills are much more severely deficient than their other cognitive skills and are out of proportion to their IQ, these children still must be considered as suffering from DLD. If one can tease out the linguistic symptoms from other "concomitant" or "associated" signs of brain dysfunction, such children may be found to be suffering from syndromes of DLD similar to those found in children with "pure" syndromes who happen to have less blatant brain dysfunctions (Ludlow, 1980).

Effects of Brain Lesions on Language

Language is a highly complex and dynamic operation that is susceptible to dysfunction at many points. It proceeds from the stimulation of the ear to a preliminary acoustic analysis of the speech signal in the various relays of the central auditory pathway. The stream of acoustic stimuli is segmented into phonemes and morphemes by complex decoding operations (Liberman, Cooper, Shankweiler, & Studdert-Kennedy, 1967). These perceptual linguistic operations and many others depend in part on availability of an acoustic short-term (working) memory store and on ready access to linguistic forms and rules in long-term storage. Further decoding operations are based on an analysis of the string of morphemes into meaningful utterances by the operation of syntactic rules and transformations and by retrieving from long-term memory semantic referents that can be attached to incoming linguistic forms.

Linguistic processing also depends on attention, a process that dictates which of many competing signals are evaluated for their significance or value at the moment, giving them a weight in the light of other ongoing processes that are also being sampled, in order to arrive at a decision as to the output (if any) they demand. Processing operations obviously vary a great deal in complexity and in the cognitive demands they place on a person. If a verbal response is decided on, it requires linguistic encoding operations (word selection, syntactic and phonologic encoding), the programming of appropriate movements by the oral–facial–respiratory muscles, and their parallel and sequential execution in order to realize the planned speech output.

Receptive problems alter speech output and result in both expressive and receptive deficiency. In contrast, a purely motor deficit affecting the muscles of articulation and phonation (*dysarthria*) may preclude speech or produce severely deficient speech articulation, but it will not interfere with language acquisition, comprehension, or receptive processing (Lenneberg, 1962). Dysarthria has to be clearly distinguished from a phonologic (linguistic) output deficit even though the two are often associated (see the following).

Phonologic encoding deficits may be "pure" although they are often associated with syntactic and word finding deficits.

Analysis of adult aphasic patients' performance on tests of reception, decoding, repetition, word findings, and speech programming has made it possible to find fairly consistent relationships between particular aphasic syndromes and particular sites of pathology (Geschwind, 1974). The definition of aphasic syndromes has been enhanced by the efforts of psycholinguists who have provided sophisticated analyses of particular patients' deficits (Goodglass & Blumstein, 1973). The fact that correlations between particular deficits and the location of underlying lesions are less than perfect is to be expected when one considers that there must be profound individual differences in the detail of brain organization among individuals. This was illustrated in a particularly striking way by the evidence that, in two bilingual patients, each of their two languages engaged the activity of somewhat different brain regions (Ojemann & Whitaker, 1978).

In general terms, the relationship between types of aphasia and location of lesions in adults is quite well known. Bilateral pathology in the superior temporal gyrus produces the syndromes of word deafness or *verbal auditory agnosia* (VAA) by interfering with the phonologic decoding of speech; dominant posterior-temporal lesions are responsible for a receptive deficit for the semantic content of language (Wernicke's aphasia); dominant prefrontal lesions interfere with the syntactic and phonologic encoding of linguistic expression (Broca's aphasia); subcortical pathology in the dominant hemisphere that interrupts the fibers connecting posterior from anterior language areas (*arcuate fasciculus*) is likely to result in a *conductin aphasia* by precluding repetition. *Word finding* is a symptom that occurs frequently with lesions in the region of the angular gyrus but is also encountered with pathology in other locations in the dominant hemisphere. The ability to repeat in the face of impaired comprehension and an inability to initiate communication suggests a lesion outside of the main peri-Sylvian language areas of the dominant hemisphere, so-called "isolation of the language area," and in some cases may result from pathology in the medial language areas (Ross, 1980). Patients with a severe aphasia may, with partial recovery, show the characteristics of a less severe syndrome. For example, global aphasia with partial recovery may take on the characteristics of Broca's aphasia, Wernicke's aphasia, or those of conduction aphasia.

The mechanisms that underlie recovery or partial recovery of language in adult aphasics are not known in detail. Some of those that may also apply to brain dysfunction in children include remodeling in remaining tissue and substitution of new behavioral strategies (Laurence & Stein, 1978). It has been shown, for example, that in very severe adult aphasia, the nondominant hemisphere is responsible for whatever little speech output remains (Kinsbourne, 1971). In normal persons the processing of *prosody*, the melody of speech, seems to depend on activity in the nondominant hemisphere (Ross & Mesulam, 1979). The degree to which language is lateralized to the left hemisphere varies. It is less strictly lateralized in many left handed or ambidextrous persons than in the right handed. The right hemisphere is capable of fairly sophisticated phonologic and semantic decoding but is deficient in syntactic and phonetic analysis skills (Zaidel, 1979). Under normal circumstances it appears to play little if any role in verbal expression, with the possible exception of singing.

We review these well-known facts here in order to provide a background for the DLD syndromes we have come to recognize in children. We are not suggesting that syndromes of DLD precisely parallel the syndromes of acquired aphasia in adults. Nevertheless, since it would not be parsimonious to think that the organization of children's brain is fundamentally different from the organization of adult brain, it is likely that similar symptoms reflect pathology in the same general systems in both children and adults. This has been demonstrated most clearly for the syndrome of verbal auditory agnosia (VAA), which is responsible for one syndrome of DLD when it occurs early enough in childhood.

DEVELOPMENTAL LANGUAGE DISORDERS: SYNDROMES

Sources of Data for the DLD Syndromes

Our attempt to delineate syndromes among children with DLD is based on data from four different sources: The clinical notes dictated at the time of consultation from the charts of approximately 100 children referred for a pediatric neurologic consultation with the chief complaint of delayed or deviant speech were reviewed. Salient data concerning the past medical history, findings on neurologic examination, neurologic test results (EEG and CT scans, when available), and descriptive statements about the child's speech, oromotor function, comprehension of language, and behavior while in the office were tabulated.

Videotape recordings obtained from approximately 20 preschool children from this sample studied longitudinally over a 1–3-year period were examined. The parents or mother were asked to play with the child in a playroom with a one-way mirror through which they were filmed. Some items from the McCarthy Scale of Children's Abilities (1972), Carrow's Test for Auditory Comprehension of Language (1973), and Menyuk's Sentences Repetition Test (1969) were administered to children who were able to cooperate. Detailed linguistic analysis of these tapes has not yet been possible, but a preliminary analysis for general features that were predictors and non-predictors of outcome has been carried out (Allen & Rapin, 1980).

A third source of information was drawn from a formal analysis of the language of 20 school-age children with severe DLD in whom a detailed neurologic and neuropsychologic investigation had been carried out. The language corpus consisted of the utterances of these children while they looked at black and white copies of pictures from the Peabody Language Development Kit (1968). Analyses of phonology, syntax, and semantics were performed.

Finally, we conducted longitudinal studies of 15 children enrolled in a therapeutic nursery for children aged 3 to 5 years who presented us with a variety of developmental disturbances, including autism. Videotape recordings of these children and their mothers were obtained twice a year for 2 years.

The richest data were derived from these longitudinal studies because we were able to obtain good naturalistic communicative interactions with parents in these videotaped sessions. In reviewing these tapes, we attended to the following linguistic parameters in the children's spontaneous productions: phonologic encoding, prosody, morphology, syntax, semantic categories, and pragmatic (communicative) use of language. Because of the nature of our data, only the expressive language could really be documented. It was not possible to test formally all subjects' capabilities for repeating words and sentences. Receptive language could only be inferred by such nonverbal behaviors as gestures, compliance with commands, verbal responses to questions, and appropriate comments in relation to the parents' utterances.

Even though we have relied heavily on the longitudinal data to identify the syndromes of DLD, we found the cross-sectional data valuable for verifying the existence of syndromes in children of different ages and in various stages of language development. In this context, we want to stress that we do *not* view the syndromes that we have isolated as being static and definitive. The symptoms of children with DLD often change over time. As a particular child's linguistic skills develop, it is often necessary to reclassify him as manifesting a different syndrome from the one originally assigned. Further longitudinal study will be required to enable us to comment on the stability of the syndromes we have isolated at this point.

The syndromes of DLD that we have identified are not intended to be exhaustive. The main purpose for delineating the syndromes is to illustrate that so-called developmental dysphasia or developmental language disability (DLD) cannot be considered to be a single diagnosis. Rather, a number of distinct (and overlapping) syndromes can be characterized by the single generic term, DLD. Although it is hypothetically possible that one might find all possible combinations of all possible deficits in phonology, syntax, semantics, and pragmatic use of language within a population of language disordered children, we opted not to begin with preconceived categories or associated symptoms. Similarly, we did not refer initially to presumed underlying neurologic or neuropsychologic dysfunction. Instead, we chose to group the children according to the most salient characteristics of their expressive language, interactive behavior, and apparent comprehension. We then defined the syndromes by determining which language features were impaired, intact, or variable within each of these more or less homogeneous subgroups of our population.

Phonologic–Syntactic Syndrome

Among language disordered children, the *phonologic–syntactic* syndrome is undoubtedly the most prevalent (Ingram, 1975; Morley, 1972). The principal impairments are in the phonological and morphology–syntax systems. Omissions, substitutions, and distortions of consonants and consonant clusters occur initially, medially, and/or finally. These disturbances of the phonologic system represent more than the simple developmental misarticulations heard in the speech of very young children (such as /f/ for /th/ or /w/ for /l/. Instead, the sounds produced are often much less predictable or are unrecognizable phones. These children may be difficult or impossible to understand. The most common disturbances in morphology and syntax include severely limited use of function words and inflections of nouns and verbs, as well as severe limitations in the number of syntactic relations expressed within a single utterance. Again, the problem is much different from that of the normally developing child in the early stages of language acquisition. For example, in normal children, we regularly hear such utterances as "baby cry," "baby crying," or "a baby crying," but not "the baby is cry," which we often find in children with this syndrome.

In those children who are not totally unintelligible, we often find that semantic categories are relatively intact. All of the other aspects of language and symbolic functioning are variable. That is, some children have adequate pragmatic functions and prosody, using their voices to indicate questions, commands, and comments, whereas others may be impaired in these functions. In most of the children, the use of gestures to make their wants known and the ability to comprehend words and short phrases or sentences are clearly ahead of expressive abilities. In some children the ability to imitate words and short sentences is vastly superior to their spontaneous production, whereas in other children aberrant phonology and syntax are reflected in sentence imitation tasks. Likewise, the cognitive skills of the children are quite variable, although performance of nonverbal tasks is uniformly better than that of verbal tasks.

Many of the children classified in this syndrome have other signs of neurologic dysfunction. The most prevalent is *oromotor* dysfunction. Mothers of some children report that their child used to have trouble sucking, chewing, and swallowing. Many still drooled or had excessively wet mouths at the time of examination, and in a few, signs of spasticity or pseudobulbar palsy included a hyperactive jaw jerk (Worster-Drought, 1974). Some but not all of the children had an oromotor apraxia and had difficulty imitating movements of the tongue (e.g., lateral displacement, elevation), jaw (e.g., lateral displacement), or lips (e.g., pursing) (Kools, Williams, Vickers, & Caell, 1971). They were unable to click their tongues and had a slow and irregular diadocokinetic rate in syllable repetition. The motor deficit influenced their ability to articulate individual consonants and consonant clusters. Although children with oromotor dysfunction tended to have worse phonologic deficits than those without, dysarthria could not account for such symptoms as substitution and inversion, let alone syntactic deficiency—even if it could be invoked to explain omissions and distortions. The fact that some of these children's phonologic skills were much better in repetition than in spontaneous production also bespeaks a deficit with phonologic programming rather than motor production. The fact that children in whom oromotor function is essentially normal have the same problems with other aspects of language as children with dysarthria suggests that they all belong to a single syndrome with wide *speech* variability within the group.

In some children, there were other neurologic signs that suggested rather widespread or bilateral cerebral dysfunction. These included motor findings such as mild spasticity in the limbs or delayed achievement of such motor milestones as sitting or independent walking. Impairment of nonverbal cognitive tasks such as building with blocks or drawing, or the occurrence of seizures were other concomitant signs of brain damage or dysfunction. Significantly, no child had severe enough focal pathology to produce a frank lateralized neurologic syndrome.

The frequency with which oromotor dysfunction occurs in children with the phonologic–syntactic syndrome supports the notion that it may reflect prefrontal pathology that, when extensive, encroaches on the motor cortex. We have no data to document this supposition nor can we venture a guess as to whether unilateral or bilateral pathology must be present to account for the occurrence of this syndrome. When repetition is superior to spontaneous production one may infer that temporal–parietal areas and their connections to prefrontal language areas are spared. Perhaps pathology in some of the subcortical connections or prefrontal cortex account for the discrepancy between production and repetition. The possibility that, in such children, a deficit in the mesial frontal language area may have occurred has not been explored. One can expect that damage to the parasagittal area may be associated with a mild spastic diparesis, manifested by toe walking, hyper-active reflexes in the legs, or difficulty with tasks such as hopping on one foot. This area is a watershed area between the circulation of the anterior middle and posterior cerebral arteries and is susceptible to damage in infants with perinatal hypoxic–ischemic injury to the brain (Volpe, 1979). When compre-hension and expression are both defective, one may suspect that temporal or temporo–parietal areas as well as frontal areas are involved. One would need to study phonemic discrimination in these children to determine whether it is in part responsible for defective production. Finally, the co-occurrence of phonologic and syntactic deficits needs to be stressed since this combination is also characteristic of adults with an acquired expressive aphasia. It should tell us something about the neurologic substrate for these linguistic opera-tions.

Severe Expressive Syndrome with Good Comprehension

The group of children with *severe expressive syndrome* are completely mute or virtually unintelligible. At best, their productions are limited to poorly articulated two-word utterances. Ferry, Hall, and Hicks (1975), borrowing a label from Critchley, called them children with "dilapidated speech." What is striking about these children is that their comprehension of language is surprisingly good. Likewise, in the absence of the ability to speak, they often invent a rich gesture language through which they can make known a wide variety of meanings. Given a more formal sign language, these children are clearly able to demonstrate their grasp of semantic relations and pragmatic uses of language, provided their cognitive skills are adequate. It is too often the case, however, that the children are not exposed to connected manual discourse, and teaching them individual signs is not sufficient to enable them to express themselves fluently. It is not at all unusual for these children to have the ability to repeat words or phrases that they are incapable of producing spontaneously, providing that their oromotor functioning is adequate. In this group, as in those described in the phonologic–syntactic syndrome, the extent of oromotor dysfunction is judged insufficient to account for the extent of expressive language disability.

The neurologic basis of this syndrome is not clear. Although it is possible that it represents but a more severe form of the phonologic–syntactic syndrome, this explanation is not entirely convincing since comprehension seems to be better than in children with severe variants of that syndrome who tend to be rather globally affected. One might remember in this context the syndrome of *aphemia* seen in some adults who are speechless or reduced to single stereotyped utterances without having a global aphasia (Geschwind,

1964). Characteristically, adults with aphemia can express themselves in writing much better than those with a Broca's aphasia whose writing faithfully reflects their oral production. The anatomic basis of aphemia is controversial as is its pathogenesis. Some argue that aphemic patients are not "aphasic" but that they have an isolated apraxia for speech: that is, that they cannot translate word images into speech. In order to show that children with the severe expressive syndrome with good comprehension resemble adult aphemic patients, it would be necessary to show that they can express themselves in fluent sign language (or learn to write).

Verbal Auditory Agnosia (VAA)

The *verbal auditory agnosia* syndrome produces as devastating a deficit in linguistic processing as deafness since it interferes with the first step in input processing, phonetic decoding, when speech is presented to the acoustic channel (Frumkin & Rapin, 1980). This block precludes all subsequent operations so that the child has no comprehension of speech and is mute or speaks a very few poorly articulated words. Such children can be readily distinguished from mute autistic children because they lack such symptoms as eye avoidance, resistance to change, and repetitive behavior. We must concede, however, that children with verbal auditory agnosia often develop severe secondary behavioral aberrations so that first impressions may be misleading. Most critically, children with VAA differ from autistic children by their ability to interpret gestures, facial expression, and tone of voice. They can and do communicate by using ad hoc gestures that may amount to an idiosyncratic sign language. Some make sophisticated drawings that they are anxious to show. Children with VAA with a high performance IQ tend not to be as obsessed with puzzles or reading as bright autistic children, possibly because their behavioral repertoire is much less restricted.

The bilateral temporal lobe pathology that is the usual basis for this syndrome evidently spares posterior temporo-parietal and frontal regions: The children can process language provided it is presented to the eye and they are capable of producing a manual linguistic output. In adults, word deafness spares reading and writing, in striking contrast to Wernicke's aphasia where comprehension of language is impaired, whether it is presented orally or by reading, and writing is precluded. Localization of dysfunction to both temporal lobes, or less often to a subcortical lesion interrupting auditory input to Wernicke's area, has been well documented in adults with strokes and in the children in whom bitemporal EEG discharges provide a signature for this syndrome (Goldstein, 1974; Rapin *et al.*, 1977). In the famous child with DLD described by Landau, Goldstein, and Kleffner (1960) both superior temporal gyri had undergone cystic degeneration. In a case from Denmark in whom the syndrome developed at 4.5 years, biopsy of the left temporal lobe revealed a chronic, presumably viral, encephalitic process that ultimately improved although verbal comprehension did not (Lou, Brandt, & Bruhn, 1977).

A number of children with VAA have histories of regression of verbal skills after reportedly normal early milestones, although in some children the problem appears to have been congenital or in any case to have developed before the start of expressive language. In this respect, histories of children with VAA are very similar to those obtained from the mothers of some autistic children who say that their child had a sizable vocabulary before the autistic process became evident. In some children with VAA the cause of the syndrome may be self-limited process since the EEG often returns to normal. The language deficit also tends to improve somewhat but the illness usually is very chronic and symptoms may persist for years. In fact it is not clear whether the improvement in language, which is rarely complete, reflects improvement in the underlying pathology or results from remedial education and increasing maturity.

Clinicians need to be acutely aware of the existence of this syndrome since it mandates a very specific intervention, supplementation of the acoustic channel by the visual channel, that is *total communication*. With this approach the children may acquire some linguistic skills, which greatly reduces their frustration. With time and training many learn to produce and understand some speech, although they may continue to require signs for clarification. Signs help them to learn to discriminate between morphemes acoustically. The children's phonology usually remains very poor and their syntax primitive, and some never achieve even marginal competence in the conversational uses of speech. Their reading and spelling reflect their limited oral skills but, like deaf children, they may do better with arithmetic. One wonders whether an earlier and more vigorous attempt to use visual language with these children would not provide them with better linguistic skills, at least for written language.

Mute Autistic Syndrome

The group of children who suffer the most profound, and usually irreversible, syndrome of DLD are the *mute autistic* children. Children suffering from this syndrome are impaired in virtually every feature of oral language and of symbolic functioning in general. These are the children who fail to participate in the most rudimentary forms of communication: making eye contact, smiling responsively, crying out in pain, and playing with toys in a meaningful way. They can be distinguished from the children who suffer from verbal auditory agnosia in that they fail to make use of gestures to

communicate or relate in other nonverbal ways. Even after intensive therapeutic intervention, which can often engender eye contact and some minimal
social skills, the prognosis for acquiring oral language remains poor for those
children who remain mute and gestureless beyond age 4.

Comprehension of language is somewhat more variable than production,
as is the level of cognitive competence. Evidence that the visual system is
much more functional than the auditory–vocal modality can be found in the
superior visual-spatial abilities of some of these children. Mute autistic
children with high levels of nonverbal intelligence sometimes learn to read
and write without formal instruction, occasionally at a very young age. Their
ability to comprehend what they read is variable but rarely normal (*hyperlexia*). Such children often become preoccupied with activities such as
reading, spelling, or doing puzzles. The high expectations resulting from such
unusual skills will not be realized if the child does not achieve some ability to
communicate, although children with such "splinter skills" tend to do better
than their more globally affected peers. Attempts to teach such children to
communicate with the use of sign language has met with variable success
(Schaeffer, 1978). DeMyer, Barton, DeMyer, Norton, Allen, and Steele
(1973) and Rutter (1979) point out that what may distinguish mute autistic
children from those who do develop language is their level of intelligence.
This is of course presumed to reflect the severity or the extent of neurologic
dysfunction.

The neurologic basis of autism is unknown. It seems plausible that autistic
behavior occurs when the function of certain critical neural systems is
impaired, whatever the etiology of the impairment. There has been much
speculation that limbic involvement can explain the lack of drive to communicate, the impaired experience of pleasure and pain, and, in some children,
the inability to learn (Damasio & Maurer, 1978; DeLong, 1979). Left
cortical pathology could explain the communication disorder. In children
with superior visual–spatial skills, right cortical function appears to be
spared. This view has received some support from a radiologic study in 17
nonverbal autistic children who were found to have left temporal lobe
atrophy affecting mesial (limbic) areas most severely (Hauser, DeLong, &
Rosman, 1975). More recent CT studies have not confirmed these findings
but have suggested that normal asymmetries between the hemispheres may
be lacking in autistic children (Hier, LeMay, & Rosenberger, 1979).
Abnormalities in biogenic amines that might reflect limbic system dysfunction have been reported but are not yet consistent enough to be
considered reliable (see Lockman *et al.*, 1979). Autistic behavior is much
more frequent in children with tuberous sclerosis, phenylketonuria, hypsa-
rythmia, and congenital rubella than in other children (Chess, Korn, &
Fernandez, 1971; Lockman *et al.*, 1979). There is no longer any doubt that

this syndrome results from an organic brain dysfunction affecting cognition, affect, and linguistic skills to varying degrees, especially since 10–20% of these children develop epileptic seizures as adults and a sizable number have paroxysmal EEG abnormalities even when they do not have seizures.

Autistic Syndrome with Echolalia

Autistic children with echolalia present quite a different picture from that of the mute autistic syndrome. These children are not totally nonverbal, even though their spontaneous production is limited. The great majority of their utterances consist of immediate echoing of the speech that they have just heard or of "canned" speech from something heard in the past. The delayed *echolalia* often consists of fairly long sequences of what appear to be syntactically well-formed utterances. Whole television commercials, nursery rhymes, songs, and pieces of overhead conversations can be observed. These productions can be very deceptive if the listener is unaware of their source since the echolalic child frequently utters them in appropriate contexts. The echoic children are more likely than the mute children to acquire the ability to speak spontaneously (Baltaxe & Simmons, 1977). Nevertheless, in their spontaneous productions, these children are impaired in virtually every aspect of expressive language.

Phonology is quite variable among verbal autistic children but is more likely than not to be defective. Their prosody is often so faulty as to result in a wooden, nonmusical, robot-like speech. Morphology is variable. Characteristically, these children do not understand the rules governing the use of "I" and "you" or refer to themselves in the third person (Baltaxe & Simmons, 1977; Bartak & Rutter, 1974; Pierce & Bartolucci, 1977; Swisher, 1979). Word retrieval is variable: The ability to label visually presented stimuli is often much superior to the production of words without visual referent. Even after they become verbal, autistic children frequently remain verbally aloof, failing to initiate conversation and being limited in their participation in extended discourse (Baltaxe, 1977). Comprehension of discourse is questionable in many children. Nonverbal intelligence is also variable. Those with higher intelligence frequently achieve at least minimal literacy skills, and some become *hyperlexic*, reading the most complex text fluently with minimal or no comprehension. Echolalia and hyperlexia both suggest deficient semantic processing of connected discourse.

One 11-year-old boy in our study had a classical history of autism with echolalia. He did not acquire spontaneous language capabilities until age 7, and remained barely intelligible. By age 11, he described a picture of a boy sharpening a pencil as follows: "This is a boy sharpen a pencil because the point of it broke and he want to sharpen it so he could write it on a piece of paper in his notebook." Although the syntax and semantics of this utterance are quite good, the morphology is faulty, his pronunciation was defective, and his prosody bizarre. It does represent, however, a considerable advance over his echolalic behavior 4 years earlier.

One reason for distinguishing this syndrome from the severe autistic syndrome is practical: Echolalic autistic children have a better prognosis and are generally brighter than mute autistic children (DeMyer et al., 1973). We suppose that they suffer from dysfunction in similar brain systems but that the dysfunction is either less severe or less extensive. The main peri-Sylvian language area of their dominant hemisphere must be spared to considerable degree since the children are verbal. Futhermore, echolalia presupposes an excellent short-term verbal memory and intact pathways between areas concerned with phonologic reception and production. Hyperlexia denotes intact visual perception and access of visual percepts processed in occipital and inferotemporal cortex to the main language areas. Impaired prosody and impaired ability to interpret facial expression and tone of voice would appear to imply nondominant dysfunction (Blumstein & Cooper, 1974; Ross & Mesulam, 1979; Schwartz, Davidson, & Maer, 1975), whereas the characteristically preserved musical abilities of some of these same children probably indicates intact function of other systems on the right (Damasio & Damasio, 1977).

Perseveration and attentional deficits of autistic children and abnormal reactions to sensory stimuli in several modalities have been attributed to frontal dysfunction; impaired drive and appetitive behavior to limbic pathology (Damasio & Maurer, 1978). Thus an analysis of the strengths and deficits of these children leads one to suspect multifocal brain dysfunction rather than impairment of a single system, even one with widespread projections.

Semantic–Pragmatic Syndrome without Autism

The *semantic–pragmatic* syndrome *without* autism is one in which the children have very fluent expressive language. In general, the utterances they produce are syntactically well-formed, phonologically intact, and, on the surface, "good language." On closer examination, however, one discovers that the language is often not really communicative. That is, there is a severe impairment in the ability to encode meaning relevant to the conversational situation, and a striking inability to engage in communicative discourse. Comprehension of the connected discourse of the conversational partner also appears to be impaired, although short phrases and individual words are comprehended. Questions are frequently answered with seemingly irrelevant responses. For example, the question "where do you go to school?" was answered by one of our children with "Tommy goes to my school because I see him in the hall everyday, but we have different teachers, and I like arithmetic but Tommy likes reading." These kinds of intrusions frequently give the appearance of "psychotic language," and it is difficult to determine whether this is a true "thought disorder" in addition to representing a communication disorder.

Frequently, young children suffering from this syndrome are echolalic. Like echolalic autistic children, they show pronominal confusions, tending to speak of themselves in the third person, as in "Leave him alone" rather than "Leave me alone." Syntax is likely to be impaired below the surface level through inversions of such categories as subject and object, or verb and locative phrase. In sentences in which these inversions occur, there is also likely to be a disruption of the sentence prosody.

We have seen this syndrome in a number of children who do not have other evidence for brain dysfunction, but it is observed most frequently in children with hydrocephalus (Dennis, 1977; Swisher & Pinsker, 1971). Some of these children will use "canned" sentences without real semantic content to maintain an interpersonal interaction. This behavior has been aptly labeled "cocktail party" conversation. In children with hydrocephalus, the site of major pathology is in the subcortical white matter. As in echolalic autistic children it is assumed that the main peri-Sylvian cortical language areas and their connections are probably spared since repetition, phonology, and syntax are intact. It is higher order processing that is impaired.

In children with hydrocephalus the syndrome may be associated with general cognitive impairment. The low IQ scores of such children often come as a surprise because their skills for repetition, their good vocabulary, and their appropriate social interactions mask their inability to deal with abstract concepts. Nonretarded children with this syndrome may become hyperlexic as well as hyperverbal, in this respect again resembling autistic echolalic children. A bright and insightful 15-year-old boy reported that he got all As in social studies despite his total lack of understanding of the subject because he could learn the book by heart. Incidentally, although he read fluently, he had been dyslexic until age 10 and his spelling was still grossly deficient.

Bright children with this syndrome are misleading: Tommy's brother, quoted previously, was diagnosed as mentally retarded when tested at age 4 with the Stanford Binet, which is heavily weighted with language items at that age. Retested with the WISC, he obtained a VIQ of 66 and PIQ of 122. Despite his superior nonverbal skills he had terrible difficulty in school and did not become a good reader, unlike his brother who was similarly though somewhat less severely affected and who was hyperlexic. Because of apparently excellent expression, lack of comprehension is rarely recognized. The teacher of this child told us "he just won't listen to me when I explain things to him!'' He got into trouble with his peers because of his inability to enter into their games. He developed severe behavior problems. Again and again those who did not understand the neurological basis of his problem viewed him as psychotic. Indeed, such children's speech often resembles that of children with childhood schizophrenia. How much of their behavioral aberration is primary and how much secondary is far from clear at this point.

One might speculate that the hemispheric pathology in children suffering from the semantic–pragmatic syndrome resembles that of echolalic autistic children without the subcortical (limbic?) pathology responsible for autistic behavior. In hydrocephalic children with this syndrome, the damage may affect intrahemispheric association pathways since in hydrocephalus damage usually involves the white matter rather than the cortex.

We have encountered this syndrome in two brothers, which suggests a genetic etiology in their case. They had presented in very early childhood with what we thought, perhaps mistakenly, was verbal auditory agnosia (Rapin *et al.*, 1977) since they made much better progress than other children with this syndrome. Therefore, we have no reason to think that the syndrome necessarily denotes brain damage. It seems more likely that it denotes dysfunction in particular systems, whatever the etiology of the dysfunction. We stress this point since we believe that this is generally true of DLD, exactly as was found to be the case for dyslexia where particular syndromes cut across etiologies (Mattis, French, & Rapin, 1975). Coming back to our discussion in an earlier section of this chapter, it is pathogenesis rather than etiology that is relevant to symptomatology.

Syntactic–Pragmatic Syndrome

Children with *syntactic–pragmatic syndrome* show grossly impaired syntax and severely limited pragmatic use of language. Comprehension of connected discourse and of the demands of interpersonal conversation are also impaired. Interestingly, these children frequently have a better grasp of prediction making, including the ability to formulate verb–complement structures, than of subject–predicate relations. Naming of pictures and objects usually presents no difficulty for them. They are also quite able to formulate and respond to simple commands, but regularly are unable to either formulate or respond to WH- questions appropriately. Function words are frequently omitted, whereas morphological inflections (particularly with verbs) remain intact. Both phonology and prosody are variable within this group of children. Isolated semantic notions and the ability to choose the right word for expressing an idea are relatively intact, although it is also not unusual for children to invent words of their own.

One such child in our study came from a bilingual background, and it was assumed that part of his language difficulty stemmed from a second language interference. On closer examination, however, it was found that in most respects he was equally impaired in both English and Spanish and that his preferred language for expression was English. We have two tapes of this child collected 6 months apart. In both instances, he was asked to tell about the Peabody pictures. Some of his utterances are shown in Table 8.1.

As can be seen, at age 8:2, Marco's descriptions of the picture of a clown juggling three balls consisted almost entirely of naming features of the picture. He also regularly introduced many of his utterances with an undecipherable /mamada/, which we originally thought to be "my mother," even though the phrase made no sense in this context. At the second taping 6 months later, Marco had dropped this introducer and appeared to have some grasp of the notion that sentences should consist of subjects and predicates; this leads us to believe that, at age 8:2, /mamada/ was a kind of place holder for the nominal. As can be seen in Marco's 8:8 sample, however, he still had not learned to formulate appropriate predications. Rather, he appeared to select isolated features from the pictures to fill the position after *is*.

We have no idea about the neurologic basis for this syndrome, which we have encountered in very few children thus far. It is the only syndrome in

TABLE 8.1
Syntactic Pragmatic Syndrome

A. Marco's Utterances at Age 8:2	
Utterances	Description of picture
1. /mamada/ is clown.	Clown juggling three balls
2. /mamada/ is clowns.	
3. What's this?	
4. Clown.	
5. /mamada/ one two three balls.	
6. /mamada/ is hats.	
7. Look at that shoes.	
8. Look.	
9. Pajamas.	

B. Marco's Utterances at Age 8:8	
Utterances	Description of pictures
1. The clown is ball.	Clown juggling three balls
2. The hammer is nail.	Man hammering a nail with a hammer
3. The car is man truck.	Man driving a truck
4. The telephone is hello.	Woman talking on the telephone
5. The comb your hair is sit chair.	Girl sitting on a chair brushing her hair

which syntax was severely affected while phonology was normal or near normal. Some children with this syndrome resemble somewhat children of the semantic–pragmatic without autism type, presumably because of the dependency of semantic operations on elaborate syntax. We speculate that it may represent a particular stage in language acquisition or "recovery" in a child who was formerly more severely affected.

PATHOLOGICAL DELAY AND "RECOVERY" OF LANGUAGE FUNCTION

There are some important generalizations that can be made about DLD children that apply to all of the syndromes we have discussed. It is a hallmark of DLD that the onset of expressive language is delayed, except in those cases in which single words and short phrases are reported to have been acquired and then lost. It is difficult to determine from parental reports whether the cooing and babbling expected in the first few months of life were normal. We do know that the children who come to us at age 2 to 3 virtually mute do not babble prosodically before they begin to speak. Most, but not all, of the "recovering" children go through at least a short period of producing single word utterances. The single words that are produced, however, are frequently quite a different kind of vocabulary from that seen in normally developing children in the second year of life. Likewise, the two-word stage may be very abbreviated or absent. It is not at all uncommon for parents to report that the child changed from being totally silent to speaking in "whole sentences."

Another aspect of the language development of DLD children that is uniformly different from that of normal children is the area of what we have termed "pragmatics": the communicative use of language. Whereas normal children use their early language to label, request, and comment on their own activities or on events that occur in the immediate environment, DLD children often confine their language to labeling and requesting alone, far beyond the time at which one would expect commenting to take place. Also, asking and answering questions, and initiating conversations regularly develop much later in these children than in normal children.

Recently, we have been studying a group of 2- to 4-year-old children who had been born prematurely. These children are also delayed in their language onset time. For this reason they provide an interesting contrast to children who are pathologically delayed. While DLD is not at all uncommon in prematurely born children, some preterm children do develop perfectly normal language, albeit on a different timetable than full-term infants. By looking at this population, we are beginning to see some striking differences between simple delay and pathological delay. We feel it is safe to say that any child who has failed to acquire any communicative use of expressive speech by the age of 3 years is pathologically delayed and can be considered to be suffering from one of the syndromes of DLD.

CONCLUSION

We have attempted to bring some order to the bewildering symptoms encountered among children whose parents' chief complaint is that their child has failed to acquire speech. We have separated children into

1. A group with three subgroups in whom an expressive disorder appears to predominate; phonologic-syntactic syndrome with or without oro-motor apraxia; severe expressive syndrome with good comprehension; syntactic–pragmatic syndrome
2. The verbal auditory agnosia (VAA) syndrome characterized by a phonetic decoding deficit that occurs at such an early stage of linguistic processing as to preclude comprehension and verbal expression, with complete or partial preservation of the ability to process visually presented language
3. An autistic group with two subgroups: severe autism with mutism; autism with echolalia, in which the disorder of communication encompasses other modalities besides the acoustic–oral channel and is associated with profound deficits in affect and cognition
4. A semantic–pragmatic syndrome that lacks the severe affective deficits of autism but is also characterized by echolalia and deficient semantic processing as well as by inappropriate use of language in certain pragmatic contexts.

Our purpose has been to group the language disorders of children into syndromes on the basis of their linguistic deficits, much as a physician diagnoses an illness according to the cluster of symptoms present and absent in that group of patients. One of the virtues of such an endeavor is to facilitate the development of hypotheses about the pathogenesis of particular symptoms. We are not yet in a position to offer hypotheses except for the syndrome of VAA where we suggest that the deficit involves a step necessary for phonetic decoding; but we are trying to understand the anatomic bases of DLD syndromes. Except in the case of VAA, we have only tentative ideas at this time about localization of dysfunction in children with DLD. We consider that the syndromes of acquired aphasia, where the localization of pathology is at least partially clear, offer clues as to where one should look for dysfunction in children with DLD. We are still in no position to resolve the frequently raised question as to whether **DLD** necessarily implies bilateral pathology; this chapter is an attempt both to provide a procedural approach for thinking about children with **DLD** based on an analysis of what it is they can do and cannot do in a communicative context and to facilitate communication among investigators.

We hope our endeavor will help fulfill the needs of investigators concerned with questions of pathogenesis. When testing hypotheses in clinical populations, investigators need to study samples of children as homogeneous as possible in order not to dilute anticipated effects and thus unwittingly weaken experimental conclusions. Although we do not claim to have offered a definitive and exhaustive classification of children with **DLD**, we hope to have taken a few steps toward achieving this goal.

REFERENCES

Ajuriaguerra, J. de, Jaeggi, A., Guignard, F., Kocher, F., Maquard, M., Roth, S., & Schmid, E. The development and prognosis of dysphasia in children. In E. M. Morehead & A. Morehead (Eds.), *Normal and deficient child language*. Baltimore: University Park Press, 1976. Pp. 345–385.

Alajouanine, T., & Lhermitte, F. Acquired aphasia in children. *Brain*, 1965, *88*, 653–662.

Allen, D. A., & Rapin, I. Language disorders in preschool children: Predictors of outcome. A preliminary report. *Brain and Development*, 1980, *2*, 73–80.

Annett, M. Laterality of childhood hemiplegia and the growth of speech and intelligence. *Cortex*, 1973, *9*, 4–29.

Aram, D. M., & Nation, J. E. Patterns of language behavior in children with developmental language disorders. *Journal of Speech and Heating Research*, 1975, *18*, 229–241.

Baltaxe, C. A. M. Pragmatic deficits in the language of autistic adolescents. *Journal of Pediatric Psychology*, 1977, *2*, 176–180.

Baltaxe, C. A. M., & Simmons, J. Q. Bedtime soliloquies and linguistic competence in autism. *Journal of Speech and Hearing Disorders*, 1977, *42*, 376–393.

Bartak, L., & Rutter, M. The use of personal pronouns by autistic children. *Journal of Autism and Childhood Schizophrenia*, 1974, *4*, 217–222.

Basser, L. S. Hemiplegia of early onset and the faculty of speech with special reference to the effects of hemispherectomy. *Brain*, 1962, *85*, 427–460.

Benton, A. The interplay of experimental and clinical approaches in brain lesion research. In S. Finger (Ed.), *Recovery from brain damage. Research and theory*. New York: Plenum, 1978. Pp. 49–68.

Bliss, L. S., & Peterson, D. M. Performance of aphasic and nonaphasic children on a sentence repetition task. *Journal of Communication Disorders*, 1975, *8*, 207–212.

Blumstein, S., & Cooper, W. E. Hemispheric processing of intonation contours. *Cortex*, 1974, *10*, 146–158.

Brodmann, K. *Vergleinchende Lokalisationslehre der Grosshirnrinde in ihren Principien dargestellt auf Grund des Zellenbaues*. Leipzig: Barth, 1909.

Carrow, E. *Test for auditory comprehension of language*. Austin, Texas: Learning Concepts, 1973.

Chess, S., Korn, S. J., & Fernandez, P. B. *Psychiatric disorders of children with congenital rubella*. New York: Brunner/Mazel, 1971.

Damasio, A. R., & Damasio, H. Musical faculty and cerebral dominance. In M. Critchley & R. A. Henson (Eds.), *Music and the brain*. Springfield, Ill.: Charles C. Thomas, 1977. Pp. 141–155.

Damasio, A. R., & Maurer, R. G. A neurological model for childhood autism. *Archives of Neurology*, 1978, *35*, 777–786.

DeLong, G. R. A neuropsychologic interpretation of infantile autism. In M. Rutter & E. Schopler (Eds.), *Autism: A reappraisal of concepts and treatment*. New York: Plenum Press, 1978. Pp. 207–218.

DeMyer, M. K., Barton, S., DeMyer, W. E., Norton, J. A., Allen, J., & Steele, R. Prognosis in autism: A follow-up study. *Journal of Autism and Childhood Schizophrenia*, 1973, *3*, 199–246.

Denckla, M. B. Language disorders. In J. A. Downey & N. L. Low (Eds.), *The child with disabling illness*. Philadelphia: W. B. Saunders, 1974. Pp. 277–304.

Dennis, M. Cerebral dominance in three forms of early brain disorder. In M. Blaw, I, Rapin, & M. Kinsbourne (Eds.), *Topics in child neurology*. New York: Spectrum, 1977. Pp. 189–212.

Dennis, M., & Whitaker, H. A. Language acquisition following hemi-decortication: Linguistic superiority of the left over the right hemisphere. *Brain and Language*, 1976, *3*, 404–433.

Dimond, S. J., & Beaumont, J. G. Experimental studies of hemisphere function in the human brain. In S. J. Dimond & J. G. Beaumont (Eds.), *Hemisphere function in the human brain*. New York: Wiley, 1974. Pp. 48–88.

Duffy, F. H., Burchfiel, J. L., & Lombroso, C. T. Brain electrical activity mapping (BEAM): A method for extending the clinical utility of EEG and evoked potential data. *Annals of Neurology*, 1979, 5, 309–321.

Eisenson, J. *Aphasia in children*. New York: Harper and Row, 1972.

Ferry, P. C., Hall, S. M., & Hicks, J. L. "Dilapidated" speech: Developmental verbal dyspraxia. *Developmental Medicine and Child Neurology*, 1975, *17*, 749–756.

Finger, S. (Ed.) *Recovery from brain damage: Research and theory*. New York: Plenum, 1978.

Frumkin, B., & Rapin, I. Perception of vowels and consonant–vowels of varying duration in language impaired children. *Neuropsychologia*, 1980, *18*, 443–454.

Galaburda, A .M., LeMay, M., Kemper, T. L., & Geschwind, N. Right–left asymmetries in the brain. Structural differences between the hemispheres may underlie cerebral dominance. *Science*, 1978, *199*, 852–856.

Gazzaniga, M. S., & LeDoux, J. E. *The integrated mind*. New York: Plenum, 1978.

Geschwind, N. Non-aphasic disorders of speech (1964). In N. Geschwind (Ed.), *Selected papers on language and the brain*. Boston: D. Reidel, 1974. Pp. 74–85.

Geschwind, N. (Ed.). *Selected papers on language and the brain*. Boston: D. Reidel, 1974.

Goldberger, M. E. Recovery of movement after CNS lesions in monkeys. In D. G. Stein, J. J. Rosen, & N. Butters (Eds.), *Plasticity and recovery of function in the central nervous system*. New York: Academic Press, 1974. Pp. 265–337.

Goldstein, M. N. Auditory agnosia for speech ("Pure word-deafness"). *Brain and Language*, 1974, *1*, 195–204.

Goodglass, H., & Blumstein, S. (Eds.). *Psycholinguistics and aphasia*. Baltimore: Johns Hopkins University Press, 1973.

Hauser, S. L., DeLong, G. R., & Rosman, N. P. Pneumographic findings in the infantile autism syndrome—A correlation with temporal lobe disease. *Brain*, 1975, *98*, 667–688.

Hier, D. B., LeMay, M., & Rosenberger, P. B. Autism and unfavorable left–right asymmetries of the brain. *Journal of Autism and Developmental Disorders*, 1979, *9*, 153–159.

Ingram, T. T. S. Speech disorders in childhood. In E. H. Lenneberg & E. Lenneberg (Eds.), *Foundations of language development. A multidisciplinary approach.* New York: Academic Press, 1975. Pp. 195–261.

Kinsbourne, M. The minor hemisphere as a source of aphasic speech. *Archives of Neurology,* 1971, *25,* 302–306.

Kinsbourne, M. Minimal brain dysfunction as a neurodevelopmental lag. *Annals of the New York Academy of Sciences,* 1973, *205,* 268–273.

Kools, J. A., Williams, A. F., Vickers, M. J., & Caell, A. Oral and limb apraxia in mentally retarded children with deviant articulation. *Cortex,* 1971, *7,* 387–400.

Krynauw, R. A., Infantile hemiplegia treated by removing one cerebral hemisphere. *Journal of Neurology Neurosurgery and Psychiatry,* 1950, *13,* 243–267.

Landau, W. M., Goldstein, R., & Kleffner, F. R., Congenital aphasia: A clinicopathologic study. *Neurology,* 1960, *10,* 915–921.

Lassen, N. A., Ingvar, D. H., & Skinhøj, E. Brain function and blood flow. *Scientific American,* 1978, *239*(4), 62–71.

Laurence, S., & Stein, D. G. Recovery after brain damage and the concept of localization of function. In S. Finger (Ed.), *Recovery from brain damage. Research and theory.* New York: Plenum Press, 1978. Pp. 369–407.

Lenneberg, E. H. Understanding language without ability to speak. *Journal of Abnormal and Social Psychology,* 1962, *65,* 419–425.

Liberman, A. M., Cooper, I. S., Shankweiler, D. P., & Studdert-Kennedy, M. Perception of the speech code. *Psychological Reviews,* 1967, *74,* 431–461.

Lockman, L. A., Swaiman, K. F., Drage, J. S., Nelson, K. B., & Marsden, H. M. *Workshop on the neurobiological basis of autism.* Bethesda, Md.: NIH Publication 79-1855, 1979.

Lou, H. C., Brandt, S., & Bruhn, P. Progressive aphasia and epilepsy with a self-limited course. In J. K. Penry (Ed.), *Epilepsy. The eighth international symposium.* New York: Raven, 1977. Pp. 295–303.

Ludlow, C. L. Children's language disorders: Recent research advances. *Annals of Neurology,* 1980, *7,* 497–507.

Mattis, S., French, J. H., & Rapin, I. Dyslexia in children and young adults: Three independent neuropsychological syndromes. *Developmental Medicine and Child Neurology,* 1975, *17,* 150–163.

McCarthy, D. *McCarthy scales of children's abilities.* New York: Psychological Corporation, 1972.

McReynolds, L. V. Operant conditioning for investigating speech sound discrimination in aphasic children. *Journal of Speech and Hearing Research,* 1966, *9,* 519–528.

Menyuk, P. A. *Sentences children use.* Cambridge: MIT Press, 1969. Pp. 137–139.

Menyuk, P., & Looney, P. A problem of language disorder: Length versus structure. *Journal of Speech and Hearing Research,* 1972, *15,* 264–280. (a)

Menyuk, P., & Looney, P. Relationships among components of the grammar in language disorder. *Journal of Speech and Hearing Research,* 1972, *15,* 395–407. (b)

Milner, B. Hemispheric specialization: Scope and limits. In F. O. Schmitt & F. G. Worden (Eds.), *The neurosciences. Third study program.* Cambridge: MIT Press, 1974. Pp. 75–89.

Morehead, D. M., & Ingram, D. The development of basic syntax in normal and linguistically deviant children. *Journal of Speech and Hearing Research,* 1973, *16,* 330–352.

Morehead, D. M., & Morehead, A. E. (Eds.). *Normal and deficient child language.* Baltimore: University Park Press, 1976.

Morley, M. E., *The development and disorders of speech in childhood.* (3rd ed.) Edinburgh and London: Churchill Livingstone, 1972.

Myklebust, H. R., Childhood aphasia: An evolving concept. In L. E. Travis (Ed.), *Handbook of speech pathology and audiology*. New York: Appleton-Century-Crofts, 1971. Pp. 1181–1202.

Ojemann, G., & Mateer, C. Human language cortex: Localization of memory, syntax, and sequential motor–phoneme identification systems. *Science*, 1979, *205*, 1401–1403.

Ojemann, G. A., & Whitaker, H. A. The bilingual brain. *Archives of Neurology*, 1978, *35*, 409–412.

Peabody language development kit. Level number P. Circle Pines, Minnesota: American Guidance Service, 1968.

Penfield, W., & Jasper, H. *Epilepsy and the functional anatomy of the human brain*. Boston: Little, Brown, 1954.

Penfield, W., & Roberts, L. *Speech and brain mechanisms*. Princeton: Princeton University Press, 1959.

Phelps, M. E., Huang, S. C., Hoffman, E. J., Selin, C., Sokoloff, L., & Kuhl, D. E. Tomographic measurement of local cerebral glucose metabolic rate in humans with (F-18) 2-fluoro-2-deoxy-D-glucose: Validation of method. *Annals of Neurology*, 1979, *6*, 371–388.

Pierce, S., & Bartolucci, G. A syntactic investigtion of verbal autistic, mentally retarded, and normal children. *Journal of Autism and Childhood Schizophrenia*, 1977, *7*, 121–134.

Rapin, I., Mattis, S., Rowan, A. J., & Golden, G. G. Verbal auditory agnosia in children. *Developmental Medicine and Child Neurology*, 1977, *19*, 192–207.

Rapin, I., & Wilson, B. C. Children with developmental language disability: Neurologic aspects and assessment. In M. A. Wyke (Ed.), *Developmental dysphasia*. London: Academic Press, 1978. Pp. 13–41.

Rees, N. S. Auditory processing factors in language disorders: The view from Procrustes' bed. *Journal of Speech and Hearing Disorders*, 1973, *38*, 304–315.

Ross, E. D. Left medial parietal lobe and receptive language functions: Mixed transcortical aphasia after left anterior cerebral artery infarction. *Neurology*, 1980, *30*, 144–151.

Ross, E. D., & Mesulam, M-M. Dominant language functions of the right hemisphere? Prosody and emotional gesturing. *Archives of Neurology*, 1979, *36*, 144–148.

Rutter, M. Definition of childhood autism. In L. A. Lockman, K. F. Swaiman, J. S. Drage, K. B. Nelson, & A. M. Marsden (Eds.), *Workshop on the neurobiological basis of autism*. Bethesda, Md.: NIH Publication 79–1855, 1979. Pp. 3–29.

Rutter, M., & Martin, J. A. M. (Eds.). *The child with delayed speech*. Clinics in Developmental Medicine #43. London: Heinemann Medical Books, 1972.

Saxman, J. H., & Miller, J. F. Short-term memory and language skills in articulation-deficient children. *Journal of Speech and Hearing Research*, 1973, *10*, 721–730.

Schaeffer, B. Teaching spontaneous sign language to nonverbal children: Theory and method. *Sign Language Studies*, 1978, *21*, 317–352.

Schwartz, G. E., Davidson, R. J., & Maer, F. Right hemisphere lateralization for emotion in the human brain: Interactions with cognition. *Science*, 1975, *190*, 286–288.

Sperry, R. W. Lateral specialization in the surgically separated hemispheres. In F. O. Schmitt & F. G. Worden (Eds.), *The neurosciences. Third study program*. Cambridge: MIT Press, 1974. Pp. 5–19.

Swisher, L. Language disorders of autistic children. In L. A. Lockman, K. F. Swaiman, J. S. Drage, K. B. Nelson, & A. M. Marsden (Eds.), *Workshop on the neurobiological basis of autism*. Bethesda, Md.: NIH Publication 79–1855, 1979. Pp. 159–189.

Swisher, L. P., & Pinsker, E. J. The language characteristics of hyperverbal hydrocephalic children. *Developmental and Child Neurology*, 1971, *13*, 746–755.

Tallal, P., & Piercy, M. Defects of auditory perception in children with developmental dysphasia. In M. A. Wyke (Ed.), *Developmental dysphasia*. London: Academic Press, 1978. Pp. 63–84.

Volpe, J. J. Cerebral blood flow in the newborn infant: Relation to hypoxic–ischemic brain injury and periventricular hemorrhage. *Journal of Pediatrics*, 1979, *94*, 170–173.

Wada, J., & Rasmussen, T. Intracortical injection of sodium amytal for the lateralization of cerebral speech dominance. Experimental and clinical observations. *Journal of Neurosurgery*, 1960, *17*, 266–282.

Walsh, R. N., & Greenough, W. T. (Eds.). *Environments as therapy for brain dysfunction*. New York: Plenum, 1976.

Weiner, P. S. The cognitive function of language deficient children. *Journal of Speech and Hearing Research*, 1969, *12*, 53–64.

Wilson, J. J., Rapin, I., Wilson, B. C., & Van Denburg, F. V. Neuropsychologic function of children with severe hearing impairment. *Journal of Speech and Hearing Research*, 1975, *18*, 634–652.

Witelson, S. F. Developmental dyslexia: Two right hemispheres and none left. *Science*, 1977, *195*, 309–311.

Woods, B. T., & Carey, S. Language deficits after apparent clinical recovery from childhood aphasia. *Annals of Neurology*, 1979, *6*, 405–409.

Woods, B. T., & Teuber, H.-L. Changing patterns of childhood aphasia. *Annals of Neurology*, 1978, *3*, 273–280.

Worster-Drought, C. Suprabulbar paresis. *Developmental Medicine and Child Neurology*, 1974, *16* (supplement 30). Pp. 1–33.

Wyke, M. (Ed.), *Developmental dysphasia*. London: Academic Press, 1978.

Zaidel, E. The split and half brain as models of congenital language disability. In C. L. Ludlow & M. E. Doran-Quine (Eds.), *The neurological bases of language disorders in children: Methods and directions for research*. Washington, D. C.: NINCDS Monograph, No. 22. U. S. Government Printing Office, 1979. Pp. 55–89.

The Developmentally Dyslexic Brain and the Written Language Skills of Children with One Hemisphere

MAUREEN DENNIS

Reading can be studied without reference to the brain. Experimental and cognitive psychologists, for example, try to isolate and formalize the operations of a normal fluent reader, without explicitly considering their neurological basis (LaBerge & Samuels, 1977; Mewhort & Campbell, 1981; Spiro, Bruce, & Brewer, 1980). In contrast, studies of alexia in brain-damaged adults invoke the brain either as a tool that induces dissociations of function in reading skill (Coltheart, Patterson, & Marshall, 1980; Saffran & Marin, 1977), or as an element in the cross mapping between different forms of brain damage and particular patterns of reading deficit (Benson, 1977; Benson, Brown, & Tomlinson, 1971; Benson & Geschwind, 1969; Geschwind, 1962). Studies of reading have provided both a functional decomposition of the reading operation and a set of hypotheses about its substrate in the brain.

Reading acquisition, too, may be studied in a manner that either disregards or includes brain function. Studies that plot the age course of particular reading operations need not make reference to the brain, although neuropsychologists interested in reading development typically do so.

NEUROPSYCHOLOGY OF
LANGUAGE, READING, AND SPELLING

A plausible neuropsychological model of reading acquisition would require a coherent developmental account of both brain function and the reading operation. Such a model does not currently exist because of an undue reliance on the paradigms of adult alexia and a failure to exploit the findings of experimental and cognitive psychology with the functional decompositions of the reading process they have utilized.

Reading pathology in the child may take the form of either developmental *dyslexia*, a failure to learn reading, or childhood *alexia*, a loss of previously acquired reading skills. The developmental dyslexic condition is much more commonly studied, and the reading skills of dyslexic children are an important part of most neuropsychological theories of reading development.

The adult alexia study has been a core paradigm for neuropsychological studies of dyslexia. Just as the former tries to relate brain damage to reading deficit, so does the latter attempt to identify the aberrant brain function in different forms of developmental reading failure. When alexic and dyslexic individuals share common reading symptoms, as must sometimes happen when each is selected for study on the basis of poor reading, it is sometimes inferred—without independent evidence—that they share common brain anomalies (Aaron, Baxter, & Lucenti, 1980).

The parallel between child and adult reading failure, however, fails in both logical and empirical ways. The brain mechanisms involved in acquiring a behavioral skill are not always those that maintain the skill, once acquired (Dennis, 1976; Goldman, 1971; Hebb, 1942). A description of the relationships among the symptoms of mature reading deficit need not provide a good framework for studying reading acquisition failure.

Over the past 20 years, experimental and cognitive psychology has begun to dissect the reading process, but the neuropsychology of developmental dyslexia has not fully exploited these analyses to create a model of reading acquisition failure. The focus on identifying a structural or functional disorder in the brain of the dyslexic child (often by analogy with brain damage in the alexic adult) has tended to preempt study of a more fundamental question: How does the dyslexic child read? In fact, speculation about brain function in developmental dyslexia has often preceded, instead of followed, an adequate analysis of its behavioral characteristics. Until the reading operations available to the dyslexic child are specified, the functional properties of the dyslexic brain must remain obscure. And specification of these properties relies more on discoveries about the cognitive basis of reading than on the heuristic neurology of adult alexia (cf. Benton, 1978).

To understand why the study of developmental dyslexia is so commonly cast in a framework of adult alexia, it is useful to consider some nineteenth-century studies of reading acquisition. Conceptualization about much behavioral and neural processing in learning to read is rooted in these early ideas.

BEHAVIORAL OPERATIONS IN LEARNING TO READ

The Nineteenth-Century Laws of Association as Explanations of Reading Acquisition

A psychology rooted in nineteenth-century concepts of learning has often been used to explain reading acquisition. The idea of a cross-modal associativeness of words and signs as the paradigmatic reading operation, particularly, invokes the laws of association. This idea is old. In 1869, Bastian explained how a child learns to read.

> The individual has already learned to associate certain objects or certain states of consciousness with certain sounds or names; he has further gained the power of articulating these names for himself; and when he begins to learn to read, he gradually builds up a still further association between a state of consciousness which he recognizes and names, and certain hieroglyphics such as the printed forms of letters are. To the original combination, therefore, there is now added a perception derived through the sense of sight; and as perceptions of this kind have what Professor Bain terms a high degree of mental adhesiveness . . . [1869a, p. 71] [I]f we consider how it is that a child learns to spell, viz. in very great part by conning, and, by dint of frequent repetition, impressing upon its mind the visual appearance and collocation of letters . . . [1869b, p. 487]

Concepts like adhesiveness and repetition are the core of an associationist psychology advanced by British empiricists like Alexander Bain. Perhaps the brain, like cognition, might be analyzed in associationist terms (see Buckingham, in press, for a discussion of the implications of this view). If the psychological laws of association could explain how reading is learned, then perhaps a failure of cerebral association might cause adult reading failure. The notion was that the child learns to read by building up a set of associations corresponding to a progressive growth of fibre tracts in the brain; and that, in adulthood, cerebral lesions could prevent these learned associations from being elicited: "And where the individual cannot read, I am inclined to think this must be owing either to some lesion of the afferent fibres to the visual perceptive centre, of the visual perceptive centre itself, or of the communication between the cells of this centre and those of the auditory perceptive centre [Bastian, 1869b, p. 484]."

Reading Involves More Than Associative Processes

The variety of operations experimental and cognitive psychology has identified in the normal fluent reader are not all obviously explicable in terms of nineteenth-century laws of association. The emphasis on the associative and cross-modal components of reading acquisition has sometimes caused nonassociative processes to be ignored.

During the initial stages of reading, the child undoubtedly learns to associate sounds and visual configurations (although this operation may be more a prerequisite for reading than the central reading operation). Were reading effected only by serially elicited associations, single words not seen before could not be read, nor could sentences and texts. Even single-letter reading is subject to a series of active operations—chunking, grouping, stacking, parsing to form higher-order units (Mewhort & Beal, 1977; Mewhort & Campbell, 1980)—that can not be characterized in associationist terms. In distributing attention to the aspects of a text critical to finding meaning, furthermore, the fluent reader scans, ignores specific lexical information, and makes inferences.

Sentences and Texts, Not Just Single Words

The goal of fluent reading is to understand a text, including all aspects of its meaning: those in single words, those in grammatical or sentential structure, and those in text construction. Much has been learned about how the normal reader performs these operations, that is, about reading fluency (Doehring, 1976; Doehring & Hoshko, 1977); inferencing and constructive prose reading (Paris & Lindauer, 1977; Paris & Upton, 1976); and mnemonic representation of discourse (Berger & Perfetti, 1977; Perfetti & Goldman, 1976; Perfetti & Lesgold, 1977).

Derivation of meaning does not depend on a complete mastery of lower-level reading operations. The identification of letters, for instance, is not necessary for word identification, nor is word identification a prerequisite for understanding meaning: On the same visual stimulus, letter identification, word identification, and the comprehension of meaning may be performed independently (Smith & Holmes, 1971). In some individuals, furthermore, the meaning of a word may be apprehended even when access to its phonemic structure is disrupted (Coltheart, Patterson, & Marshall, 1980).

Studies of developmental dyslexia have tended to emphasize single-word decoding rather than sentence and text comprehension. As a result, certain reading operations, such as inferencing, are rarely investigated and some important questions about dyslexia—as, for example, how does a dyslexic reader derive meaning from a word, sentence, or text when single-word decoding is impaired and Why are some dyslexic individuals able to read single words but not sentences and texts?—have not been part of systematic research investigations.

THE BEHAVIORAL MANIFESTATIONS OF DEVELOPMENTAL DYSLEXIA

The Argument from Analogy with Adult Alexia: The Search for the Word-Blind Child

One illustration of how reading acquisition has been viewed in terms of adult alexia is the word-blind child. Congenital word blindness was emphasized in early studies of developmental reading failure, because these cases, however rare, were the pediatric version of the adult word-blindness Kussmaul described.

Schilder's (1944) interest in developmental dyslexia was explicitly in terms of the adult model: He sought to study the developmental reading failure that corresponded most closely to the behavioral manifestations of adult alexia. "Investigation on seven cases have (sic) been made on the nature of congenital word blindness *from the point of view of its position in the system of aphasias and agnosias* [p. 67; italics added]."

One might ask why this particular form of developmental reading failure should be studied, and also why its position in the adult scheme should be emphasized rather than its properties as one of a set of functional lacunae in the development of reading competence. In the early studies, certain types of developmental reading failure were studied to the exclusion of other, perhaps more common, forms. As a result, early theories about brain function in reading acquisition tended to be based on a limited subset of the various manifestations of developmental reading failure (Orton, 1937). Some dyslexic children are word blind, others are not: Of itself, this particular behavioral deficit cannot provide the basis for a comprehensive theory of reading acquisition failure.

Dyslexic Syndromes

Dyslexia is not a homogeneous condition. Reading involves many operations, failure to perform any one of which will delay the acquisition of normal fluent reading. The search for dyslexic typologies or syndromes (Boder, 1973; Mattis, French, & Rapin, 1975) is important as part of the attempt to characterize both the diversity of reading deficit and some of its electrophysiological correlates (Fried, Tanguay, Boder, Doubleday, & Greensite, 1981).

The creation of a dyslexic typology does not, of itself, enhance understanding of dyslexia. The methodological flaws in many studies have been outlined by Satz and Morris (1980): Broadly, the problems include the use of intuitive a priori assumptions about the nature and number of subtypes; attempts to "eyeball" typologies from data sets that more properly require a multi-dimensional analysis if their internal structure is to be revealed; and a failure to validate subtypes through data manipulation techniques or on variables external to the subtypes themselves. A dyslexic typology or syndrome, furthermore, is only as useful as the functional decomposition on which it is based. In some instances, this is neurological rather than behavioral, so that it provides little insight into the dyslexic reading operation; in no instance does the typology encompass sentence and text comprehension. At best, the existing typologies provide a heuristic for the further study of single-word decoding in dyslexic populations.

Reading Changes throughout Its Course of Acquisition

Although much attention has been given in recent investigations to deriving dyslexic syndromes and typologies, an equally salient feature of reading has also come to be emphasized: the fact that reading itself changes throughout its course of acquisition. If typologies have focussed on differences among dyslexic children, other studies have emphasized differences over time in the functions any child must master in order to read successfully (Bakker, 1973; Fletcher, 1981; Fletcher & Satz, 1979; Fletcher, Satz, & Scholes, 1981).

This research makes less plausible theories of dyslexia that emphasize a unitary impairment. In addition, it complicates the picture of reading failure by requiring that any deficit be seen in the context of total reading mastery. This problem finds discussion in the current evaluations of "lag" and "deficit" constructs in dyslexia (Rourke, 1976; Satz, Fletcher, Clark, & Morris, 1982). Failure to master a primitive component of the reading operation may or may not be compensated for over time; a separate issue is whether, in addition, early failure prevents the child from acquiring a later stage of reading or from developing the normal sequence of skills (Fletcher, 1981). Any plausible account of reading failure must encompass the broad developmental base over which normal reading is acquired.

The Behavioral Correlates of Dyslexia

The dyslexic child often shows a variety of behavioral anomalies, whether frank neurological symptoms, neurological "soft signs," or delays in attaining age-appropriate performance on psychological tests. Analysis of these deficits has long been made (Schilder, 1944) in an attempt to clarify the behavioral attributes of different forms of developmental dyslexia (Benton, 1975; Lachmann, 1960).

This approach, however, does not reliably signal the kinds of neural or cognitive processing deficits underlying impaired reading. For instance, the observation that some dyslexic children are impaired on perceptuo-motor tests (Silver & Hagin, 1970) gives no indication of either brain or behavioral anomalies in children showing such impairments. Associated symptoms are correlates of dyslexia, not necessarily signs or causes.

One might also question whether the energy expended in searching for the correlates of dyslexia has been well directed. At one time or another, almost every type of behavioral anomaly has been proposed as a dyslexic correlate. Unless some constraints on how to evaluate associated symptoms are accepted, the interpretation of dyslexic correlates is so random as to be meaningless.

Perhaps more important is the fact that many associated symptoms are far removed from the act of reading. It seems unprofitable to list yet more behavioral correlates of dyslexia while we have imperfect understanding of how normal and dyslexic children differ in constructing supraletter units from printed matter, in analysing syllabic structure, in applying morphophonemic rules to the decomposition of graphemes, and so on.

The most effective use of associated behavioral symptoms in the study of reading acquisition failure has been to evaluate them, not as correlates, but as predictors of reading deficit (Satz, Friel, & Goebel, 1975; Satz, Friel, & Rudegeair, 1974). By assessing the predictive and concurrent validity of these behavioral correlates, such investigations have made the correlates interpretable by showing their value in predicting the child's reading status.

NEURAL OPERATIONS IN DEVELOPMENTAL DYSLEXIA

Agenetic Cortical Defects: Failure of the Dyslexic Child to Develop Reading Centers in the Brain

The neurology of the late nineteenth century was replete with brain "centers"—for articulate speech, auditory comprehension, and reading. It is not surprising, then, that early students of developmental dyslexia saw their task as a search for the defective brain centers in the child that corresponded to those centers known to be damaged in adult alexics.

The brain was assumed to be a tabula rasa at birth, with centers that became functional as they were needed. Inability to learn to read was seemingly caused by a failure to develop the appropriate brain centers. The conclusion was drawn that in the developmental dyslexic, there was a primary dysgenesis, structural or functional, of the centers that normally mediated reading.

In early dyslexia research, the idea was made explicit that a brain insult in similar regions was involved in the adult alexic and developmental dyslexic. Morgan's 1896 case of congenital word-blindness was cast in terms of this analogy: "This case is . . . due most probably to defective development of that region of the brain, disease of which in adults produces practically the same symptoms—that is, the left angular gyrus [p. 1378]."

In 1900, Hinshelwood published two cases of congenital word-blindness, and proposed an agenetic cortical defect as their basis. Fisher (1905, 1910) added new cases and asserted that the disease may be both hereditary and familial, advancing at the same time the idea that word–blindness arose because of a congenital defect in the left cerebral cortex. Fisher described two subgroups of congenital word-blindness: one with a congenital failure of the visual memory center for words in the left angular and supramarginal gyrae to develop, and a second with the same center injured by birth damage. Further, because male children were more prone to birth palsies, he was able to explain the greater incidence of congenital word-blindness in males.

Direct evidence for left hemisphere atrophy in word-blind children was generally missing—none of Fisher's cases, for example, had a right hemiparesis—but the view was advanced vigorously. Even when only cursory examination of a child was made, congenital word-blindness was resolutely attributed to a congenital dysgenesis of brain centers: "I have not been able to study their cases as carefully as I wish, and am compelled to present my views after a more or less imperfect investigation. I do not doubt, however, that in these two boys there is a congenital deficiency, or at least a tardy development of the word memory centres . . . [Claiborne, 1906, p. 1813]."

The concept of agenetic cortical defects was extended in various ways. Variations in the rate at which a child learned to read were supposedly due to differential development of those parts of the brain necessary for reading, just as the congenital reading disability itself was held to arise from an incomplete functional development of the brain centers for reading.

Agenetic Cortical Defects in Dyslexia?

Most dyslexic children do not have demonstrable defects in those brain areas that produce adult alexia. To assume that they do so, on the basis only of behavioral anomalies, is to make an unjustified inductive leap, as in the following instance:

> If we analyse the perceptual defects found in children with reading disabilities . . . the defect may be interpreted as a defect in spatial or temporal orientation. . . .The finding . . . that the function of visual spatial organization resides primarily in the lesser hemisphere, suggests that these children with reading disabilities have functioning defects in the lesser hemisphere . . . [Silver & Hagin, 1970, p. 454].

Some constraints are needed on conceptualization of brain function in the developmental dyslexic. The issue is not whether the dyslexic brain is well-organized for learning to read—it presumably is not—nor even whether discrete malfunction in the brain might account for subtypes of dyslexia, a reasonable hypothesis (Denckla, 1972). The question, rather, is whether the case for atypical brain organization in dyslexia should be based on an analogy with the structural lesions that cause adult alexia; whether, as Benton (1978) claims, the acquired alexia model is likely to advance understanding of developmental reading failure.

Disturbances of Cerebral Dominance in Dyslexia

Not all early research accepted that agenetic cortical defects were responsible for dyslexia. Orton, for example, noted several problems with this view.

> In the first place, such areas of agenesis are of comparatively rare occurrence and are not met with in a general autopsy service with anywhere near the frequency with which the cases of reading disability are to be encountered among children. Secondly, if it be true as Marie reported that there is no higher incidence of speech disorders in children born with a right hemiplegia than in those with a left, and if Marie's assumption from this, that when one hemisphere is damaged before speech is learned the other can take its place, is correct, it would then require a lack of development in the angular gyri of both hemispheres to satisfy Hinshelwood's hypothesis, and such bilateral agenetic defects are exceedingly rare [1937, p. 70]."

Orton reasoned about the dyslexic brain by analogy with the damaged adult brain, as had earlier researchers, but he assumed that intergrading between the brain areas critical for reading, with a resulting failure to develop a clear hemispheric dominance, was responsible for dyslexia.

> [T]he very close parallelism which exists between the symptoms to be seen in adults who have suffered a loss in language as a result of brain injury and those to be seen during the development of the language faculty in some children suggests very strongly that we are dealing with a disturbance of the same physiological process in

both instances and, since in the adult such a loss occurs only when the lesion is in the master hemisphere, our attention is naturally directed to those factors, open to our observation and study, which tend to determine the choice and establishment of unilateral brain control. For reasons which are too technical to be reviewed in detail here, the hypothesis that these developmental disorders in acquiring the language functions are the result of faulty development of particular brain areas (agenetic cortical defects) is no longer tenable, while the existence of demonstrable mixtures between right and left motor preferences with a strong familial background implies that comparable intergrading may exist between the critical areas for the various fractions of the language faculty in the two hemispheres of the brain, thus giving rise to a series of developmental disorders in language . . . [1937, pp. 66–67].

Orton's ideas involve some strong assumptions about brain function. The first is that some properties of the child's brain are not identical to those of the adult, although one may hypothesize certain features of the former by analogy with the latter. The second is that a direct relationship exists between peripheral and cerebral laterality, so that the magnitude of one measures the magnitude of the other. The third is that language-related brain areas are intergraded in individuals with poor lateral preferences.

Cerebral Dominance in the Child and in the Adult

To support his view of "Language Losses in the Adult as the Key to Developmental Disorders in Children [1937, p. 21]," Orton analyzed the adult aphasias in considerable detail (1937, Chapter 1). He stressed, not only that these symptoms occurred after left-sided rather than right-sided injury in right-handed individuals (1937, p. 40), but also that focal rather than diffuse brain damage was responsible.

[T]he locus of an area of brain destruction is of much greater import in determining a language disorder than is the amount of brain tissue destroyed. Thus a very small area of damage in the angular gyrus region may result in a complete loss of the ability to read and write and a marked disturbance in speech as well, while a much greater destruction of tissue in, for example, the frontal region of the brain may give no demonstrable disorder in language [p. 26].

In reasoning from these adult data to developmental reading disorders, Orton made an assumption that appears incongruous with his emphasis on focal left-hemisphere lesions in the production of reading pathologies. He stressed that side of cerebral dominance in the child was unimportant, provided that one side be dominant. It was the absence of any dominance, he thought, that put the child at risk for dyslexia; "there is reason to believe that a high degree of specialization in either hemisphere makes for superiority and that the good left-hander is therefore not only not abnormal but is apt to be better equipped than is the indifferent right-hander [p. 50]."

The assertion that the left hemisphere is not itself critical for language and reading in the child is a strong assumption. Although he relied on the adult aphasia literature to a large extent in formulating his views about dyslexia, Orton also incorporated Marie's view that the two hemispheres were equipotential at birth.

> The infant at birth starts with no unilateral superiority in control of either hand or language as far as we can determine. This is supported by the entire indifference with which a very young infant uses either hand and by Pierre Marie's observation that there is no greater incidence of speech disorder in children who have suffered a birth paralysis involving the right hand than when it involves the left. Marie inferred from this that neither the right nor the left hemisphere is exclusively predestined for control of speech at birth . . . [p. 48].

Whether or not they were confirmed by later research (Dennis & Whitaker, 1977), Orton did hypothesize characteristics of the child's brain other than those directly inferred from analogy with the adult.

Peripheral Laterality and Cerebral Laterality

Although Orton was aware that peripheral laterality might not be a perfect index of cerebral laterality, he saw it as the only evidence available: "[T]he only guide we have as to whether the right or left hemisphere of the brain is operating as the master half in the normal individual is his sidedness as shown by his handedness, footedness and eyedness [1937, p. 68]."

Some of the peripheral laterality measures proposed as indices of cerebral dominance by Orton and others bear a questionable relationship to brain structure or function. McFie (1952) noted, for example, that eye preference could not indicate hemispheric dominance, since each retina has a bilateral cerebral projection.

Orton considered that anomalous peripheral laterality was an indication of developmental brain immaturity rather than of brain injury. He excluded from his discussion, although not necessarily from his data, anomalies of handedness caused by disease or damage to the young brain. As Satz (1972) has suggested, however, it may be the brain damage associated with some types of left-handedness—rather than anomalous peripheral laterality—that is responsible for impaired function.

Perhaps the major problem in Orton's reasoning is the logical inductive error involved in assigning individuals to "cerebral dominance" groups on the basis of disturbances of peripheral laterality, in using the magnitude of peripheral laterality to signal the magnitude of cerebral dominance (Satz, 1977). This problem is still present in studies that measure competing laterality by dichotic, dichaptic, or visual half-field techniques (rather than the direct measures of motor preference that Orton used) and propose anomalous brain organization in those individuals who show something other than a right ear, hand, or eye superiority for language-related tasks.

Peripheral laterality may indeed be an indication of cerebral dominance as Orton suggested. It is questionable, however, that this is a simple, quantitative relationship such that the extent of lateral preference signals the extent of cerebral dominance. A quantitative relationship is as doubtful for competing laterality measures as for Orton's peripheral motor preferences.

Motor Intergrading and Cerebral Intergrading

For Orton, the particular cerebral anomaly that prevented the child from learning to read was cerebral intergrading, an intermixing of the brain areas responsible for language-related tasks. Cerebral intergrading is one hypothesis about brain function that derives directly from lateral motor preferences: A diffuse rather than a focal representation of language within the tertiary zones of the cortex is inferred from the absence of lateralized peripheral motor preferences.

> Since the principle of functional superiority of one brain hemisphere is operative in the control of the language function in the normal adult as well as in determining a greater capacity for the acquisition of skilled acts on one side of the body, we may safely assume that a variability exists in the establishment of the unilateral patterns in language development in the child comparable to the demonstrable variation found in the motor patterns [p. 68].

As Satz (1976) notes, the intergrading construct is little more than a label describing unobservable events referable to dyslexic children. Furthermore, the notion of cerebral intergrading finds little empirical support. Many proficient readers have no clear lateral preferences, as Orton himself admitted (pp. 62–63). The incidence of bilateral cerebral speech representation is low (Milner, Branch, & Rasmussen, 1966)—much lower than the incidence of incompletely established lateral preference.

Some researchers, who continued to reason in Orton's manner, have compounded the problem by attempting to predict individual cerebral laterality from a knowledge of group motor preferences. Zangwill (1960), for example, interpreted the anomalous handedness in his poor readers to mean a less lateralized, more diffuse, cerebral representation of reading- or language-related functions. But, of course, left handedness need not entail a diffuse linguistic representation in the brain (Milner, Branch, & Rasmussen, 1966) even if left handers as a group show less established left-hemisphere language dominance. In a sample of 20 left-handed aphasics, for instance, half may have left-sided lesions, and half right-sided; it is not the case that each individual has diffuse language representation.

Changing Peripheral Laterality and Altering Brain Function

One questionable heritage from the early research on developmental dyslexia is the view that enforced changes in lateral preference will alter brain efficiency for reading. As early as 1906, Claiborne drew pedagogic implications from his observations of anomalous peripheral laterality in word-blind children: "When symbol or auditory amblyopia exists in such children, it is a reasonable idea that they may be taught to be left-handed. It is improbable that the corresponding cells on the right side are similarly affected, and thus the speech center and the symbols and sounds may be transferred entirely to that side, or the right side be so educated that it takes command [p. 1816]."

There is no evidence that such manipulations, particularly in mid- or late-childhood, would alter speech representation. The main factor in right hemisphere speech seems to be left-sided birth lesions (Rasmussen & Milner, 1977). The idea of altering brain function through manipulations of peripheral laterality did not die out in 1906; it is present today in the form of procedures that stimulate the right ear with tones of a particular frequency in order to enhance left hemisphere operations.

Pathologies of the Dyslexic Brain

In searching for the neural substrate of dyslexia, early studies emphasized structural alterations in a given area, whereas later research implicated the failure to develop a normal physiological pattern of action in that region. Some of the later work did serve to broaden the range of putative mechanisms for developmental behavioral functions. For instance, Orton's (1937, 1966) account of how memory images are "elided" from one hemisphere during normal reading, if implausible today, at least suggested the notion that suppressive or inhibitory mechanisms might be important for skill acquisition (Dennis, 1976).

There is no doubt that the developmentally dyslexic brain is not functioning optimally. The pathologies sometimes ascribed to it, whether structural or functional, were (and are) often implausible. Brain models constructed on the basis of peripheral laterality measures are logically poor: A left-hand superiority, for instance, is not sufficient evidence to hypothesize a brain with two right hemispheres. In some instances, the empirical evidence does not support the proposed pathology: Deficits on visuospatial tests do not indicate a right hemisphere lesion. At best, the physiological mechanisms proposed are relevant to only a limited subset of reading processes. For example, Orton thought that the visual engrams in one hemisphere needed to be suppressed in order to permit their "facile associative linkage [1966, p. 96]" with auditory engrams, that is, that the brain's task in reading was to mediate cross-modal associations.

Perhaps the fundamental problem with many dyslexia-based brain models goes beyond errors of fact, inference, or construct formation. The brains hypothesized, wherever and whatever their suggested pathology, have no specific mechanism to deal—well or ill—with the range of operations performed by the fluent or dysfluent reader.

LEARNING TO READ WITH HALF A BRAIN: WHICH OPERATIONS DOES EACH HEMISPHERE ACQUIRE?

Subject Material

Studies of the failure to acquire reading normally begin from a behavioral deficit—dyslexia—and then speculate about the kind of brain that cannot learn to read. The answer to this question has been sometimes useful, sometimes implausible, depending in large measure on the depth of under-standing of the reading process. Surprisingly, few studies consider the obverse relationship by beginning from a condition of know developmental brain pathology and considering which reading operations such a brain can learn to perform. This type of investigation represents a virtually untapped source of information about the neuropsychology of dyslexia. If conducted with reference to modern analyses of the reading operation, it could both enhance understanding of how children learn to read with particular forms of brain damage and limit the more implausible speculations about brain pathology in dyslexia.

One approach to the problem of cerebral dominance and reading acquisi-tion is to take children with pathology in one hemisphere and to ask how this particular congenital aberration limits the ability to read single words, sentences, and texts. Such an investigation would reveal what each hemisphere, developing in isolation, contributes to the acquisition of written language. Such pathology is rare, so what the left hemisphere performs in isolation need not be identical to its role during normal or unsuccessful reading acquisition for individuals possessing two hemispheres. The single-hemisphere case, nevertheless, provides an opportunity to explore the limits of hemispheric asymmetry for the processing of written language.

The children studied are three cases of *Sturge–Weber syndrome*, each with one hemisphere removed in infancy to control intractable seizures. Although of similar intelligence, the children with only a right hemisphere are less sensitive than the right hemidecorticate to the grammatical structure of English (Dennis & Whitaker, 1976), to aspects of meaning derived from the form of an utterance (Dennis, 1980b), and they even have different strategic modes for processing sentential structure (Dennis, 1980a). The left hemidecorticate children show the syntactic defects of older left-hemidecorticate infantile hemiplegics (Dennis & Kohn, 1975).

Results of Reading and Spelling Tests

The following section summarizes the written language skills of the hemidecorticate children; more detail may be found in Dennis, Lovett, and Wiegel-Crump (1981).

The ability to decode nonsense words was assessed (Goldman, Fristoe, & Woodcock, 1974) on two occasions, 3 years apart (ages 10–11 and 13–14). In reading or spelling nonsense words, the right hemidecorticate child was superior to the left operates at both ages. The left hemidecorticate decoding failure was not due to inability to make cross-modal associations, because these children performed better than the right operate in learning the nonsense names for a set of random patterns, suggesting that the cross-modal operation in reading and spelling was not specifically difficult for them. Further, the oral and written spelling of two left hemidecorticates were equally poor.

When the children performed various forms of decomposition on heard nonsense words—segmenting, blending, reauditorizing—the right hemidecorticate was again superior. Each left-hemidecorticate child experienced difficulty with some (if not all) aspects of sound analysis. The right hemisphere appeared to be a poorer substrate than the left for manipulating the internal structure of words, heard or seen.

Because producing a word in written form increased the left hemidecorticate's difficulty in attacking unfamiliar words, it was important to study the children's knowledge of English orthography. This involves two types of regularities: The first is concerned with the allowable sequence of letter classes (graphotactics); the second, with the rules relating graphemes to sound (Venezky, 1967). The children were asked to judge if pseudowords varying in order of approximation to English (Hirata & Bryden, 1971) were possible words, when the higher-order approximations resemble closely normal English words. Although each child could perform the task, the right hemidecorticate proved more sensitive than either left operate to the statistical structure of permissible letter sequences in English. More important, when the children's reading and spelling errors were analyzed, the right hemidecorticate was considerably more adept in applying markers, geminate consonants, morpheme and phonotactic rules. The error analysis showed how rules had been generalized from years of experience with written English to the decoding of unfamiliar nonsense words. The right hemidecorticate, unlike the left operates, extracted not only information about the specific phone–letter matchings to which he had been exposed, but also morphophonemic and phonotactic rules that represent generalizations about the way graphemes map to and from sound.

The decoding tests revealed the right hemisphere to be inferior to the left in manipulating fundamental components of the reading operation. The next question was whether (Perfetti & Lesgold, 1977) or not (Smith & Holmes, 1971) such lower-order deficits prevented comprehension of more extended prose units.

In adolescence, the hemidecorticate children were tested for various skills in prose comprehension: extracting meaning from single sentences, integrating information across successive sentences, deriving implied information from text, and recalling the main ideas of a prose passage. The first question was whether they differentiated the different kinds of information in a sentence. When tested for recognition of semantic, syntactic, or specific lexical change in a sentence (Lovett, 1979), each child not only identified the no-change sentences but was also able to respond selectively to different kinds of sentential information. The second question considered story comprehension. Text comprehension requires that semantic operations relate information both within and between sentences. When the children were asked to judge the truth of an inferential statement based on intersentence semantic constraints (Note 1), to appreciate implications based on specific lexical information, to understand inferences of a presuppositional and consequential nature (Paris & Upton, 1976), or to recall the gist of a story (Mandler & Johnson, 1977), no clear hemispheric asymmetry was found.

A difference between the two left hemidecorticates on the text comprehension and memory tasks suggested that some isolated right hemispheres may have a poor memory for text. The basic result, however, was clear: The lower-order decoding deficits in the left hemidecorticates do not necessarily prevent them understanding what they read, particularly in individual sentences. It is the case, however, that selective left-hemidecorticate comprehension deficits may appear when the task demands include the discrimination of fine detail within a story or the simultaneous use of information from several different sentences in the text.

Reading accuracy is often a sufficient demonstration of reading competence, but the extent to which reading skills are automatized may be equally important (LaBerge & Samuels, 1974). The hemidecorticate children's reading fluency was assessed. The Denckla and Rudel (1974) automatized naming test showed the two hemispheres to be equally rapid at reading letters, colors, or animal pictures, but the mechanics of automatization to be more poorly developed in the right hemisphere (as indicated by a greater number of pacing, perseveration, and anticipation errors). The automaticity of sentence processing was assessed by a cloze procedure (Doehring, 1976; Doehring & Hoshko, 1977) that required an omitted word (either a semantic or a syntactic deletion) to be provided. Although all children understood the sentences, the right-hemidecorticate child assessed meaning most rapidly. The final study revealed the reason for the left hemisphere superiority in automaticity. When sentences were scrambled so that either the lexical content or the syntactic structure is removed (Notes 1 and 2), the right hemidecorticate's accuracy and speed were more disrupted than those of the left operates by the absence of sentence structure and textual constraints. The poorer development of decoding and automaticity in the isolated right hemisphere is associated with a failure to capitalize on written syntax, the higher-order structures that relate words in texts.

Written Language Processing in Each Hemisphere

As a substrate for the acquisition of written language, the left hemisphere was superior to the right in reading and spelling unfamiliar words, and in exploiting the structure of sentence units and grammar to achieve fluency. In relation to the right, the left hemisphere read texts with a higher level of fluency and accuracy, and retained meaning more successfully. An atypical lateralization of language affects, not only the decoding of single words, but also the integration of textual material over units larger than the sentence.

The left-hemisphere superiority in written language was not due to an enhanced capacity for relating sounds to signs. In the right hemisphere, proficiency at learning names for signs was associated with deficits in blending and segmenting words, in applying morphophonemic and phonotactic rules to the decoding of unfamiliar words, and by deficient prose reading; whereas, in the left hemisphere, relatively inefficient logograph learning did not prevent the acquisition of skilled and fluent single word and prose reading.

The acquisition of effective decoding depends not so much on mastery of the cross-modal associations of written language as on the ability to manipulate and exploit the rules of English orthography. How does implicit or explicit knowledge of such rules account for the degree of automaticity a reader achieves? Do the same rules explain differences in the extraction of textual meaning? What is the relation between automaticity and comprehension?

Written English captures facts about meaning, sound, and symbol (Gleitman & Rozin, 1977) rather than transcribing any one level. The three hemidecorticate children can be contrasted in terms of their access to each of three systems concerned with representing meaning, sound, and symbol: phonemic (phone–letter correspondences), morphophonemic, and logographic (Figure 9.1).

Left-hemidecorticate C. A. was a logographic decoder, as shown by her poor reading of unfamiliar words and also, perhaps, in her tendency to normalize new words to familiar ones. Despite poor access to the phono-

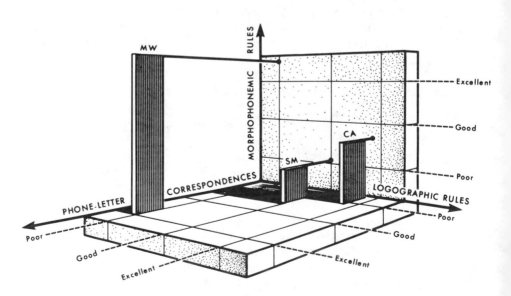

FIGURE 9.1. Schematic representation of written language systems available to the left and right hemispheres.

logical structure of new words, she decoded overlearned words fluently, learned logograph names rapidly, and readily read symbol-like material such as animal pictures or color swatches. Such a logograph-based reading system provides enhanced automaticity for single words, but not for larger textual units, with the result that the automatization and comprehension of texts are deficient.

The other left hemidecorticate, S. M., was a less-skilled logographic learner, and his decoding was poorly automatized. But because he had a more complete roster of phone–letter correspondences, his decoding accuracy and gist comprehension were generally greater. The limitations of his reading system concerned fluency rather than text comprehension.

Written language for the right hemidecorticate, M. W., was anchored securely in the morphophonemic structure of English. His reading system was a generative one that allowed him to read and spell words he had never encountered. He was disrupted to a greater extent than either right hemisphere by the removal of sentential structure or textual constraints, demonstrating the extent to which the left hemisphere uses higher-order linguistic structures to guide comprehension of sentences and texts (see also Dennis & Kohn, 1975; Dennis & Whitaker, 1976). Much more than the right, the left hemisphere capitalizes on large units of written syntactic textual structure.

These studies on the acquisition of written language in a single hemisphere provide clues, not about a particular alexic or dyslexic syndrome or typology, but about the processing characteristics each hemisphere develops for decoding and extracting meaning from words, sentences, and texts. It is not so much that one hemisphere reads better than the other—although true, this observation is hardly new—as that each has developed different information-processing systems to analyze written material. An understanding of these systems reveals both how and what each isolated hemisphere can read.

DISCUSSION

In studying how children learn to read, neuropsychologists have proposed abstractions about the immature brain that might explain reading success or reading failure. Any abstraction about the brain will be based on a selection of facts about its structure or function. In the case of reading, there are a number of potentially important facts; the neuropsychologist's task is to select reading-relevant from reading-irrelevant ones, and to shape the former into a coherent abstraction.

One might think that facts about reading behavior would guide selection of facts about its neural basis, but this has not been the case. Neural models of dyslexia have been based on facts about the brain selected by analogy or temporal correlation, rather than by an analysis of reading.

Sometimes a brain structure has been highlighted because of its importance for adult reading. In assuming that immature brain mechanisms can be
elucidated by analogy with the adult brain, one ignores other features of the
child's brain of equal or greater importance for reading. Undoubtedly,
similarities exist between the heuristic neurology of reading in alexic and
dyslexic populations; there is reason to doubt, however, that the a priori
characterization of dyslexic pathology should be an alexic brain.

When the immature rather than mature brain has been considered, brain
facts used to form an abstraction have often been selected by temporal
correlation rather than an analysis of behavior. Orton (1937, p. 20) argued
that the features of brain maturation important for reading might be those
most active at the time the child began to learn to read. This is not an
abstraction or neural model, of course, since the only evidence for it is the
temporal patterning of the neural and behavioral events. The issue here is not
whether certain facts about brain maturation (such as the late myelination of
commissural and association cortices) are important for any abstraction
about reading—undoubtedly, they are—but rather which functional systems
in the immature brain might subserve various transformations of print that
are required of the beginning reader.

The plausibility of speculations about brain pathology in dyslexia has
rarely been tested against the reading skills of children with known cerebral
insult. The proposed anomalies of cerebral dominance in dyslexic children,
for instance, might profitably be evaluated in light of findings about the
written language skills of children with known perturbations of normal
hemispheric dominance. In children with early hemidecortication, for instance, each hemisphere is proficient at somewhat different reading operations. For the left hemisphere, those operations concern the morphophonemic and grammatical structure of English, whereas the right hemisphere contribution to reading acquisition involves fewer linguistic operations and more learned cross-modal associations. When only one hemisphere
learns to read and spell, each hemisphere makes a different contribution to
reading, with the left being more important than the right for the fluent
reading of sentences and syntactically complex texts.

The problem with the constructs purporting to characterize brain pathology in developmental dyslexia is not just that they refer to unobservable
events (Satz, 1976)—many brain events can be operationalized in some
manner—but that they are untestable in relation to formal analyses of the
reading operation. Research into dyslexia has not yet succeeded in constructing a brain that can account for learning to derive meaning from print, in large
measure because to date the analysis of reading in dyslexic and brain-
damaged children has been descriptive rather than formal, unlike current

analyses of normal readers (Mewhort & Campbell, 1981). If the behavior cannot yet be formalized, then abstractions about the brain mechanisms that subserve it are unlikely to be valid.

ACKNOWLEDGMENT

Work on this chapter was supported by an Ontario Mental Health Foundation Scholarship and by Ontario Mental health Foundation Research Grant #763. I am grateful to Martha Denckla for her critical comments on the chapter.

REFERENCE NOTES

1. Lovett, M. W. 1977. Early reading competence: The perception and memory of sentential information. Unpublished doctoral dissertation, McGill University.
2. Lovett, M. W., & Rabinovitch, M. S. A study of early reading competence: Linguistic structure and the eye–voice span. Paper presented to 38th annual meeting of the Canadian Psychological Association, Vancouver, British Columbia, June 1977.

REFERENCES

Aaron, P. G., Baxter, C. F., & Lucenti, J. Developmental dyslexia and acquired alexia: Two sides of the same coin? *Brain and Language*, 1980, *11*, 1–11.
Bakker, D. J. Hemispheric specialization and stages in the learning-to-read process. *Bulletin of the Orton Society*, 1973, *23*, 15–27.
Bastian, H. C. On the physiology of thinking. *Fortnightly Review*, 1869, 5, 57–71. (a)
Bastian, H. C. On the various forms of loss of speech in cerebral disease. *The British and Foreign Medico-Chirurgical Review*, 1869, *49*, 209–236, 470–492. (b)
Benson, D. F. The third alexia. *Archives of Neurology*, 1977, *34*, 327–331.
Benson, D. F., Brown, J., & Tomlinson, E. B. Varieties of alexia. *Neurology*, 1971, *21*, 951–957.
Benson, D. F., & Geschwind, N. The alexias. In P. J. Vinken & G. W. Bruyn (Eds.), *Handbook of clinical neurology Volume 4*. Amsterdam: North-Holland, 1969. Pp. 112–140.
Benton, A. L. Developmental dyslexia: Neurological aspects. In W. J. Friedlander (Ed.), *Advances in neurology*. New York: Raven Press, 1975. Pp. 1–47.
Benton, A. L. Some conclusions about dyslexia. In A. L. Benton & D. Pearl (Eds.), *Dyslexia*. New York: Oxford University Press, 1978. Pp. 453–476.
Berger, N. S., & Perfetti, C. A. Reading skill and memory for spoken and written discourse. *Journal of Reading Behaviour*, 1977, *9*, 7–16.
Boder, E. Developmental dyslexia: A diagnostic approach based on three atypical reading–spelling patterns. *Developmental Medicine and Child Neurology*, 1973, *15*, 663–687.
Buckingham, H. W. Early development of association theory in psychology as a forerunner to

connection theory. In H. A. Whitaker, R. Joynt, & S. Greenblatt (Eds.), *Historical studies in neuropsychology and neurolinguistics.* New York: Academic Press (in press).

Claiborne, J. H. Types of congenital symbol amblyopia. *Journal of the American Medical Association,* 1906, *47,* 1813–1816.

Coltheart, M., Patterson, K., & Marshall, J. C. *Deep dyslexia.* London: Routledge & Kegan Paul, 1980.

Denckla, M. B. Color-naming defects in dyslexic boys. *Cortex,* 1972, *8,* 164–176.

Denckla, M. B., & Rudel, R. Rapid "automatized" naming of pictured objects, colors, letters and numbers by normal children. *Cortex,* 1974, *10,* 186–202.

Dennis, M. Impaired sensory and motor differentiation with corpus callosum agenesis: A lack of callosal inhibition during ontogeny. *Neuropsychologia,* 1976, *14,* 455–469.

Dennis, M. Capacity and strategy for syntactic comprehension after left or right hemidecortication. *Brain and Language,* 1980, *10,* 287–317. (a)

Dennis, M. Language acquisition in a single hemisphere: semantic organization. In D. Caplan (Ed.), *Biological studies of mental processes.* Cambridge: MIT Press, 1980. Pp. 159–185. (b)

Dennis, M., & Kohn, B. Comprehension of syntax in infantile hemiplegics after cerebral hemidecortication: Left hemisphere superiority. *Brain and Language,* 1975, *2,* 472–482.

Dennis, M., Lovett, M. W., & Wiegel-Crump, C. A. Written language acquisition after left or right hemidecortication in infancy. *Brain and Language,* 1981, *12,* 54–91.

Dennis, M., & Whitaker, H. A. Language acquisition following hemidecortication: Linguisitic superiority of the left over the right hemisphere. *Brain and Language,* 1976, *3,* 404–433.

Dennis, M., & Whitaker, H. A. Hemispheric equipotentiality and language acquisition. In S. Segalowitz & F. Gruber (Eds.), *Language development and neurological theory.* New York: Academic Press, 1977. Pp. 93–106.

Doehring, D. G. Acquisition of rapid reading responses. *Monographs of the Society for Research in Child Development,* 1976, *41,* Serial Number 165.

Doehring, D. G., & Hoshko, I. M. A developmental study of the speed of comprehension of printed sentences. *Bulletin of the Psychonomic Society,* 1977, *9,* 311–313.

Fisher, J. H. A case of congenital word blindness (inability to learn to read). *Ophthalmic Review,* 1905, *24,* 315–318.

Fisher, J. H. Congenital word blindness (inability to learn to read). *Transactions of the Ophthalmological Society of the United Kingdom,* 1910, *30,* 216–225.

Fletcher, J. M. Linguistic factors in reading acquisition: Evidence for developmental changes. In F. J. Pirozzolo & M. Wittrock (Eds.), *Neuropsychological and cognitive processes in reading.* New York: Academic Press, 1981. Pp. 261–294.

Fletcher, J. M., & Satz, P. Has Vellutino led us astray? A rejoinder to a reply. *Journal of Learning Disabilities,* 1979, *12,* 168–171.

Fletcher, J. M., Satz, P., & Scholes, R. J. Developmental changes in the linguistic performance correlates of reading achievement. *Brain and Language,* 1981, *13,* 78–90.

Fried, I., Tanguay, P. E., Boder, E., Doubleday, C., & Greensite, M. Developmental dyslexia: Electrophysiological evidence of clinical subgroups. *Brain and Language,* 1981, *12,* 14–22.

Geschwind, N., The anatomy of acquired disorders of reading. In J. Money (Ed.). *Reading disability.* Baltimore: Johns Hopkins Press, 1962. Pp. 115–129.

Gleitman, L. R., & Rozin, P. The structure and acquisition of reading. I: Relations between orthographies and the structure of language. In A. S. Reber & D. L. Scarborough (Eds.), *Towards a psychology of reading.* Hillsdale, N. J.: Lawrence Erlbaum Associates, 1977. Pp. 1–53.

Goldman, P. S. Functional development of the prefrontal cortex in early life and the problem of neuronal plasticity. *Experimental Neurology,* 1971, *32,* 366–387.

Goldman, R., Fristoe, M., & Woodcock, R. W. *Goldman–Fristoe–Woodcock sound–symbol tests*. Circle Pines, Minn.: American Guidance Service, 1974.

Hebb, D. O. The effect of early and late brain injury upon test scores, and the nature of normal adult intelligence. *Proceedings of the American Philosophical Society*, 1942, *85*, 275–292.

Hinshelwood, J. Congenital word-blindness. *Lancet*, 1900, *i*, 1506–1508.

Hirata, K., & Bryden, M. P. Tables of letter sequences varying in order of approximation to English. *Psychonomic Science*, 1971, *25*, 322–324.

Kussmaul, A. Les troubles de la parole (trad. par A. Rueff, Paris, 1884).

LaBerge, D., & Samuels, S. J. *Basic processes in reading: Perception and comprehension*. Hillsdale, N. J.: Lawrence Erlbaum Associates, 1977.

LaBerge, D., & Samuels, S. J. Toward a theory of automatic information processing in reading. *Cognitive Psychology*, 1974, *6*, 293–323.

Lachmann, F. M. Perceptual–motor development in children retarded in reading ability. *Journal of Consulting Psychology*, 1960, *24*, 427–431.

Lovett, M. W. The selective encoding of sentential information in normal reading development. *Child Development*, 1979, *50*, 897–900.

Mandler, J. M., & Johnson, N. S. Remembrance of things parsed: Story structure and recall. *Cognitive Psychology*, 1977, *9*, 111–151.

Mattis, S., French, J. H., & Rapin, I. Dyslexia in children and young adults: Three independent neuropsychological syndromes. *Developmental Medicine and Child Neurology*, 1975, *17*, 150–163.

McFie, J. Cerebral dominance in cases of reading disability. *Journal of Neurology, Neurosurgery and Psychiatry*, 1952, *15*, 194–199.

Mewhort, D. J. K., & Beal, A. L. Mechanisms of word identification. *Journal of Experimental Psychology: Human Perception and Performance*, 1977, *3*, 629–640.

Mewhort, D. J. K., & Campbell, A. J. The rate of word integration and the overprinting paradigm. *Memory and Cognition*, 1980, *8*, 15–25.

Mewhort, D. J. K., & Campbell, A. J. Toward a model of skilled reading: An analysis of performance in tachistoscopic tasks. In G. E. MacKinnon & T. G. Waller (Eds.), *Reading research: Advances in theory and practice Volume 3*. New York: Academic Press, 1981. Pp. 39–118.

Milner, B., Branch, C., & Rasmussen, T. Evidence for bilateral speech representation in some non-right-handers. *Transactions of the American Neurologoical Association*, 1966, *91*, 306–308.

Morgan, W. P. A case of congenital word blindness. *British Medical Journal*, 1896, *2*, 1378.

Orton, S. T. *Reading, writing and speech problems in children*. New York: W. W. Norton, 1937.

Orton, S. T. *"Word Blindness" in school children and other papers on strephosymbolia (specific language disability—dyslexia) 1925–1946*. Pomfret, Conn.: The Orton Society, 1966.

Paris, S. G., & Lindauer, B. K. Constructive aspects of children's comprehension and memory. In R. V. Kail & J. W. Hagen (Eds.), *Perspectives on the development of memory and cognition*. Hillsdale, N. J.: Lawrence Erlbaum Associates, 1977. Pp. 35–60.

Paris, S. G., & Upton, L. R. Children's memory for inferential relationships in prose. *Child Development*, 1976, *47*, 660–668.

Perfetti, C. A., & Goldman, S. R. Discourse memory and reading comprehension skill. *Journal of Verbal Learning and Verbal Behavior*, 1976, *14*, 33–42.

Perfetti, C. A., & Lesgold, A. M. Discourse comprehension and sources of individual differences. In M. Just & P. Carpenter (Eds.), *Cognitive processes in comprehension*. Hillsdale, N. J.: Lawrence Erlbaum Associates, 1977. Pp. 141–183.

Rasmussen, T., & Milner, B. The role of early left-brain injury in determining lateralization of cerebral speech functions. *Annals of the New York Academy of Sciences*, 1977, *299*, 355–369.

Rourke, B. P. Reading retardation in children: Developmental lag or deficit? In R. M. Knights & D. J. Bakker (Eds.), *The neuropsychology of learning disorders*. Baltimore: University Park Press, 1976. Pp. 125–137.

Saffran, E. M., & Marin, O. S. M. Reading without phonology: Evidence from aphasia. *Quarterly Journal of Experimental Psychology*, 1977, *29*, 515–525.

Satz, P. Pathological left-handedness: An explanatory model. *Cortex*, 1972, *8*, 121–135.

Satz, P. Cerebral dominance and reading disability: An old problem revisited. In R. M. Knights & D. J. Bakker (Eds.), *The neuropsychology of learning disorders*. Baltimore: University Park Press, 1976. Pp. 273–294.

Satz, P. Laterality tests: An inferential problem. *Cortex*, 1977, *13*, 208–212.

Satz, P., Fletcher, J., Clark, W., & Morris, R. Lag, deficit, rate and delay constructs in specific learning disabilities: A re-examination. *Bulletin of the Orton Society*, 1982.

Satz, P., Friel, J., & Goebel, R. Some predictive antecedents of specific reading disability: A three-year follow-up. *Bulletin of the Orton Society*, 1975, *25*, 91–110.

Satz, P., Friel, J., & Rudegeair, F. Differential changes in the acquisition of developmental skills in children who later became dyslexic: A three-year follow-up. In D. Stein, J. Rosen, & N. Butters (Eds.), *Plasticity and recovery of function in the central nervous system*. New York: Academic Press, 1974. Pp. 175–202.

Satz, P., & Morris, R. The search for subtype classification in learning disabled children. In R. E. Tartar (Ed.), *The child at risk*. New York: Oxford University Press, 1980.

Schilder, P. Congenital alexia and its relation to optic perception. *Journal of Genetic Psychology*, 1944, *65*, 67–88.

Silver, A. A., & Hagin, R. A. Visual perception in children with reading disabilities. In F. Young & D. Lindsley (Eds.), *Early experience and visual information processing in perceptual and reading disorders*. National Academy of Science, Washington, D. C., 1970. Pp. 445–455.

Smith, F., & Holmes, D. L. The independence of letter, word, and meaning identification in reading. *Reading Research Quarterly*, 1971, *6*, 394–415.

Spiro, R. J., Bruce, B. C., & Brewer, W. F. *Theoretical Issues in Reading Comprehension*. Hillsdale, N. J.: Lawrence Erlbaum Associates, 1980.

Venezky, R. L. English orthography: Its graphical structure and its relation to sound. *Reading Research Quarterly*, 1967, *2*, 75–105.

Zangwill, O. *Cerebral dominance and its relation to psychological function*. Edinburgh: Oliver and Boyd, 1960.

10

Reading and Spelling Disabilities: A Developmental Neuropsychological Perspective

BYRON P. ROURKE

A selective overview of our research program in the neuropsychology of learning disorders is presented in this chapter. The review focuses on the results of developmental studies of reading and spelling disabilities that are both cross-sectional and longitudinal. In addition to presenting our research findings, some tentative conclusions that we feel are warranted are discussed and some indications of the directions that our future research in this area will take are outlined.

Before beginning this review, it would be best to establish at the outset that the children whom we have investigated and whom we have dubbed "learning disabled" were chosen because they meet a specific set of criteria that describe a group of clinical disorders that, although quite common, is not well understood. This is not an appropriate forum within which to consider the many criticisms of these criteria, but it is essential that the reader understand that the learning disabled children employed in the studies to be discussed in this chapter have been chosen with reference to them. These children have full scale IQs on the WISC that fall roughly within the normal range; they

[1] The studies by the author that are reported in this chapter were supported by grants from the Ontario Mental Health Foundation (#195 and #933) and from the Ontario Ministry of Education Grants-in-aid Educational Research and Development Programme.

were not judged to be in need of psychiatric intervention because of socioemotional disturbances; they spoke English as their primary language at home and in school; they were not suffering from uncorrected visual acuity problems or significant hearing losses; they had attended school regularly since approximately the age of 6 years; and, they were not judged to be "culturally deprived." In spite of the fact that none of these factors could be considered to be causative, their performances in at least one—and usually more than one—school subject were rated as seriously deficient.

Although it may be the case that the conclusions that we have arrived at on the basis of our investigations of such children apply to a greater or lesser extent to children who are mentally retarded, emotionally disturbed, multilingual, afflicted with debilitating visual or hearing impairments, deprived of adequate academic instruction, or who are either culturally or linguistically unprepared to benefit from ordinary classroom instruction, there is certainly no empirical evidence that we have generated that would speak to these issues. Hence, it would seem best to assume, until shown to be otherwise, that such generalizations are not justified.

This issue of definition having been dealt with, at least for the purpose of this chapter, we are now in a position to review some of our early developmental studies in which children with undifferentiated learning disabilities were investigated. Our reasons for beginning with an examination of a rather heterogeneous population of learning disabled children should become evident as we proceed, but it would be well to bear in mind that our principal purpose in conducting these studies was to determine whether and to what extent a neuropsychological model for the explanation of such disorders would prove to be meaningful and heuristic.

STUDIES OF CHILDREN WITH UNDIFFERENTIATED LEARNING DISABILITIES

Verbal–Performance Discrepancies

Age 9–14 years

In the first cross-sectional study in this series (Rourke, Young, & Flewelling, 1971), 90 learning disabled children between the ages of 9 and 14 years were divided equally into three groups on the basis of their WISC verbal and performance IQ scores: a high-performance IQ–low-verbal IQ group (HP–LV); a verbal IQ equal to performance IQ group (V = P); and, a high-verbal

IQ–low-performance IQ group (HV–LP). The groups were equated for age and full scale IQ; the range of full-scale IQ was 79 to 119. The performance of these subjects on 12 dependent variables revealed a very marked superiority of the HV–LP group on most measures of verbal and auditory–perceptual abilities, and clear superiority of the HP–LV group on those tasks that primarily involved visual–perceptual skills. For the most part, the V= P group performed at levels that were roughly intermediate to those of the other two groups.

These results indicated that WISC verbal–performance discrepancies could be used to predict rather consistent differential performances in a number of areas for children with learning disabilities. For example, the superiority of the HV–LP group was evident in such areas as word-recognition, spelling, speech-sounds perception, and auditory discrimination, and the superiority of the HP–LV group was evident on tests involving visual–spatial sequencing and short-term visual memory. It is also of interest to note that these results suggested rather strongly that "learning disabilities" constitutes a heterogeneous clinical classification. We will return to a fuller discussion of this issue later in this chapter.

If one assumes that language-related abilities are very likely to be subserved primarily by the left cerebral hemisphere, whereas visual–spatial abilities are likely to be subsumed primarily by the right cerebral hemisphere, the results of this study might suggest that the HV–LP group had relatively intact left hemisphere systems within a context of relatively dysfunctional right hemisphere systems, and that the opposite state of affairs obtained for the HP–LV group. By the same token, no differential superiority of the systems of one cerebral hemisphere over the other would be suspected in the case of the V=P group.

In order to shed further light on this issue, 45 right-handed learning disabled boys who were between the ages of 9 and 14 years were divided into HP–LV, V=P, and HV–LP groups and their performance on 25 measures of motor and psychomotor abilities were examined (Rourke & Telegdy, 1971). The groups were equated for age and full-scale IQ; the WISC full-scale IQ range was 85 to 115. The dependent measures used in this study were chosen so as to reflect varying degrees of both complexity and of the visual–spatial skills that are necessary to complete them successfully. For example, there were some very simple motor tasks (such as strength of grip and speed of tapping) and some relatively complex psychomotor tasks (such as one that involves the timed placement of grooved pegs into holes).

The results of this study indicate that the performances of the HP-LV group on most measures of complex motor and psychomotor abilities were superior to those of the HV–LP group, regardless of the hand employed. These results, together with those of the Rourke et al. (1971) study, indicated that the HV–LP group exhibited relative superiority on tasks thought to be subserved primarily by the left cerebral hemisphere (reading, spelling, speech-sounds perception) and relative inferiority on tasks thought to be subserved primarily by the right cerebral hemisphere (spatial visualization, visual memory, and complex visual–motor coordination), whereas the opposite pattern of relative superiority and impairment characterized the performance of the HP–LV group.

Regardless of one's interpretation of these results, it is clear that the separation of the groups was quite marked in both of these studies. In the Rourke and Telegdy (1971) study, for example, the only ambiguous results related to the absence of significant differences that might have been expected in the differential hand superiority of the HP–LV and HV–LP groups. It is this fairly clear differentiation of children with undifferentiated learning disabilities, who have been classified solely on the basis of these WISC criteria, that contrasts markedly with the pattern of performance evident among younger children who have been chosen in terms of these same WISC criteria and whose performance on the same dependent measures have been analyzed.

Age 5–8 years

In a study carried out by Rourke, Dietrich, and Young (1973), 5- to 8-year-old children with undifferentiated learning disabilities were divided into three groups on the basis of WISC criteria identical to those used in the previously mentioned studies. The three groups were equated for age and full-scale IQ; the full-scale IQ range was 79 to 120. The performance of these subjects on measures of verbal, auditory–perceptual, visual–perceptual, problem-solving, motor, and psychomotor abilities did not yield the same clear-cut differences that were observed in the aforementioned studies with older children. The reasons for the differences in results between the older and younger learning disabled children are, in terms of our present concerns, of more than passing importance.

As can be seen (Figure 10.1) in the comparison of the 5- to 8-year-old data with that for the 9- to 14-year-olds in the Rourke *et al.* (1971) study, the *pattern* of relationships for the verbal, auditory–perceptual, problem-solving, and visual–spatial measures tended to be somewhat similar, but the differences in *levels of performance* were not nearly as clear-cut. In the case of the comparison of the 5- to 8-year-old data with that of 9- to 14-year-olds in the Rourke and Telegdy (1971) investigation, it is evident that not even the pattern of scores is similar, with the only possible exception being in the case of performance on the Pegs measure.

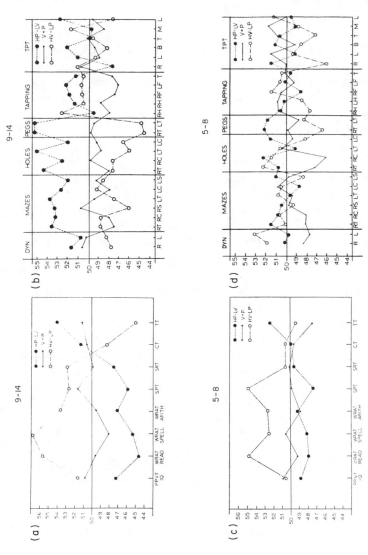

FIGURE 10.1. (a & c): (Left side) Mean *T* scores for each group on the verbal, auditory–perceptual, visual–perceptual, and problem-solving tasks. Abbreviations: PPVT (Peabody Picture Vocabulary Test); WRAT (Wide Range Achievement Test); READ (Reading subtest); SPELL (Spelling subtest); ARITH (Arithmetic subtest); SPT (Speech-Sounds Perception Test); SRT (Seashore Rhythm Test); CT (Category Test); TT (Target Test). (b & d): (Right side) Mean *T* scores for each group on the motor and psychomotor tasks. Abbreviations: R (Right hand); L (Left hand); T (Time); C (Counter); S (Speed); F (Foot); B (Both hands); M (Memory); L (Location). (Adapted, with permission of the *Journal of Clinical Psychology* © 1971 and *Perceptual and Motor Skills* © 1971, from Rourke and Telegdy, 1971).

Variable Performance: Older and Younger Children

The absence of significant intergroup differences on the great majority of motor and psychomotor measures may reflect a general lag in sensorimotor development in younger children with learning disabilities, as has been proposed by Kephart (1960). Another dimension that may have been responsible for the differences in the performance of these two age groups is the fact that the standard deviations for the dependent variables for the older subjects were considerably lower than were those for the young subjects. There was much more intrameasure variability among the younger subjects. Also,there was probably a high incidence of cerebral dysfunction in this younger group (the records of 45 of the 58 subjects in this group who had received EEG examinations were described as "borderline" or "abnormal"). This state of affairs would also be expected to contribute to higher levels of variability. Furthermore, it would be expected that younger children with learning disabilities would exhibit much higher levels of variability in their WISC verbal and performance IQs than would older subjects.

In any case, for our present purpose these comparisions of younger with older children should serve to illustrate that the differentiation of abilities that is expected to occur with advancing years in normal children would certainly seem to be the rule rather than the exception for learning disabled children as well. Although we have not conducted a study that has been designed to deal specifically with such an issue, it is likely that a comparison of the performances of younger learning-disabled children with those of normal children would demonstrate that there is considerably more variability evident in the performances of the learning disabled. This degree of variability and a lack of clear-cut differences among groups would certainly suggest that the clinician should exercise considerable caution when drawing inferences about patterns of performance in young learning-disabled children on the basis of the sort of psychometric instruments that were used in these investigations.

At the same time, it should be pointed out that there would seem to be rather more marked differentiations among language-related and visual–spatial skills than among motor and psychomotor abilities in this younger learning-disabled population. Although it may be too extreme to suggest that there is little predictability possible on the basis of the latter sets of measures for this group, it would certainly seem clear that one is likely to gain more information from the analysis of verbal, auditory–perceptual, visual–perceptual, and visual–spatial abilities among younger learning-disabled children than from the analysis of their motor and psychomotor performances. Even at these tender ages, the languaged-related and visual–spatial abilities of learning disabled children would seem to be sufficiently well-developed (or differentially developed) to allow for some reasonably reliable observations to be made.

Two additional points concerning the results of this series of studies should also be made. First, it is clear that inferences regarding 9- to 14-year-old children that are based on results obtained from adults with well-documented lateralized and nonlateralized cerebral lesions are at least possible. However, adult-based models would seem to fare rather more poorly when one attempts to use them as a way of interpreting the performances of younger children. These observations, based on the results of the first three studies, will be raised almost to the status of principles as we proceed to examine the results of subsequent investigations in this area that have focused on children with more "specific" deficiences in learning.

Comparisons with Brain-Damaged Children

Before proceeding with an analysis of such studies, however, one further series of investigations of a cross-sectional sort should be discussed. These investigations (Czudner & Rourke, 1972; Rourke & Czudner, 1972) employed brain-damaged children as subjects and visual and auditory reaction times as the dependent variables. We were concerned with determining whether children with apparently mild, chronic cerebral dysfunction would exhibit the same degree of attentional deficit at older and younger age levels that were roughly equivalent to the age levels compared in the Rourke et al. (1973) study. The results of an earlier investigation (Czudner & Rourke, 1970) had suggested that this would be the case. The finding of interest in these two subsequent investigations was that, for both visual and auditory reaction time measures, younger brain-damaged subjects exhibited longer latencies than did their normal age-mates, whereas there were no differences between these two groups at the older age levels. We took these results to mean that the older brain-damaged subjects had either overcome their attentional deficit or had learned to compensate for it in such a way that it no longer affected adversely their capacity to maintain a state of readiness to respond.

What is of particular interest within the present context is that the results of these reaction time studies stand in marked contrast to those dealing with verbal IQ–performance IQ discrepancies. Setting aside for the moment the rather obvious differences in subject populations employed in these two sets of studies and the limitations imposed by cross-sectional data of this sort, the possibility remains that the lessening of attentional deficit with advancing years may very well be the crucial factor that allows deficiencies in more basic information processing differences to emerge with greater clarity. The implication here is that attentional deficiencies evident at younger age levels may mask information processing differences among groups of children who are suffering from different brain-related deficiencies. In order to illustrate this point, an analogy with the temporal sequence of the psychological sequelae of head injury may be instructive.

Immediately following fairly severe head injury, it is often the case that the symptoms of brain-stem concussion predominate. The usual reason given for this is that there is a certain amount of brain edema or swelling after serious mechanical trauma of the head, and that this essentially prevents one from seeing with any degree of clarity the focal symptoms due to damage at higher (cortical) levels of damage that would otherwise be evident. With time, recovery usually takes place in the sense that edema subsides, the person becomes more alert, the symptoms of brain-stem concussion disappear, higher cortical control is more evident and, of particular importance within the present context, previously masked signs of focal cortical involvement begin to emerge. After several months, when the person's condition is said to have "leveled off" or become stable, we often see only rather focal, circumscribed deficiencies that, although present from the time of the head injury, were hidden or masked by the more pervasive effects of brain-stem concussion and edema.

The analogy between this temporal sequence and the previously mentioned verbal IQ–performance IQ discrepancy and attentional deficit studies is fairly straightforward. It may be the case that attentional deficit is a type of "psychic edema," in the sense that it can mask specific information-processing deficiencies under an umbrella of very compelling problems such as hyperactivity, distractibility, and disruptiveness. It is only after this "psychic edema" subsides, that is, after the maturation and learning that accompany advancing years have had their effects, that we are able to see clearly the rather specific central processing deficiencies that have been present all along and that have been "hidden" by the more generalized and diffuse effects of attentional deficit.

One consequence of this is that, although we often see children recover from their attentional deficit with advancing years, this seems not to have anything approaching a very general positive effect on their academic learning abilities. For example, it is quite common to see a child who makes some advances in arithmetic calculation, which requires attention to detail and persistence, after his or her attentional deficiencies subside. But this same child may still have very serious deficiencies in reading and spelling, in spite of the fact that he or she is now quite capable of attending to the matters at hand. In such cases, we usually find that the child has very serious problems in phonemic hearing and phonemic segmentation and that language-related skills are severely deficient. In other words, the child has a fairly circumscribed set of deficiencies that hamper information processing through the auditory mode, within the context of adequate attentional, nonverbal concept formation, and visual–spatial abilities that allow for advances to be made in mechanical arithmetic competencies. It is investigations of these sorts of variable competencies and specific deficiencies in academic skills to which we will now turn our attention.

STUDIES OF CHILDREN WITH READING DISABILITIES

Sex Differences

In a study (Canning, Orr, & Rourke, 1980), which bears certain similarities to that of Rourke *et al.* (1973), we compared the performances of male and female retarded readers at two age levels (6.5–8.5 years and 10.5–12.5 years) on a number of perceptual, visual–motor, linguistic, and concept-formation abilities. We did so because there were suggestions in the literature dealing with reading disorders in children (Witelson, 1976) to the effect that the brain might be a "sex organ." This assertion suggests that the brains of males and females are organized differently, and that this difference is important with respect to the etiology and treatment of developmental dyslexia. We wanted to see if a deduction based on this view could stand up to empirical test. In addition, since sex differences are an important consideration in the development of a great many abilities in normal children (Maccoby & Jacklin, 1974), it seemed reasonable to determine whether and to what extent similar sex differences in adaptive abilities would be evident in groups of learning disabled children.

Eighty subjects were employed in this investigation: 20 male and 20 female retarded readers at each of the two age levels. All of the subjects obtained reading centile scores below 30 on the Wide Range Achievement Test (WRAT) (Jastak & Jastak, 1965). The subjects were chosen such that there were no significant differences between (*a*) the four groups on the WRAT Reading subtest, (*b*) the four groups in WISC full-scale IQ, and (*c*) the two groups at each age level in age. It was thought that there might be sex differences in at least some of the perceptual, psychomotor, linguistic, and concept-formation abilities on which the boys and girls at each age level were compared. It was also thought that at least some of these differences, if found, would vary as a function of age. The results were quite clearly contrary to both of these expectations.

These results were in sharp contrast to the findings of most previous developmental research in this area that has demonstrated fairly marked sex differences within populations of normal children on dependent measures of the sort that were employed in this study. Also, since performances on some of the measures used are known to be sensitive to the integrity of the cerebral hemispheres in children at these ages (Boll, 1974; Rourke, 1975), the virtually identical performances of the boys and girls at each age level would suggest very strongly that there are no differences in brain status among the retarded readers of each sex at each of these two age levels. Finally, these results offer no support for the view that male and female retarded readers require quite different modes of remedial intervention if they are to make advances in reading. On the contrary, the results would suggest that a far more reasonable educational tack to take would be to disregard the sex of retarded readers and to focus on their particular patterns of adaptive abilities and deficits in order to design useful modes of intervention (see Rourke, 1976a, 1981, for suggestions along these lines).

With respect to the developmental considerations that are the focus of concern in this chapter, there are some features of this study that should be pointed out. For example, it should be emphasized that this was a cross-sectional study that employed children at ages where sex differences in the abilities in question are known to be present among normal children. In addition, the measures were chosen to reflect a broad range of adaptive abilities that would seem to do some "justice" to the general categories of abilities that are known to be subserved by the brain and that have been found to be impaired when one or more of the systems within the brain are dysfunctional. For these reasons, it is possible to assert with a certain degree of confidence that sex differences, at least in the case of reading disorders, at these two age levels, are not relevant neuropsychological considerations. In fact, it would appear that the condition or conditions that lead to reading disorders have the effect of "erasing" sex differences that are known or thought to be present in normal children at these ages. Among other things, this might suggest that the neuropsychological deficits that are thought by some to underlie disorders in reading have a kind of "leveling" effect on the interactive product of genetic and environmental factors that ordinarily eventuate in sex-based differences in adaptive functioning in normal children. This issue of neuropsychological deficits and their relationship to reading retardation was the focus of another series of investigations of a longitudinal nature that were carried out in our laboratory. These studies are discussed next.

Developmental Lag or Deficit

Paradigms

In one of the investigations in this series (Rourke, 1976b), the relative merits of the "developmental lag" position and the "deficit" position with respect to the explanation of reading disorders in children were examined. In order to do this, the results of a study conducted by Paul Satz and his colleagues (Satz, Friel, & Rudegeair, 1974) and data from our own longitudinal investigation of reading disabled and normal readers were scrutinized in the light of seven "developmental lag"–"deficit" paradigms. These paradigms were developed in an attempt to characterize various types of lag and deficit results that are obtained in developmental studies of learning disabled subjects. These types are presented in Figure 10.2. Although these paradigms are not viewed as completely exhaustive, they are felt to characterize the principal sorts of results that are usually obtained in studies such as those under consideration. In point of fact, one result of this investigation was that it was quite easy to structure the data from Paul Satz's laboratory and from our own in terms of them.

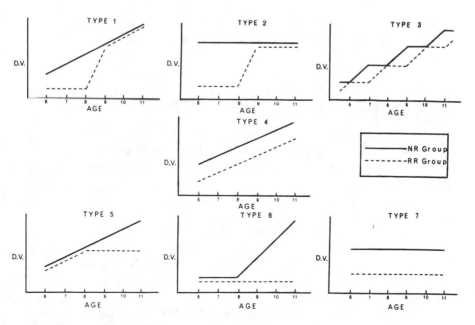

FIGURE 10.2. Seven developmental lag–deficit paradigms. Abbreviations: DV, dependent variable; NR, normal reading; RR, retarded reading.

These paradigms illustrate age–performance interactions over time that can accommodate both longitudinal and cross-sectional data. It would take us too far afield to describe them in detail, but it should be pointed out that 1, 2, and 3 represent "lag" paradigms; 5, 6, and 7 "deficit" paradigms; and 4 an essentially ambiguous state of affairs. This is so because the developmental lag position, at least as espoused by Satz and Van Nostrand (1973), maintains that the skills of disabled readers will develop more slowly than will those of normal children, but that the disabled readers will eventually "catch up" to their normal reading age-mates in reading-related skills and, by implication, in reading itself. Types 1, 2, and 3 are pictorial representations of three possible ways in which this can happen. Type 5, 6, and 7 illustrate age-related modes of development where neither a slow, steady rate of development nor eventual catching up over time is implied. Rather, the states of affairs outlined in these paradigms are those wherein rather persistent—if not permanent—states of disability are envisioned. Type 4 represents a situation that is ambiguous with respect to the lag–deficit dichotomy because eventual catching up may occur (lag), or the performance of the disabled reader may plateau while that of the normal continues to advance (deficit).

Implications

Although there were several very obvious differences between the two studies that were subjected to this analysis (including age differences, size of samples, and methods of subject selection), a number of conclusions could be drawn on the basis of this analysis that are relevant to our current discussion. For example, the data that fit the developmental lag paradigms were, for the most part, those relating to early emerging and less complex abilities. In addition, some of the measures that best fit into the lag paradigms had very obvious ceiling effects, which virtually assured that a developmental lag interpretation could characterize the data. Furthermore, the abilities that tended to fit the developmental lag paradigms, in that the "catch-up" phenomenon was clearly evident, are those that are ordinarily thought of as being subserved primarily by the right cerebral hemisphere. On the other hand, the abilities that seemed to be best characterized by the deficit paradigms were, for the most part, complex skills that are ordinarily thought to be subserved primarily by systems within the left cerebral hemisphere. In other words, the abilities that seem to catch up are primarily those that are subserved by the right hemisphere, whereas those that do not, that is, those that fit the deficit paradigms, are thought to be subserved primarily by the left hemisphere.

In this connection, it should also be noted that measures sensitive to language-related abilities were in the minority in the Satz *et al.* (1974) investigation, especially at the younger ages where their absence could lend spurious support to some aspects of the Satz and Van Nostrand (1973) notion of developmental lag. Furthermore, the inadequate "floors" for some of the tests that were used would have the similar effect of offering spurious support for the notion that sensorimotor abilities are more crucial during the early stages of learning to read, whereas higher-order conceptual and linguistic abilities are more salient at more advanced reading levels. Recent studies by Satz and his colleagues (Fletcher & Satz, 1980) would certainly suggest that this point of view has been taken into consideration in the interpretation of their data vis-à-vis the development lag issue, and that issues of predictive and concurrent validity are now of more immediate concern to this group than are tests of the developmental lag theory.

With respect to the aims of this chapter, it was the developmental context that brought to light the neuropsychological significance of the results of these two studies. It goes without saying that one must carry out a developmental study in order to determine how well the concept of a developmental lag interpretation fits the phenomena of interest. What may not be so obvious is that, when this is done, the utility of a neuropsychological model for the interpretation of learning disorders can emerge. For example, by looking at the results of these studies in terms of the hypothesized lateralization of abilities that are thought to reflect a developmental lag as opposed to a deficit, new light is shed on a set of phenomena that might otherwise tend to defy meaningful characterization.

Predictive Capacity

There is another way in which longitudinal data of this sort can be used to test hypotheses regarding the neuropsychological foundations of learning disorders in children, that is, by determining the relative predictive accuracy of various measures in the case of normal and disabled readers. One study in our laboratory (Rourke & Orr, 1977) yielded results that indicated that there were some very accurate predictive measures of reading and spelling achievement levels over the course of our 4-year longitudinal study. One very noteworthy aspect of the results of this study was that, especially in the case of retarded readers, performance on the Underlining Test (Rourke & Gates, 1980; Rourke & Petrauskas, 1978) was a much more accurate predictor of eventual achivement levels in reading and spelling than were tests of reading, spelling, or psychometric intelligence. The results of this investigation suggested that performance on the Underlining Test is a far more potent means of identifying retarded readers who are "at risk" (at ages 7–8) with respect to eventual reading and spelling achievement (at ages 11–12) than are the standard measures of psychometric intelligence, reading, or spelling that were used.

Another interesting aspect of the results of this study was that only approximately 25% of the retarded readers made any appreciable gains in reading over the 4-year period. The remaining 75% made little or no progress. One way of viewing this particular finding is that the developmental lag model may "fit" marginally well in the case of those retarded readers who improved, but that a deficit interpretation would be more appropriate in the case of the three-quarters of the group that did not show any appreciable degree of progress.

A Working Hypothesis

The differences evident in the relative predictive accuracy of these various measures for the normal and reading disabled groups should serve to highlight the possibility that a neuropsychological method of analysis could explain the deficiences exhibited by the disabled reader. The working hypothesis is, quite simply, that some form of cerebral dysfunction underlies these deficiencies. A corollary of this position is that one would not expect disabled readers to develop their skills in a manner that would parallel developments in their normal age mates. Quite the contrary, one would expect that a "normal" pattern of development would be the *exception* rather than the rule; that advances in reading and at least some reading-related skills would take place only with very special attention; and then only with considerable effort and good fortune; and that there is no guarantee that such disabled readers would ever catch up in either reading-related skills or in reading itself.

From time to time this particular view of reading disability has been criticized because it is not "optimistic." Although we should not grace this rather romantic position with anything but the sort of fleeting attention that it deserves, it might be well to point out that it is the role of a scientist to tell the truth. Having done this, most scientists would then assume that this truth will, at least in the long run, be beneficial to those who are seemingly given short shrift by the more immediately apparent aspects of such truth. It is doubtful that this particular scenario, however, complete with all of the elements of very bad theatre, obtains, in this instance. Rather, the principal corollary of the neuropsychological deficit position, at least as espoused in this chapter, is that the child with a reading disability is likely to develop a qualitatively distinct manner of dealing with the processing of print.

Among other things, the deficit position of the neuropsychologist implies that the reading disabled child, in order to adapt to the (school) environment, will adopt *different* means for handling information (Usprich, 1976). There is no guarantee that these qualitatively distinct information-processing strategies will lead to better reading. In fact, these attempts at adaptation may be counterproductive. The clinical or practical significance of this situation is that it is incumbent on those who would plan a program for such a child (*a*) to determine the precise parameters of this difference, and (*b*) to provide the sort of habilitational and rehabilitational experiences that are consistent with this difference. In a word, to bury one's head in the sand of a developmental lag position merely because it seems to provide a more comfortable and optimistic view of the reading disabled child does nothing more than forestall the development of appropriate educational techniques for teaching children whose manner of processing information cries out for different, unique, and special forms of intervention.

Subgroups

It should be clear that the results of the latter two investigations, when viewed within the context of other research in this area (Rourke, 1978a, b), suggest that retarded readers are not a homogeneous group. It would seem reasonable to believe that there are rather distinct subgroups of retarded readers, and that attempts to define these subgroups in terms of their neuropsychological ability structure would prove fruitful. Two studies conducted in our laboratory would suggest that this is, indeed, the case.

Age 7–9 years

The first study (Petrauskas & Rourke, 1979) involved the classification of retarded readers between the ages of 7.0 and 8.9 years by means of the technique of *Q* factor analysis. Three reliable subtypes of retarded readers were found at this age level, and a fourth subtype was delineated that was composed primarily of normal readers. It was also found that the three subtypes of retarded readers that were isolated were rather similar to subtypes of retarded readers that had been suggested in the literature (Mattis, French, & Rapin, 1975).

Age 9–14 years

Since this attempt at classification seemed to be useful, we decided to carry out a developmental investigation of a cross-sectional nature that would allow us to determine if subtypes of learning disabled children could be identified between the ages of 9 and 14 years. We were also interested in whether or not the persistence of any subtypes might be found across the age groups. This study (Fisk & Rourke, 1979) involved 264 right-handed children between 9.0 and 14.9 years of age, all of whom had obtained WISC

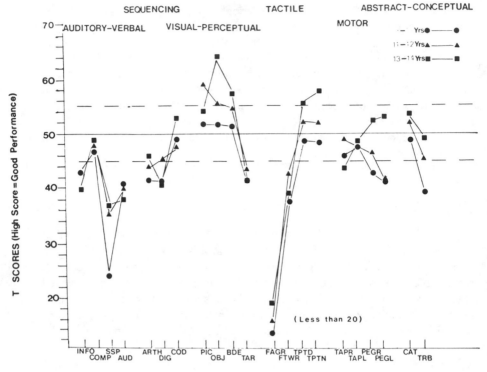

FIGURE 10.3. Graphic illustration of one of the "replicated" subtypes in the Fisk and Rourke (1979) investigation. The words at the top of the graph denote the six categories of dependent variables that were used; the abbreviations for the dependent variables within each category (e.g., INFO = WISC Information) are indicated along the bottom of the graph. (With permission of the *Journal of Clinical Neuropsychology* © 1979).

full-scale IQs within the 86 to 114 range. All of the children had centile scores equal to or less than 30 on all three subtests (reading, spelling, and arithmetic) of the WRAT. From the total sample of subjects, three subsamples that were based on 2-year age intervals were composed, and each age-based sample was equated for WISC full-scale IQ.

Each age-based sample was subjected to a separate Q-factor analysis; this yielded a classification of 80% of the learning disabled children at the three age levels. The most interesting aspect of this study was that two of these subtypes were found at all three age levels, and a third was in evidence at the two older age levels. Figure 10.3 contains an example of one of these replicated subtypes. It should be noted that the correlations between the subtypes that were replicated across age levels were, by definition, very high (in the 80s and 90s), as were the visual configurations for each of their sets of scores on the dependent variables. Of particular interest was the fact that the correlations between the three subtypes that were replicated across either two or three of the age levels were nonsignificant. This would certainly suggest that these replicated subtypes of retarded readers are quite independent of one another, and that they represent very stable configurations of neuropsychological abilities and deficits that tend to persist across the age span from 9 to 15 years.

Implications for Remediation

With respect to the present discussion, the principal point to be made is that, once again, it is clear that a developmental analysis of the neuropsychological abilities and deficits of learning disabled children can yield very specific and potentially very useful information about such children. At the present time, we are designing studies that will enable us to test the relative effectiveness of various remedial programs for these subtypes of learning disabled children. In the design of these studies, we are attempting to use a "challenge" procedure, similar to that employed in studies in psychopharmacology. That is, we are designing remedial education programs of two types: (a) those that we feel would be very compatible with and good for children of each subtype; and (b) those that would constitute "challenge" programs in the sense that they should eventuate in limited progress, no progress, or even regression for the children of specific subtypes. By alternating in a systematic fashion the application of these intervention strategies, it should be possible to demonstrate predictable gains and losses in learning. In this way, we can test our notions about the way in which the brains of children within these various subtypes are organized and, at the same time, offer ways for dealing with these differences in an educationally therapeutic fashion.

STUDIES OF CHILDREN WITH SPELLING DISABILITIES

In this section, three related studies dealing with younger and older disabled spellers will be discussed. The principal dimension of interest in our study of retarded spellers has been the extent to which their misspellings are accurate from a phonetic point of view.

The first study in this series (Sweeney & Rourke, 1978) involved the comparison of normal spellers and two groups of retarded spellers at different age levels. The children were equated with respect to their level of deficient performance in spelling, but they differed markedly in their percentages of phonetically accurate misspellings. The normal group was equated for age and WISC performance IQ with the two groups of disabled spellers.

Phonetic Accuracy or Inaccuracy

This study was designed to circumvent some of the shortcomings that were evident in much of the previous research in the area of spelling retardation in children. Most earlier studies had relied almost exclusively on a level-of-performance approach: that is, straightforward comparisons of groups of normal and retarded spellers. A notable exception to this general trend was the study of Nelson and Warrington (1976). Our investigation was similar to this study in that it involved a comparison of two types of retarded spellers who, on the basis of research results with brain-damaged adults (Kinsbourne & Warrington, 1964; Newcombe, 1969), would be expected to exhibit differences in their psycholinguistic skills. The younger groups were composed of children who were approximately 10 years of age; the older groups were approximately 13.5 years old. At both younger and older age levels there were 8 subjects (5 males and 3 females) in each of the three groups examined. One younger and one older group were composed of retarded spellers who rendered 40% or less of their misspelled syllables on the WRAT spelling subtest in a phonetically accurate manner; we refer to these as the phonetically inaccurate disabled spellers (PIs). In addition, one older and one younger group were composed of retarded spellers who rendered at least 60% of their misspelled syllables on the WRAT spelling subtest in a phonetically accurate manner, the phonetically accurate disabled spellers (PAs). There were no statistically significant differences in degree of spelling retardation between PIs and PAs at either age level. Also, the differences in degree of phonetic accuracy of misspelled syllables between the normal group (Ns) and the PAs at each age level were not statistically significant. Phonetic accuracy was determined on a syllable-by-syllable basis in a fashion that obviated the use of raters. (This sytem is available from the author.)

Age Differences

A graphic illustration of the results of this study is contained in Figure 10.4. The *T*-score means are arranged such that good performance is represented in one direction (above 50) and poor performance is represented in the opposite direction (below 50). As can be seen, the separation of the groups was much more dramatic at the older than at the younger age level. There were a great many significant differences evident at the 13.5-year age level between these groups, but there were only two significant differences at the younger age level.

With respect to differences on specific tests at the older age level, the lack of a significant difference on the Goldman–Fristoe–Woodcock Test of auditory discrimination would certainly suggest that the limiting feature responsible for the poor spelling performance of the PAs and PIs is something other than the type of selective attention deficit suggested by several researchers (Dykman, Ackerman, Clements, & Peters, 1971). The significant differences favoring the normal spellers and the PAs on the sentence memory, auditory closure, and WISC digit span-backward measures at the older age level would suggest that the language abilities of the older PIs "break down" even in the case of tests that involve the comprehension of rather short word strings, the synthesis of sounds, and sequence reversals. The absence of significant differences between the normal spellers and the PAs on the sentence memory, auditory closure, and WISC digit span-backward tests would suggest that the PAs are as adept as are the normals in the application of relatively basic operations to word strings. In addition, there was no evidence that the PAs had any deficiencies relative to their normal counterparts in immediate memory.

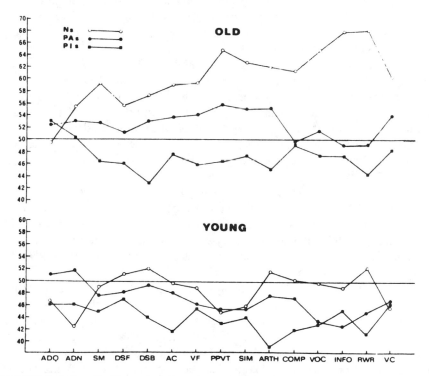

FIGURE 10.4. Graphic illustration of mean standardized T scores for Ns (Normal Spellers), PAs (Phonetically Accurate Retarted Spellers), and PIs (Phonetically Inaccurate Retarded Spellers) at each age level (Sweeney & Rourke, 1978).

On the remainder of the dependent measures, the older PIs performed at levels inferior to those of the normal spellers. However, it is interesting to note the changing relationship of the performance of the PAs vis-à-vis the normal spellers and the PIs at the older age level. The performance of the PAs was not significantly different from those of normal spellers and was superior to that of the PIs on the verbal fluency test and the WISC arithmetic and similarities subtests; their performance was inferior to that of normals and superior to that of the PIs on the Peabody Picture Vocabulary Test. Their performance was inferior to that of the normal spellers and not significantly different from that of the PIs on the WISC information, comprehension, and vocabulary subtests.

It may very well be the case that the dimension of novelty required in the answers to the latter three WISC subtests constituted the feature that limited the performance of the PAs. Indeed, it would appear that the amount of "new" information that is required for a response is the dimension that limits the performance of the PAs. Even on the particular test for verbal fluency that was employed, which involves generating words to a phonological cue, the absence of differences between the normal spellers and the PAs may very well be accounted for in terms of the very good phonemic hearing and, possibly, rhyming skills of the PAs.

In general, the PIs at the older age level performed in a fashion very similar to that which would be expected from an impairment in linguistic systems that are thought to be subserved primarily by the temporal (and, possibly, adjacent) cortical regions of the left cerebral hemisphere. It is clear that the picture is far different in the case of the PAs. If they are, indeed, suffering from limitations imposed by cerebral dysfunction, the data would certainly indicate that the locus and the degree of impairment would have to be considerably different than that hypothesized for the PIs.

As we found in another longitudinal study (Burgher & Rourke, Note 1), in which retarded readers exhibited a significantly greater number of phonetically inaccurate spelling errors as compared to normal readers in Grades 2, 4, 5, and 6, the PIs in the current study were quite deficient in reading (word recognition). It should also be noted that this difference in reading skills was especially evident at the older age levels.

This would certainly seem to indicate that, within the constraints imposed by a cross-sectional study of the sort under consideration, the older PIs are suffering from a deficit that has a progressively more debilitating effect on their reading skills; that is, rather than catching up in reading skills, they appear to fall further behind in them. Overall, there is little doubt that the linguistic deficiencies of the two retarded spelling groups are more marked at the older age level, a result quite contrary to one that would be predicted on the basis of a developmental lag view of learning disabilities.

There is a possibility that the significant difference evident at the younger age level on the WISC arithmetic subtest reflects a deficiency of the PIs to develop, through instruction, the ability to perform complex operations on stimuli. Among other things, this would imply that the PIs may encounter considerable difficulty in inducing rules for processing linguistic information. For this reason, we examined the logical–grammatical reasoning abilities of these younger PIs relative to their normal spelling and PA age-mates (Sweeney, McCabe, & Rourke, Note 2).

In order to test the major hypothesis of this study, we compared the performances of the three groups of subjects at the younger age level in the Sweeney and Rourke (1978) study on the Logico–Grammatical Sentence Comprehension Test (Wiig & Semel, 1974). The results indicated that, as predicted, younger children, who are deficient in spelling ability, show deficiencies in certain aspects of linguistic processing. Overall, the phonetically inaccurate spellers were poorest in logical–grammatical ability as measured by this test.

Thus, the results of this study led to the conclusion that retarded spelling ability appears to be related to deficiencies in logical–grammatical ability, particularly for children whose spelling is predominantly phonetically inaccurate. These findings are consistent with the view that phonetically inaccurate retarded spelling is a reflection of a more general difficulty in developing strategies and rules for the processing of information.

Linguistic Components

Finally, in a recent study (Coderre, Sweeney, & Rourke, Note 3), we compared the performance of 24 children, ages 9- to 11-years who had been divided into 3 groups of spellers similar to those discussed in the preceding studies. The dependent measures were spelling recognition, visual closure, visual memory, and phonemic segmentation. These tests were devised to place stringent linguistic demands on the 3 groups of subjects at this younger age level.

The results of this study suggested that these younger PAs do poorly in spelling because they experience difficulty both in going beyond the phonemic information present in words and in utilizing visual gestalts. Visual memory did not seem to be the primary limiting feature for the performance of the PAs, since they did not differ from the normals on the visual memory test. It was also apparent that the PAs had very well-developed phonemic segmentation abilities, as would be expected. It may very well be the case that, when attempting to spell, however, they devote too much attention to phonemic analysis at the expense of other skills. This, in turn, would suggest that remedial programs for PAs should focus on an appreciation of orthographic relationships over and above those conveyed by phonemic information. Certainly, further instruction in phonemic segmentation would not seem to be advisable for this group of children.

The ability pattern of the PIs on the spelling recognition test, the visual cloze procedures, and the phonemic segmentation test in the Coderre *et al.* study (Note 3) would certainly suggest that they have deficiencies in basic linguistic operations, such as phonemic segmentation, phonemic retrieval, and phonemic synthesis. In addition, relative to the normal spellers, they were deficient in visual memory. These very poor performances suggest that PIs are in need of remedial aid in a much wider range of areas than is the case for the PAs.

With respect to the aims of this chapter, it is important to note that the attempt to place greater "demands" on the linguistic processing capacities of the younger groups in this series of studies brought to light differences that were not apparent in the initial Sweeney and Rourke (1978) investigation. In addition, these differences serve to illustrate that, even at fairly tender ages, the dimension of phonetic accuracy–phonetic inaccuracy in the misspellings of retarded spellers is an extremely important index of very crucial differences in neuropsychological abilities for children who can be classified into distinct groups by this dimension.

CONCLUSIONS

There are some generalizations regarding these research results and speculations that would seem to be in order. In summary form, these are as follows.

1. Younger (5- to 8-year-old) learning disabled children pose problems with respect to the determination of their neuropsychological abilities. These problems are probably the result of some combination of the following: the relative unreliability of neuropsychological instruments at these tender ages; the variability in performance that seems to typify these youngsters; and, their relatively undifferentiated ability structures. In addition, there is sometimes the added complication of an attentional deficit (*psychic edema*) that can serve to mask basic information processing deficiencies at these age levels.

2. There are, however, some ways of getting around these problems. For example, Rourke and Orr (1977) and Fletcher and Satz (1980) were able to show that fairly accurate predictions can be made from data obtained on young learning disabled children. In fact, it would seem

likely that the neuropsychological dimensions of reading and spelling disabilities at these younger ages will, in the future, be revealed through the use of measuring techniques that build on these rather encouraging findings.

3. As learning disabled children approach late childhood and early adolescence, their patterns of abilities and deficits begin to allow for analyses that are based on models developed for use with brain-damaged adults. This should come as no surprise. For the record, however, it is necessary to point out that the results of the studies reviewed in this chapter would certainly indicate that this particular principle has now been demonstrated.

4. There is considerable evidence that learning disabilities in children are a heterogeneous group of clinical disorders. Whether one chooses to divide children into subtypes on the basis of a priori considerations, as in the Sweeney and Rourke (1978) study, or on the basis of empirical subtyping strategies, as in the Petrauskas and Rourke (1979) investigation, the same conclusion emerges: There are very marked differences between children who exhibit equally impaired levels of performance on academic tasks. These differences seem to be related to quite distinct modes and patterns of brain-related information processing capacities. In this connection, it might also be of interest to note that an identical conclusion has been reached with respect to arithmetic disabilities in children (Rourke & Finlayson, 1978; Rourke & Strang, 1978).

5. There is evidence that at least some of the subtypes of learning disabilities in children persist across the age span from 9 to 14 years (Fisk & Rourke, 1979). It is clear that developmental investigations of this type should be continued because of the light that they will probably shed on the natural history of central processing deficiencies and the impact they could have on the planning of remedial intervention programs for such children.

6. There are some sets of deficiencies that serve to "mark" subtypes of learning disabled children (e.g., phonetic inaccuracy of misspellings) that seem to have particularly debilitating consequences for the children who exhibit them. Among other things, this would seem to suggest that the use of a priori classification techniques that are based on sound neuropsychological models should be pursued with even greater vigor than is now the case.

7. The uniqueness evident among the reading- and spelling-disabled populations should serve to reinforce efforts among educators to promote individualized programming for learning disabled children. The principal prerequisite for such programming would seem to be a neuropsychological assessment procedure that is sufficiently sophis-

ticated to reveal the unique features of the child's central processing deficiencies. To do any less is simply to ignore the neuropsychological realities that continue to emerge in the sorts of investigations outlined in this chapter.

ACKNOWLEDGMENT

The author wishes to express his gratitude to John L. Fisk, John D. Strang, Robert D. Gates, and Joan Daly for their helpful comments on the manuscript.

REFERENCE NOTES

1. Burgher, P., & Rourke, B. P. A comparision of the phonetic accuracy of spelling errors of normal and retarded readers—second through sixth grade. Prepublication manuscript.
2. Coderre, D. J., Sweeney, J. E., & Rourke, B. P. Word analysis, visual memory, spelling recognition, and reading in children with qualitatively distinct spelling errors. Prepublication manuscript.
3. Sweeney, J. E., McCabe, A. E., & Rourke, B. P. Logical–grammatical abilities of retarded spellers. Prepublication manuscript.

REFERENCES

Boll, T. J. Behavioral correlates of cerebral damage in children aged 9 through 14. In R. M. Reitan & L. A. Davison (Eds.), *Clinical neuropsychology: Current status and applications*. Washington, D. C.: V. H. Winston, 1974. Pp. 91–120.
Canning, P. M., Orr, R. R., & Rourke, B. P. Sex differences in the perceptual, visual-motor, linguistic and concept-formation abilities of retarded readers. *Journal of Learning Disabilities*, 1980, *13*, 563–567.
Czudner, G., & Rourke, B. P. Simple reaction time in "brain-damaged" and normal children under regular and irregular preparatory interval conditions. *Perceptual and Motor Skills*, 1970, *31*, 767–773.
Czudner, G., & Rourke, B. P. Age differences in visual reaction time of "brain-damaged" and normal children under regular and irregular preparatory interval conditions. *Journal of Experimental Child Psychology*, 1972, *13*, 516–526.
Dykman, R. A., Ackerman, P. T., Clements, S. D., & Peters, J. E. Specific learning disabilities: An attentional deficit syndrome. In H. R. Myklebust (Ed.), *Progress in learning disabilities* (Vol. 2). New York: Grune & Stratton, 1971.
Fisk, J. L., & Rourke, B. P. Identification of subtypes of learning disabled children at three age levels: A neuropsychological, multivariate approach. *Journal of Clinical Neuropsychology*, 1979, *1*, 289–310.
Fletcher, J. M., & Satz, P. Developmental changes in the neuropsychological correlates of reading achievement: A six-year longitudinal following. *Journal of Clinical Neuropsychology*, 1980, *2*, 23–37.
Jastak, J. F., & Jastak, S. R. *The Wide Range Achievement Test*. Wilmington: Guidance Associates, 1965.

Kephart, N. C. *The slow learner in the classroom*. Columbus, Ohio: Merrill, 1960.

Kinsbourne, M., & Warrington, E. K. Disorders of spelling. *Journal of Neurology, Neurosurgery, and Psychiatry*, 1964, *27*, 224–228.

Maccoby, E., & Jacklin, C. *The psychology of sex differences*. Palo Alto: Stanford University Press, 1974.

Mattis, S., French, J. H., & Rapin, I. Dyslexia in children and young adults: Three independent neuropsychological syndromes. *Developmental Medicine and Child Neurology*, 1975, *17*, 150–163.

Nelson, H. E., & Warrington, E. K. Developmental spelling retardation. In R. M. Knights & D. J. Bakker (Eds.), *Neuropsychology of learning disorders: Theoretical approaches*. Baltimore: University Park Press, 1976. Pp. 325–332.

Newcombe, F. *Missile wounds to the brain*. London: Oxford University Press, 1969.

Petrauskas, R. J., & Rourke, B. P. Identification of subtypes of retarded readers: A neuropsychological, multivariate approach. *Journal of Clinical Neuropsychology*, 1979, *1*, 17–37.

Rourke, B. P. Brain–behavior relationships in children with learning disabilities: A research program. *American Psychologist*, 1975, *30*, 911–920.

Rourke, B. P. Issues in the neuropsychological assessment of children with learning disabilities. *Canadian Psychological Review*, 1976, *17*, 89–102. (a)

Rourke, B. P. Reading retardation in children: Developmental lag or deficit? In R. M. Knights & D. J. Bakker (Eds.), *Neuropsychology of learning disorders: Theoretical approaches*. Baltimore: University Park Press, 1976. Pp. 125–137. (b)

Rourke, B. P. Neuropsychological research in reading retardation: A review. In A. L. Benton & D. Pearl (Eds.), *Dyslexia: An appraisal of current knowledge*. New York: Oxford University Press, 1978. Pp. 139–171. (a)

Rourke, B. P. Reading, spelling, arithmetic disabilities: A neuropsychologic perspective. In H. R. Myklebust (Ed.), *Progress in learning disabilities* (Vol. IV). New York: Grune & Stratton, 1978, Pp. 97–120. (b)

Rourke, B. P. Neuropsychological assessment of children with learning disabilities. In S. B. Filskov & T. J. Boll (Eds.), *Handbook of clinical neuropsychology*. New York: Wiley-Interscience, 1981. Pp. 453–478.

Rourke, B. P., & Czudner, G. Age differences in auditory reaction time of "brain-damaged" and normal children under regular and irregular preparatory interval conditions. *Journal of Experimental Child Psychology*, 1972, *14*, 372–378.

Rourke, B. P., Dietrich, D. M., & Young, G. C. Significance of WISC verbal–performance discrepancies for younger children with learning disabilities. *Perceptual and Motor Skills*, 1973, *36*, 275–282.

Rourke, B. P., & Finlayson, M. A. J. Neuropsychological significance of variations in patterns of academic performances: Verbal and visual–spatial abilities. *Journal of Abnormal Child Psychology*, 1978, *6*, 121–133.

Rourke, B. P., & Gates, R. D. *The Underlining Test (preliminary norms)*. Windsor, Ontario: Author, 1980.

Rourke, B. P., & Orr, R. R. Prediction of the reading and spelling performances of normal and retarded readers: A four-year follow-up. *Journal of Abnormal Child Psychology*, 1977, *5*, 9–20.

Rourke, B. P., & Petrauskas, R. J. *Underlining Test (revised)*. Windsor, Ontario: Author, 1978.

Rourke, B. P., & Strang, J. D. Neuropsychological significance of variations in patterns of academic performance: Motor, psychomotor, and tactile–perceptual abilities. *Journal of Pediatric Psychology*, 1978, *3*, 62–66.

Rourke, B. P., & Telegdy, G. A. Lateralizing significance of WISC verbal–performance discrepancies for older children with learning disabilities. *Perceptual and Motor Skills*, 1971, *33*, 875–883.

Rourke, B. P., Young, G. C., & Flewelling, R. W. The relationships between WISC verbal–performance discrepancies and selected verbal, auditory-perceptual, visual-perceptual, and problem-solving abilities in children with learning disabilities. *Journal of Clinical Psychology*, 1971, *27*, 475–479.

Satz, P., Friel, J., & Rudegeair, F. Differential changes in the acquisition of developmental skills in children who later became dyslexic: A three-year follow-up. In D. Stein, J. Rosen, & N. Butters (Eds.), *Plasticity and recovery of function in the central nervous system*. New York: Academic Press, 1974. Pp. 175–202.

Satz, P., & Van Nostrand, G. K. Developmental dyslexia: An evaluation of a theory. In P. Satz & J. J. Ross (Eds.), *The disabled learner: Early detection and intervention*. Rotterdam: Rotterdam University Press, 1973.

Sweeney, J. E., & Rourke, B. P. Neuropsychological significance of phonetically accurate and phonetically inaccurate spelling errors in younger and older retarded spellers. *Brain and Language*, 1978, *6*, 212–225.

Usprich, C. The study of dyslexia: Two nascent trends and a neuropsychological model. *Bulletin of the Orton Society*, 1976, *25*, 34–48.

Wiig, E. H., & Semel, E. M. Development of comprehension of logico–grammatical sentences by grade school children. *Perceptual and Motor Skills*, 1974, *38*, 171–176.

Witelson, S. F. Sex and the single hemisphere: Right hemisphere specialization for spatial processing. *Science*, 1976, *193*, 425–427.

11

The Organization of Visual, Phonological, and Motor Strategies in Learning to Read and to Spell

LYNETTE BRADLEY

THE DILEMMA

Children and adults with problems in reading, writing, and spelling have difficulties that vary from one individual to another. It is not surprising to find that when disabled learners are grouped together as, for example, aphasic, slow learning, or dyslexic, the boundaries between the groups are often unclear, and the groups themselves are obviously heterogeneous.

Examples of the way backward readers write demonstrate this quite clearly. In some cases, the complex and abstract relationships between alphabetic writing and speech seem to present a major problem (Rozin & Gleitman, 1977). An example of this is evident in the sample displayed in Figure 11.1. The writer seems to have made little connection between spoken and written language, for the written words are not presented as spatially distinct wholes.

Other backward readers seem aware that speech can be represented on paper by groups of letters that are spatially distinct. Nevertheless, they are unable to reproduce a meaningful representation of the word in writing, as Figure 11.2 clearly shows. Still others produce strings of correctly written words but fail to generate a meaningful sentence (see Figures 11.3, and

235

NEUROPSYCHOLOGY OF
LANGUAGE, READING, AND SPELLING

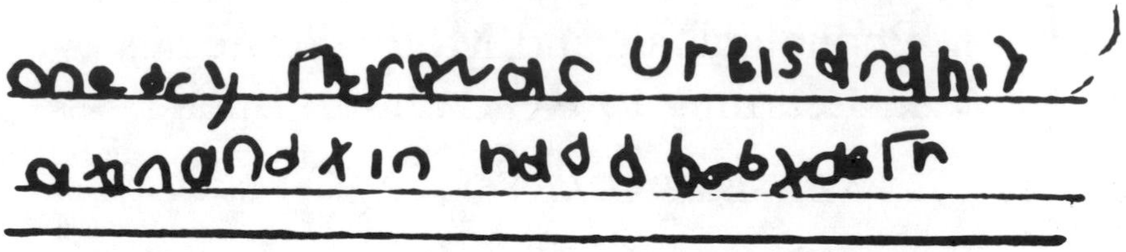

FIGURE 11.1. Words not represented as spatially distinct units (written by boy age 8:10).

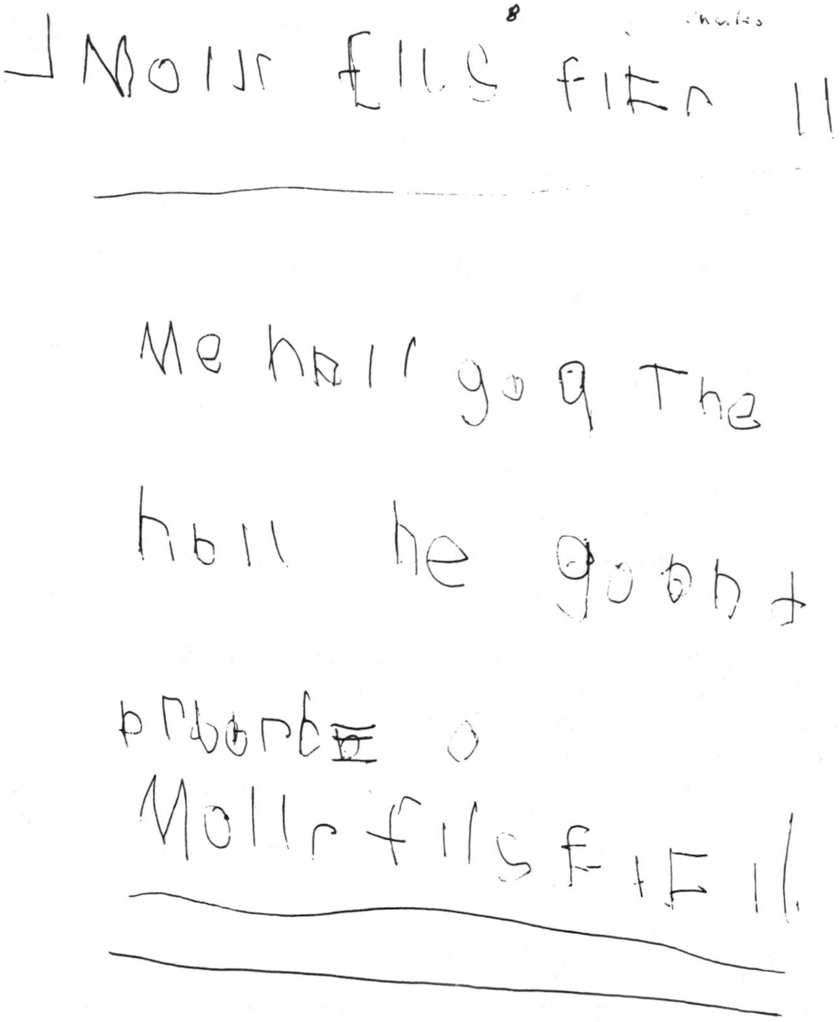

FIGURE 11.2. Spatially distinct written units that are not meaningful words (written by boy, age 8:0).

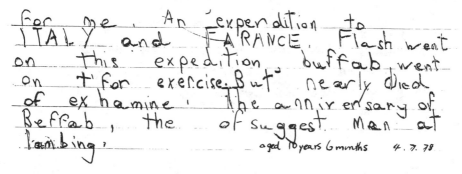

FIGURE 11.3. Correctly written words not used to represent the correct spoken word (boy, age 10:6).

11.4). Thus, some backward readers can learn to read but cannot express their thoughts in writing. It may be that they do not know how to begin, or they are unable to organize what they want to say, or they do not know how to translate spoken language into written language. Possibly they do not know how to organize the spelling patterns into words (Bradley, 1980b). For a different reason, a number of children and adults learn to read but fail to master spelling (Frith, 1980).

Differences among backward readers are also apparent in their oral reading. One boy looked at the word *pasteurization* and said, "I don't know. Boil it." Clearly, he knew the meaning of the word, but he could not decode it either by phonemic analysis or by connecting it with a similiar word, as for example, *pasture*. Another backward reader, confronted with the word, *orchestra*, made several abortive attempts: "or . . . stra; or . . . ches . . . t; I can't *pronounce* it but I know what it means. It's a band that plays music." He was able to use a phonetic strategy, but he could not synthesize well enough to say the word. A third backward reader correctly read the word, *forfeit*, but failed to recognize it as a meaningful unit in language saying, "Forfeit. Is that a word?"

The fact that retarded readers vary so much poses a problem for the development and implementation of training programs. Many investigators have tried to solve the problems associated with backwardness in reading by looking at individual profiles. Because the profiles are so variable, little progress has been made using this approach. In addition, training programs developed as a result of such studies proved to be effective for some subjects but not for others (Boder, 1976).

Let us look at the problem another way: The one thing that all backward readers have in common is that they cannot read or that they find reading difficult. If, instead of looking at individual readers, we ask what it is about the reading and spelling processes that cause so many individuals to fail, we

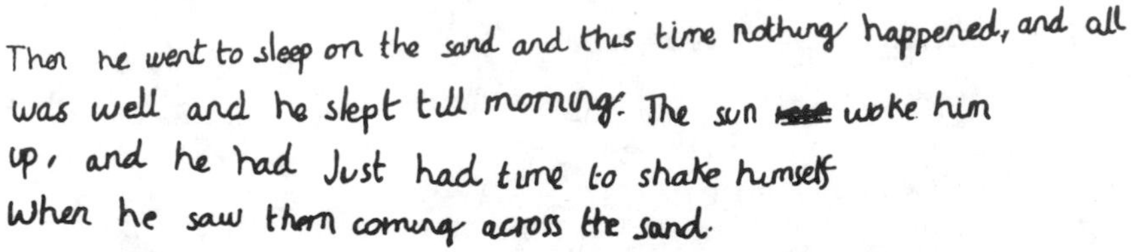

Then he went to sleep on the sand and this time nothing happened, and all
was well and he slept till morning. The sun ~~was~~ woke him
up, and he had just had time to shake himself
when he saw them coming across the sand.

Copying by an older control group normal reader, aged 9 years 8 months.

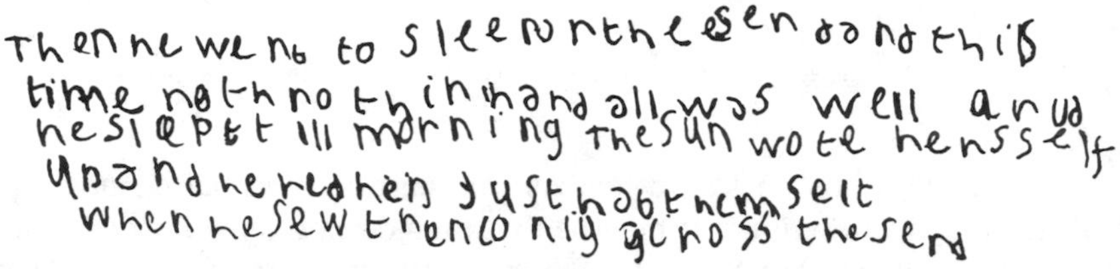

Thenne went to sleenrthe sen sond this
time nothno thin hand all was well anus
heslepet ill mornıng Thesun wote hensself
upond he redhen just hobk nem selt
when he sew then co nig gcno ss thesend

Copying by a backward reader, aged 9 years 8 months;
reading age 6 years 9 months.

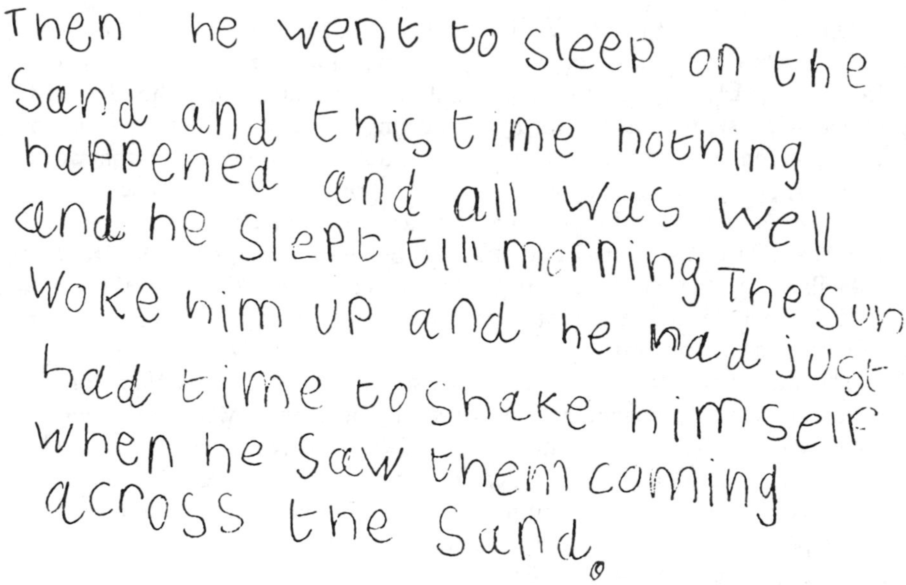

Then   he went to sleep on the
Sand and this time nothing
happened and all was well
and he slept till morning The Sun
Woke him up and he had just
had time to shake himself
When he saw them coming
across the Sand.

FIGURE 11.4. (A): Copying by an older control group normal reader, aged 9:8. (B): Copying by a backward reader, aged 9:8; reading age 6:9. (C): Copying by a young normal reader, aged 6:6; reading age 6:9.

might find an answer. Since both reading and spelling involve working with alphabetic script to encode or to decode spoken language, we might begin by examining the relationship between these two skills. How do normal readers learn to read and to spell? Do they use the same strategies and cues for reading and spelling? Do their strategies differ from those of retarded readers? How is it that backward readers can write words that they can not read? Before addressing these questions, some comments on experimental design are in order.

Methodological Considerations

Although many studies have confirmed that backward readers have a variety of problems, the precise nature of these problems has not been established. Backward readers have frequently been asked to perform tasks that seem to have only the most tenuous links to reading and writing. If we are to discover the cues that backward readers use to read and to spell, the tasks they are asked to perform must involve words.

A further problem arises when backward readers are compared with each other. Since their approach to reading and writing can vary in subtle ways, it is impossible to evaluate the effectiveness of a strategy by comparing one backward reader to another. This problem can be avoided if each reader serves as his or her own control and performance using one strategy is compared with performance using another. Finally, studies contrasting backward with normal readers have traditionally compared children of the same age and intellectual level who differed only in their ability to read. With this type of design, differences between groups might just as well be due to the backward readers' limited experience in reading as to their reading problem itself. The experiments reported in this chapter involve two control groups: One is a group of normal readers matched for age to the backward readers; the other is a group of younger normally reading children matched for reading level with the backward readers. With this design, if backward readers do less well than the younger normal readers, their failure cannot be merely the result of a lack of reading experience.

Major Issues

What follows is an attempt to answer some of the questions that were raised earlier. Three major issues are addressed. The first concerns the *strategies* young children and backward readers employ when they read and when they spell. If their strategies are the same, why do backward readers fail? Can we identify areas of failure? If their strategies are not the same, how and in what way do they differ?

The second concerns *remediation*. If particular areas of difficulty are identified, are there ways of improving performance? Can experimental evidence of improved performance be produced, which will provide a rationale for training programs? The third and final issue is a more speculative one. Clinical observation of a large number of normal and disabled learners suggests that individuals must organize various aspects of their behavior in order to function competently. The ability to organize could be a major factor that is operative in cognitive development. The importance of *organization* is evident in both verbal and nonverbal behavior. Perception, muscle control, and the development of visuomotor skills as well as spoken language and retrieval of words from memory require organization. Individuals may have difficulty in organizing one aspect of their behavior, or more than one aspect, in varying combinations and degree. The third major issue addressed in this chapter, therefore, is whether or not the inference that backward readers have difficulty with various aspects of organization can be demonstrated.

INDEPENDENCE OF READING AND SPELLING
IN BACKWARD AND NORMAL READERS

In order to understand the connection or lack of connection between reading and spelling problems, it is necessary to examine the performance of normal children and retarded readers and to determine whether they use the same strategies and cues when they spell as when they read. A simple way of addressing this problem is to give backward and normal readers the same words to read and to spell on different occasions. If children read and spell in the same way, they should read and spell more or less the same words. It should be borne in mind, of course, that reading is generally easier than spelling and, therefore, there may be words that can be read but not spelled. If the cues used in reading are not those employed in spelling, children will probably spell some words and read others. If they read some words that they do not spell but also spell some words that they cannot read, the discrepancy would indicate that the two skills are, to some extent, independent. This could have important practical implications: Finding a solution to the reading problems could still leave the spelling difficulties untouched (Yule, 1976).

Sixty-two children of normal intelligence, but 18 months or more behind the average reading skill for their age, were compared with a group of younger children also of normal intelligence, whose reading skills were normal for their age (Bradley & Bryant, 1979). Although the backward readers were, on average, more than three years older than the other group, both groups read at the same level. The young normal readers did not have the benefit of more

TABLE 11.1
Success in Reading and Spelling the 18 Words

	Number	Number of words read correctly (mean)	Number of words spelled correctly (mean)	Children reading more words than they spelled (%)	Children spelling more words than they read (%)
Backward readers	62	10.8	10.0	50	29
Normal readers (Young controls)	30	12.7	12.0	50	23

reading experience than the backward readers as happens in the more traditional design when backward readers are compared with children of the same chronological age.

All the children were given the same 18 words to read in one session and to write in another. The words were: *pin, leg, bed, rub, cot, fit, hunt, grab, flap, dent, crop, slid, upset, sunlit, content, oldest, upon, pretend.* All the words were regular in that they could be constructed on a letter by letter basis from the sounds typically associated with their individual letters. The results of the study showed that children in both groups read more words than they could spell (see Table 11.1). Many children in both groups, however, actually spelled more words correctly than they read correctly—a surprising result. In fact, 79% of the backward readers and 63% of the young normal readers spelled at least one word that they did not read.

In order to measure the extent of this pattern we counted the number of words each child both read and spelled properly (RS words), how many were neither read nor spelled ($\overline{RS}$ words), how many were read but not spelled ($R\overline{S}$ words) and the number of words spelled but not read ($\overline{R}S$ words). The first two categories reveal very little about the relationships between reading and spelling, since children may or may not be using the same cues when they can both read and spell a word (RS), or when they fail to read and spell the same word ($\overline{RS}$). The discrepant categories are more valuable for, if children read some words that they cannot spell ($R\overline{S}$), and spell other words without being able to read them ($\overline{R}S$), we can be reasonably certain that the two skills are, to some extent, independent.

The discrepant categories ($R\overline{S}$ and $\overline{R}S$) occurred in both groups but were observed more often in the backward reading group. This indicates that 6- and 7-year-old children and backward readers, whose reading ability is around 7 years, do not always use the same cues when they read and when they spell. We also examined the discrepant categories developmentally and found that age made a difference. The reading without spelling category ($R\overline{S}$) occurred at every level. The number of words spelled correctly but not read ($\overline{R}S$) varied with age, however. Among older children with normal reading ability and backward readers with higher reading levels, the tendency to spell words and not to read them was minimal. The performance of a second control group of 30 children who were matched with the backward readers for chronological age was similar: 29 children successfully read and spelled all 18 words. One child read all the words correctly but spelled one word incorrectly. It appears then, that this disconnection between reading and spelling is a temporary phenomenon confined in most children to the early stages of their reading and writing.

In order to discover the cues the children used to read and to spell these words, the pattern of errors was examined. The words used in the experiment could all be constructed on a phonological basis. Thus, errors were divided into those that had no connection with the correct word, those that had one sound in common with it, and those that had more than one sound in common with the correct word. The results of this analysis showed a clear difference between reading and spelling. The phonological connections were far greater when the children spelled than when they read. There was no significant difference between retarded readers and young normal readers in any of the three categories of error.

Here, then, is evidence that backward readers and young children at the beginning stages of reading rely primarily on phonological cues when they spell but not when they read. This is not really surprising. Because young children have a very limited experience of written language, it must be natural for them to use what they know about sounds to construct a word they wish to write when they cannot remember what it looks like. Further analysis showed that, although both groups used phonological strategies for spelling from the very beginning, young normal readers who had reached a reading

TABLE 11.2
Phonological Connections between Reading and Spelling Errors and Correct Words

	Errors with no phonological connection to correct word (%)	Errors with one sound in common with correct word (%)	Errors with more than one sound in common with correct word (%)
Backward readers			
Reading	9.4	10.9	79.7
Spelling	3.4	3.6	93.0
Normal readers			
Reading	10.0	14.6	75.4
Spelling	4.6	4.6	90.8
Young controls			

level of about 7 years began to use phonological connections in reading also. When we looked at the number of misread words that had more than one sound in common with the correct word, children reading above the 7-year-old level differed significantly from children reading below that level ($\chi^2 = 58.39, p < .001, df\,3$). Young normal readers and a good number of the more advanced backward readers who could read above the 7-year-old level applied a phonological strategy to reading as well as to spelling. Yet, the children with the lower reading levels in both groups used a phonological strategy for spelling but not for reading even when they were asked to read words that they had successfully spelled. The question was raised, could they apply a phonological strategy to reading also?

To discover the answer to this question the experiment was repeated with 50 children, age 6:6 to 7:6, using a wider variety of words (Bryant & Bradley, 1980). Similiar results were obtained. Both of the discrepant categories occurred among the younger children ($R\overline{S}$ and $\overline{R}S$); instances of words being spelled without being read ($\overline{R}S$) declined with age and with increasing reading skill.

In the second part of this experiment, the words that each child had failed to read were embedded in a list of nonsense words. Thus, this list varied from child to child Among the nonsense words were all the words that the child had not read in the first part of the experiment (the $\overline{R}S$ words and the $\overline{R}S$) words). Each child was shown how to read the nonsense syllables, such as *WEF* and *BIP* phonologically. Upon testing, the children read more of the words that they had previously failed to read but had spelled successfully. There was no change in their ability to read words that they had previously been unable to spell.

This supports the inference that young children often read and spell in different ways. Initially, they depend on phonological cues for spelling; when they are encouraged to use phonological codes for words that they can spell but not read, they can, in fact, read them.

VISUAL FACTORS IN READING AND SPELLING

Recognizing Visual Patterns

At the level of the individual letter, English orthography is highly variable. Particular letters often signify different sounds in different words (Donaldson, 1978). This variability is reduced as the chunk of letters that the child takes in gets larger. Thus, more information is available from *ought* than from *ough, oug, ou, or o,* if children can remember common patterns and detect differences between them. There is, indeed, evidence that very young children can go to the meaning of a word without using a phonological code (Barron & Barron, 1977). But how important are visual cues in reading?

To examine this question, the same backward and young normal readers were asked to select the odd word out of four words that were presented on a card (Bradley, 1979). There were six trials in each of three series. In one series, the last letter of the odd word differed: *fed, ten, den, hen*. In the other two series, either the first letter, *but, bad, lop, big*, or the middle letter, *nod, rod, pod, mud*, differed. The children were not asked to read the words. Thus, selection of the odd word could be made on the basis of visual similarities and differences in the written words.

Although the performance of backward readers was worse than that of young normal readers reading at the same level, 86.60% of the former and 92.26% of the latter made no errors at all. This difference was not significant. The majority of children in both groups had no problem detecting visual similarities and differences in these written words. A second control group of normal readers of the same chronological age as the backward readers made no errors indicating that normal readers become fully efficient at this task as their reading improves with age. Nevertheless, detecting visual similarities and differences in written words will not help readers if they are unable to name the visual sequence that represents the word. If they cannot label the pattern, then they cannot generalize from a pattern that they recognize to one that they do not, as, for example, from *and* to *hand* (Bradley, Hulme & Bryant, 1979).

Remembering Visual Patterns

Is there a difference in the way backward readers and normal readers remember visual patterns that they see? This question was explored by asking the same groups of children to complete four tasks: a within modality visual-memory task, an auditory–auditory task, and two cross-modal tasks: one, auditory–visual (spelling) and the other, visual–auditory (reading). In the first task (visual–visual), the children were shown words that were printed on a card one after the other. The words were of regular construction: *clam, limp, grip, next.* After looking at a word for 5 sec the child was asked to construct it using letters that were printed on small cards that were available on the table. Each child was required to reproduce four words in this manner. The backward readers were not quite as efficient as the younger normal readers. Backward readers made more errors at the ends of words and inverted and reversed more letters than the younger children. The number of words reproduced correctly by the two groups did not differ, however (Bradley, 1979). There was no difference between the groups in the auditory control condition that required the children to repeat four words.

Nevertheless, the backward readers did less well than the younger normal readers in both cross-modal conditions in which they were asked either to read the four words (visual–auditory) or to spell the four words using letter cards (auditory–visual). There was a significant difference in both the auditory–visual condition (spelling: $\chi^2 = 8.096$; df, 2; $p < .02$) and the visual to auditory condition (reading: $\chi^2 = 10.795$; df, 2; $p < .01$) condition. This was a surprising result, indeed, since the groups could reproduce the words from memory and repeat them equally well. It may be that the young normal readers used the alternative phonological strategy to help them to read and to spell the words they did not know, while the backward readers did not. Again, being able to reproduce a visual pattern does not help you to read if you do not know its name.

Visual Memory in Reading and Spelling

Let us look now at the relationship between the performance of these backward and young normal readers on the visual memory task and their performance on standardized tests of reading and spelling. Each child was given the Neale reading test and the Schonell spelling test. In the Schonell spelling test, only the first 12 words may be worked out phonetically. Success on these words yields a spelling age just above 6 years. Above this level many of the words are irregular and must, therefore, be remembered visually. The backward readers and younger children reading at the same level were subdivided into those children who made errors in the visual memory for a sequence of letters task (VSE) and those who did not (VSO). The results are presented in Table 11.3. As can be seen, poor visual memory for words seems to have a particularly harmful effect on spelling in both groups (young normal readers, $t = 3.603$; df, 30; $p < .01$; backward readers, $t = 4.187$; df, 60; $p < .001$). Some children in both groups spelled only the first phonetically regular words correctly. Among these children, those who also made errors on the visual memory task failed at the point on the Schonell test where irregular words are introduced (age 6:7). This strongly suggests that, in addition to a phonological strategy, memory for a visually presented sequence of letters is important in learning to spell, particularly for the spelling of irregular words. A similar, but not so strong a relationship, can be observed for reading. Correlations between the visual memory scores and

TABLE 11.3
Division of the Two Groups into Those Children Making No Errors (VSO) and Those Children Who Did Make Errors (VSE) on the Visual Memory Task

	Backward readers			Young normal readers		
	No errors VSO	Errors VSE	t test of the difference	No errors VSO	Errors VSE	t test of the difference
N	21	41		12	18	
Mean age	10:7	10:2	1.59 N.S.	7:3	6:7	2.07*
Mean IQ	110.62	107	1.38 N.S.	112.67	104.72	3.68***
Mean reading age	7:10	7:4	2.22*	7:11	7:2	2.32*
Mean spelling age	7:5	6:7	4.19***	8:1	6:7	3.6**

$*p < .05$
$**p < .01$
$***p < .001$

those on the standardized tests of reading and spelling confirmed this. In the backward reading group the correlations were .55 and .73 respectively. In the normal reading group the equivalent correlations were .60 and .67.

AUDITORY FACTORS IN READING
AND SPELLING

The younger, but normally reading children, appeared to use a phonological strategy for spelling. This implies that they were able to discriminate between words, to segment speech sounds (Liberman, Shankweiler, Fischer, & Carter, 1974), to group together different words which have sounds in common, and to generalize from a known word (*fight*) to an unknown word (*sight*). To examine the degree of auditory organization characteristic of young normal and backward readers and to assess its importance for reading and spelling, the following experiment was carried out.

Auditory Organization

The children were asked to detect the odd word in a group of four spoken monosyllabic words. Three series of words were presented, each with six trials (18 trials in all). In one series, the words had a common opening sound: *pen, pig, hat, pup;* in the second, a common middle sound: *cat, hot, lot, pot;* in the third, a common final sound: *peg, leg, hen, beg* (Bradley & Bryant, 1978). Two backward readers, who failed to recall some of the words, were excluded from the study. Although few of the young normal children could remember all the words in each trial, none was excluded.

The results showed that young normal readers were far superior to the older backward readers on this task: 91.6% of the backward readers made errors; 85.0% made more than one error. Only 53.3% of the young normal readers made mistakes. Of these, 26.6% made more than one. A clear developmental trend was observed among the young normal readers. Those who made one or no errors were older and had significantly higher scores on measures of intelligence, reading, and spelling. No such trend was found among the backward readers.

For the first time, then, we can demonstrate a clear difference between the backward readers and the young normal readers, who were reading at the same level, in the processes associated with reading and spelling. Since these two groups of children had reached the same reading level, the backward readers' failure on this auditory organization task cannot be due to a lack of reading experience. We strongly suspect, instead, that these backward readers were held back by a particular difficulty in auditory organization.

Alternate Strategies

Taking these experiments together, it is possible to see why the young normal readers were more successful than backward readers in the cross-modal conditions of reading and spelling, If we look at the children in each group who were not successful in the visual memory condition, we find a surprising difference: 55% of the young normal readers who were not successful on the visual memory task were successful on the auditory organization task, whereas only 4.9% of the backward readers (2 out of 41 children) who failed on the visual memory task were successful in the auditory organization experiment. This suggests that although the two groups appear to be equivalent as far as visual memory is concerned, more than half the young normal readers whose visual memory is poor can adopt an alternative strategy. The backward readers cannot.

Because auditory organization implies not only the use of a phonological strategy but also the ability to generalize from one spoken word to another and to analyze speech units, this capacity can assist children to read both regular and irregular words.

WRITING AND SPELLING

As children write, certain strings occur and recur and become familiar. For many children, spelling eventually becomes automatic. We might ask how children learn to spell irregular words such as *fought*. Because visual memory was shown to be important for learning these irregular sequences, it may be this factor that underlies poor spelling. On the other hand, poor spellers may lack adequate motor skill. To discover whether or not writing is important for spelling a pilot study was undertaken with a group of 10 children who were backward in reading and spelling. The mean age of this group was 9:8 and the mean IQ was 100 (as measured by the WISC). One child was in the dull-normal range; another was epileptic. In addition, the children had a variety of problems with motor control, as well as with visual and auditory perceptual processing. The method selected to train the children in spelling was an adaptation of Gillingham and Stillman's Simultaneous Oral Spelling (1977).

In this adaptation, the word to be learned is presented on a card. The child names the word, and then writes it down, naming each letter of the word as it is written (simultaneous oral spelling—SOS). When the whole word has been written in this way, the word is named again. The child then checks to see if the word was written correctly. This is done three times. The stimulus word is covered or disregarded as soon as the child is able to manage without it. This procedure is the same whether or not the student is familiar with all the sound–symbol relationships, and can read or write.

The children were taught to spell 4 words using this adaptation of the SOS method. In a control condition, the 4 words were taught by using letters printed on cards; the words were not written. As a further control 4 words were presented for the children's inspection; these words were not taught. Each child served as his or her own control. The 12 words were varied systematically between conditions, and the children received training for 4 consecutive days. Spelling was tested at the end of the training sessions and again 4 weeks later. At the second testing period, 80% of the words learned by means of writing were spelled correctly; only 21% of these words learned in the first control condition were retained.

To explore further the contribution of writing, another experiment was designed. The subjects were nine children attending a remedial reading centre. The mean IQ score of the group was 100 (as measured by the WISC), but the range within the group varied by 40 points. The mean age of this group was 11 years. Histories of delayed speech, dyspraxia, disturbed behavior, poor language skills, and epilepsy characterized the group. Each child in the group acted as his or her own control. There were four conditions. In each, the words to be learned were presented written on a card, and the subject named the word. In condition 1, simultaneous oral spelling (SOS), the subjects wrote the word naming each letter as they wrote it. In condition 2, visual auditory motor (VAM), the subjects wrote the whole word as they named the word. In condition 3, visual auditory (VA), the subjects constructed the word using printed letters on cards taken from a box on the table. Each letter was named as it was placed, but it was not written. In condition 4, the words were presented by not taught (UT) Sixteen words, which none of the subjects could spell, were varied systematically across conditions and between subjects. Each day subjects were trained on the words selected to be taught. Sessions were held on 4 consecutive days. There were three posttests: one on the fifth day; the other tests were given after intervals of 2 and 4 weeks.

The results showed that at the first posttest the children remembered the three groups of words that had been taught better than those that had not been taught. By the third posttest, however, only the SOS condition was superior to the untaught condition ($p < .01$). It was also superior to each of the other conditions, $p < .01$ in each case (Bradley, 1981).

We may ask why this adaption of Gillingham and Stillman's method is so effective. Clearly, writing the words is not sufficient to promote learning. The answer seems to lie again in the complex and abstract relationship between speech and alphabetic writing. When backward readers use this method, it does not matter if they cannot analyze the syllabic unit. They may not be able to decide that there are two written units in *un*, three written units in *der*, and five written units in *stand*. The use of SOS appears to establish a *one-to-one* relationship between the spoken and the written symbol. For these children, writing and naming appears to be a must; simply naming and seeing the units proved to be ineffective.

Although this method may establish a first link between written and spoken language when all else has failed, auditory analysis and organization are still necessary if backward readers are to make progress in reading and spelling. Because the spoken word is abstract and transitory, this can be very difficult. One way of helping to make this task tangible and to demonstrate how difference words can share common units is to use plastic script letters. This tactile method of learning to generalize from one word to another has proved effective with the most resistent backward readers (Bradley, 1980b).

COPYING AND THE BACKWARD READER

A large part of children's time in school is spent in copying words from the blackboard, from work cards, and from books. One recent survey suggested that 7- and 8-year-old children spend almost 20% of the school day recording information from a variety of sources. Because backward readers cannot read on their own, they are often given work to copy to keep them occupied. It is thought that copying can be done without help and that it is unrelated to the level of reading skill.

As our previous experiments show, the backward reading group pays less attention to detail in words than younger normal readers, even when they only have to reproduce words one at a time using printed letters. Although they are not significantly worse than the younger children on this immediate visual memory task, (backward readers 64.9% correct; young normal readers 72.5% correct), they are not as proficient as the normal readers of their own age, who make no errors at all. So it seems possible that backward readers might be at a particular disadvantage when they have to copy prose.

Therefore, the following questions were asked. Do backward readers take longer than normal readers to copy prose? Do they make more errors than normal readers? Does the use of a marker have an effect on the time taken and the number of errors that are made? Does the marker have a different effect for backward and for normal readers? Do backward and normal readers make the same kind of errors when they copy prose; and do they retain the meaning of the text irrespective of errors? Do backward and normal readers copy prose in the same way: phrase by phrase, word by word; or letter by letter?

Three groups of children participated in this study: 62 backward readers, 30 young normal readers matched with them on reading level, and 30 normal readers matched with the backward readers on chronological age. The readability level of the passages to be copied was age 7:6. Six passages, closely matched for degree of difficulty, were typed in a large print on a white card. Each card was presented in a vertical position. The marker was long enough to underline one word of the text at a time, but narrow enough so that it did not cover any part of the text. Because the marker was metal, it could be moved by sliding a magnet along the back of the card. This proved to be very effective, and did not obscure the text in any way.

Each child was seen individually. The two groups of older children copied six prose passages, three with the marker and three without. The marker was moved in the marker condition so that it kept pace with each child's speed of writing. Half the children in each group used the marker first; the other half used it last. The order in which the six passages were presented was varied systematically between condition and across children. The young control group copied only the first card in each condition. Because many of these young children had been in school for a short time and their experience of writing was limited, they were unable to complete the six cards.

When the children copied without the marker, the experimenter recorded on an identical passage each time the child looked up and what the child subsequently wrote down. In this way a record was made of the way the words were copied. The time required to copy each card under the different conditions was noted. Between trials the children either rested or played games.

Results of analyses of variance showed that the backward readers are significantly slower than their peers in copying prose, (F (1,56) = 21.534, p < .001). These differences were significant under both conditions: when the marker was used and when it was not (F (1,56) = 15.014, p < .001). Although the backward readers were much slower in both conditions (Tukey, HSD p < .01), their performance improved considerably when a marker was used (p < .01). The backward readers also made many more errors than their peer control group (See Table 11.4)

Analysis of variance also revealed a highly significant difference in the number of errors made by children in the two groups whether they copied without the marker (F (1,56) = 46.551, p < .001), or with the marker (F (1,56) = 56.878, p < .001). Tukey's HSD test indicated that the marker made a significant difference in the performance of backward readers (p < .01) but did not affect that of the normal readers. A detailed analysis of the way in which the two groups copied showed that the normal readers copied words and phrases whereas the backward readers copied letter by letter. The finding that backward readers copy one letter at a time could explain why

TABLE 11.4
The Number of Errors Made by the Backward Readers and by the Older Control Group in Each Category in the Two Conditions (with or without Marker) over 6 Cards

Categories	Backward readers $n = 62$		Older control group $n = 30$	
	Number of errors with marker	Number of errors without marker	Number of errors with marker	Number of errors without marker
Letter omission	75	130	13	13
Word omission	11	190	6	13
Letter substitute	73	86	1	1
Word substitute	6	11	8	7
Alteration	175	339	23	30
Misspelling	42	72	6	12
Reversed letter	8	8	0	0
Reversed word	4	11	0	0
Inversion	14	25	0	0
Repetition of word	7	93	1	2
Total number of errors	415	965	58	78

they were so slow, made so many errors, did not leave spaces between words, lost their place, and lost the meaning of the text. The marker must have provided structure and organization that was not otherwise available to the backward readers.

The performance of the backward readers was similar to younger normal readers in that both groups copied letter by letter, made similar types of errors, and copied more accurately when a marker was used (F (1,56) = 33.65, $p < .001$). The groups differed in significant ways however: Younger children were slower than retarded readers but they were also more accurate; young readers gradually began to copy larger meaningful units, but backward readers did not (see Figure 11.4); poor readers persist at the level of the letter while the copying of normally reading children becomes organized around words and phrases as they grow older and become more skilled in reading.

It is evident, then, that backward readers experience great difficulty in copying prose. There can be no doubt at all about their predicament. The source of their difficulty appears to lie in an inability to organize their written copy into meaningful, spatially distinct units.

CONCLUSIONS

This chapter set out to explore several issues. The experimental design of the studies proved beneficial in all aspects. It enabled us to answer questions about the reading and spelling processes. We found that young children and backward readers often spell words in one way and read them in another. This relative independence between reading and spelling appears to be a temporary phenomenon in normal reading development. Children initially rely primarily on phonological segments when they spell and visual wholes when they read.

We were able to demonstrate that organization plays an important role in normal skill development. Young normal readers appear to organize their visual, auditory, and motor skills as they grow older and more skilled in reading and spelling. Visual memory becomes more important for spelling, and auditory organization for reading.

Backward readers begin to read and write in the same way as the normal readers, but they do not seem to organize their skills in the same way as they grow older. This cannot be due to lack of reading experience, at least as far as auditory organization is concerned. The backward readers were far worse at this task than a group of much younger normal readers who were reading at the same level. It seems possible, therefore, that many backward readers fail to make progress because they have such difficulty in generalizing from one speech unit to another.

Two remedial strategies, SOS and the use of plastic script letters, were shown to be effective in helping backward readers and spellers to establish the relationship between spoken language and the alphabetic script. The strategies appeared to be successful in spite of the differences found among backward readers both because they are related to the reading and spelling processes themselves and because they enable the backward reader to relate the alphabetic code to speech.

Finally, it is clear that copying prose presents a serious problem to backward readers. The crucial element seems to be their inability to organize written copy around meaningful units such as the word. Backward readers are slow and inaccurate when they copy writing, but they copy more quickly and accurately when they have some form of marker on the passage they have to copy. This is an issue that requires further investigation.

REFERENCES

Barron, R., & Barron, J. How children get meaing from printed words. *Child Development*, 1977, *48*, 587–594.
Boder, E. School failure—Evaluation and treatment. *Paediatrics*, 1976, *58*, 394–403.
Bradley, L. *Perceptual and cognitive difficulties experienced by able backward readers.* Unpublished doctoral dissertation, University of Reading, 1979.
Bradley, L. Reading, writing and spelling problems. In N. Gordon & I. McInlay (Eds.), *Helping clumsy children*. Edinburgh: Churchill Livingstone, 1980. (a)
Bradley, L. *Assessing reading difficulties: A diagnostic and remedial approach.* Basingstoke: Macmillan Education, 1980. (b)

Bradley, L. The organisation of motor patterns for spelling: An effective remedial strategy for backward readers. *Developmental Medicine and Child Neurology*, 1981, *23*, 83–91.

Bradley, L., & Bryant, P. Difficulties in auditory organisation as a possible cause of reading backwardness. *Nature*, 1978, *271*, 746–747.

Bradley, L., & Bryant, P. The independence of reading and spelling in backward and normal readers. *Developmental Medicine and Child Neurology*, 1979, *21*, 504–514.

Bradley, L., Hulme, C., & Bryant, P. The connexion between different verbal difficulties in a backward reader: A case study. *Developmental Medicine and Child Neurology*, 1979, *21*, 790–795.

Bryant, P., & Bradley, L. Why children sometimes write words which they do not read. In U. Frith (Ed.), *Cognitive processes in spelling*. New York: Academic Press, 1980. Pp. 355–370.

Donaldson, M. *Children's minds*. Glasgow: Fontana, 1978.

Frith, U. Unexpected spelling problems. In U. Frith (Ed.), *Cognitive processes in spelling*. New York: Academic Press, 1980.

Gillingham, A., & Stillman, B. W. *Remedial training for children with specific disability in reading, spelling and penmanship* (7th ed.). Cambridge, Mass.: Education Publishing Service, 1977.

Liberman, I., Shankweiler, D., Fischer, F., & Carter, B. Reading and the awareness of linguistic segments. *Journal of Experimental Psychology*, 1974, *18*, 201–212.

Rozin, P., & Gleitman, L. The structure and acquisition of reading 11: The reading process and the acquisition of the alphabetic principle. In A. Reber & D. Scarborough (Eds.), *Toward a psychology of reading*. Hillsdale, N. J.: Lawrence Erlbaum Associates, 1977. Pp. 55–142.

Tukey, J. W. The problem of multiple comparisons. Unpublished manuscript. Princeton University, 1953.

Yule, W. Issues and problems in remedial education. *Developmental Medicine and Child Neurology*, 1976, *18*, 674–682.

V CONCLUSION

12 Language and the Brain: Implications for Education

URSULA KIRK

What information about the developing brain can neuropsychological research offer to education that might influence approaches to teaching and learning? What insights can education provide that might advance our understanding of the "working brain" in the process of development? Are there critical problems and educational dilemmas that the experienced teacher can identify that might be examined by research? Do these issues differ from those currently being studied?

This book contributes to the understanding of the relationship between language and the brain at different stages of development and affirms the part that education can play in extending this knowledge. Widely divergent investigations of how the brain mediates language are presented here. Despite these differences, the recurrence of certain themes reflects considerable convergence of thought and points to a conceptual change in the way that language, reading, and spelling are described and explored. A number of themes that are particularly relevant to education are identified and discussed in this chapter.

Two related themes will be considered together at the outset. Both are concerned with the inadequacy of the constructs currently used to explain the processes involved in learning to talk, to read, and to spell. The first theme

NEUROPSYCHOLOGY OF
LANGUAGE, READING, AND SPELLING

focuses on the source of these outdated constructs and the limitations they impose on the search for neural substrates. The second has to do with the realization that because the acquisition and the proficient use of language skills are different tasks, they are mediated by different brain mechanisms, and require different investigatory paradigms.

Dennis in Chapter 9 of this volume discusses the extent to which a philosophy, rooted in nineteenth-century concepts and emphasizing the laws of association, has influenced neuropsychological thought. The view that language is developed by building up associations and its widely accepted corollary that, once acquired, language is mediated by circumscribed and primarily cortical regions of the brain are two cases in point. Dennis maintains that these somewhat limited views have led neuropsychologists to focus on the search for structural or functional dysgenesis of specific neural tissue to explain developmental disorders of language, reading, and spelling. In addition, models have been constructed to account for the relationship between brain and language in children that are based on analogies drawn from alexic or aphasic adults to the exclusion of more dynamic developmental considerations. In criticizing these trends, Dennis does not argue against the idea that specific brain regions make specific contributions to function. Rather, she argues against two rather common approaches to neuropsychological research: an effort to discover a unitary basis for one or the other developmental disorder and a tendency to delimit the brain mechanisms involved in these disorders to connections among restricted areas of neural tissue.

Dennis cites two additional consequences of an uncritical reliance on nineteenth-century concepts: an almost exclusive preoccupation of neuropsychological research with failure at the early stages of the learning process and a neglect of the total context within which normal language skills are acquired and used.

The contributors to this book propose that an adequate understanding of oral and written language requires that these capacities be viewed within a broader conceptual framework. Kirk suggests that when language, reading, and spelling are considered as instances of skill, both commonalities and critical differences among them become apparent. Morever, the distinction between the task that faces the beginner and the task that is posed to the accomplished reader stands out clearly. Denckla in Chapter 2 emphasizes the crucial role of learning-to-learn skills and of metalinguistic awareness in the process of becoming a proficient language user. Rapin and Allen in Chapter 8 call for an examination of language disorders that takes into account the total communicative interaction rather than emphasizing only the presence or absence of speech. Dennis in Chapter 9 and Trevarthen in Chapter 3 point to recent research findings that demonstrate the role of constructive, inferential, predictive, attentional, mnemonic, and motivational factors in the acquisition and proficient use of language-related skills. In different ways, these researchers challenge both prevailing neuropsychological concepts of language, reading, and spelling and the models of brain–behavior relationships that have been proposed to account for them.

The research reported in this book suggests that language, reading, and spelling are complex, interactive, multilevel functions that require for their expression the integrated contribution of multiple neural systems and subsystems. In this regard, Denckle speculates about the involvement of left frontal convexity systems. She draws on evidence from two sources to support this inference: blood flow studies and the results of brain electrical activity mapping (BEAM). The first set of studies demonstrates that frontal areas, and in particular the supplementary motor area, are highly activated during tasks that involve naming or reading. The BEAM studies uncovered the presence of unusual alpha activity while 10-year-old dyslexic boys were performing a variety of language-related cognitive tasks. During a routine EEG, when someone is resting quietly with eyes closed, the electrical activity recorded from posterior, but not frontal, regions of the brain falls within the alpha range. Thus, alpha rhythm is thought to represent the resting or idling state of the brain. Typically, when cognitive activities are undertaken, marked changes of rhythm occur. These changes are referred to as alpha blocking and are thought to represent the working state of the brain. The BEAM studies revealed the unexpected presence of alpha activity in both frontal and posterior regions while the dyslexic boys were reading, listening to speech, and learning to associate visual patterns with nonsense syllables. Denckla concludes that the evidence from both sets of studies provides adequate grounds for speculating that dysfunctional frontal systems are related to some types of dyslexia.

Ojemann's findings in Chapter 7 suggest that lateralized mechanisms at cortical and thalamic levels participate in linguistic, mnemonic, and attentional components of verbal behavior. He reports that the disruptive effect of electrical stimulation on language can be observed at discretely localized sites in peri-Sylvian cortex. Stimulation interferes with naming at some sites and with reading at others. At some sites, stimulation interrupts both sequential facial movements and phoneme discrimination whereas at others, short-term verbal memory is affected. With regard to thalamus, Ojemann suggests that it acts as a gate or specific alerting mechanism to control access to or from short- and long-term memory for verbal material. Rapin and Allen identify seven distinct syndromes within the more general classification of developmental language disorders. Because of the variety of linguistic, cognitive, social, and emotional deficits that are associated with these syndromes, they speculate that prefrontal, temporal, and mesial limbic regions as well as intra- and interhemispheric pathways may be selectively involved.

Kirk (in Chapter 1), Trevarthen, and Dennis point out that the neural systems subserving acquired skills in the adult may differ from those that participate in the acquisition of skill during infancy and childhood. In addition, they discuss the possibility that the contributions of neutral systems may differ as a function of the age at which a new skill is acquired and the stage of the learning process itself. Commenting on his findings that a second language is disrupted by stimulation in wider areas of the brain than is the first, more competent language, Ojemann suggests that acquiring a new skill may involve the cooperation of more extensive systems than does the execution of a practiced skill. Baken in Chapter 4 provides evidence that the ability to talk does not rely solely on neural mechanisms. Anatomincal changes that gradually restructure the infant's vocal tract, increased precision of phonatory–motor control, and the maturation of the respiratory system combine to make the production of adultlike speech possible. Clearly, systems other than those traditionally described as language zones participate in the complex task of acquiring and making use of language.

Perhaps the most important inference that can be drawn from these findings is that the accuracy with which brain mechanisms mediating oral and written language can be identified is as much a function of our conceptualizations as it is of the technological tools with which we work. Only to the degree that the researcher is cognizant of recent theoretical advances in understanding the nature of language, reading, and spelling, the processes involved in acquiring skill, the principles and practices of teaching and learning, can the search for brain mechanisms take into account the complexities inherent in these tasks. It may well be that the ability to apply neuropsychological research findings to problems in education will depend on the extent to which the researcher and the educator communicate and collaborate. The implication is clear. Within each domain, professionals are needed who, because they are conversant with the language, methodology, and theoretical constructs of the other domains, can generate a more adequate conceptual framework within which to explore brain–behavior relationships. The more closely models of brain–behavior relationships approximate the way the system actually functions, the greater the possibility that research findings can be translated into educational practice.

A third theme that emerges from the research that is discussed in this book reflects a fundamental shift in the way that the nature of the central nervous sytem is conceived of and described. Earlier views portray the system in passive terms as reacting to and, to a certain extent, being controlled by incoming sensory stimulation. Trevarthen comments that the very terminology that is currently used to describe the bulk of brain tissue mediating complex, multimodal, coordinative processes implies a reactive system engaged in making cerebral associations between what is seen and heard and what is felt and done. The term "association" all too often connotes passive responsivity. A different concept appears to lie behind the investigations that are reported here. Whether the emphasis is placed on the capabilities of the developing infant, the processes involved in the acquisition and use of skill, analyses of the task to be performed, or the neural substrates that mediate function, the underlying concept appears to be that the system is designed for action.

Trevarthen's position is quite clear. He views the nervous system as specifically constituted to benefit from, that is, to learn from, interactions with the environment. He suggests that powerful "motives" for communication are inherent in the developing system. These motives are translated into the infant's search for and regulation of face-to-face encounters with adults. By means of conversation-like exchanges, which are gradually extended to include shared experiences of objects and events in the environment, infants outline in their behavior, in gesture, facial expressions, and vocalizations, what will become the syntax and semantics, the mood and prosody of speech. Trevarthen suggests that these inherent motives for language, arising from core structures of the brain, mediate the infant's rudimentary forms of cognition, action, and response that will in time, engender linguistic communication. He suggests, further, that these core structures contribute to the growing proficiency in the use of language that can be observed in the child and in the adult.

Kirk's analysis of cognition, language, and the acquisition of skill in the young child is consistent with this view of the active, learning infant. She points out that the problem-solving, rule-governed, constructive activity of the child generates two kinds of knowledge: increased understanding of complex relations and more effective strategies for learning and doing. Both kinds of knowledge are necessary; both contribute to the child's ability to solve new and more difficult problems as the demands made by academic tasks and by the environment become increasingly complex.

Denckla underscores the importance of learning-to-learn skills for success in academic tasks. She asserts that the most efficient learners are not passive absorbers. Rather, they are active participants in the process. She notes further that the ability to create order and to pose questions may be more crucial to academic learning than the ability to master preorganized, redundant information.

Beyond behavioral indices, what evidence is there that the fundamental bias of the nervous system is for action? As mentioned earlier, the BEAM studies described by Denckla revealed the presence of alpha waves in frontal regions and the absence of alpha blocking in posterior regions while dyslexic boys worked on a variety of tasks. These curious signs of cortical "idling" were not evident in the recordings from age-matched control boys performing the same tasks. Because the absence of appropriate cortical activation marked the performance of the dyslexic, but not the normally reading boys, even in the face of considerable sensory stimulation, one can speculate that ordinarily, an intrinsic mechanism readies the system so that it can benefit from interactions with the environment. Denckla urges that future research be directed toward uncovering the contributions that frontal systems might make to learning, language, and reading.

Trevarthen presents related findings from electrophysiological recordings in adults. He reports the presence of anticipatory neural activation in regions of intermediate (association) cortex both prior to the onset of speech and one quarter of a second after hearing a word. Noting that the mature language user is far from passive but is engaged in "elaborate motor preparation, cognitive prediction, and covert inference regarding the acts of communication," Trevarthen speculates that this type of anticipatory neural activation may reflect these preparatory cognitive operations.

Ojemann's findings suggest that motor systems and language systems are linked at cortical and subcortical levels. In addition to a common mechanism for orofacial movements and phoneme discrimination, he speaks of a final motor pathway located in posterior, inferior frontal cortex. All aspects of language behavior are disrupted when electrical stimulation is applied to specific sites in this area of cortex. Of even greater interest is the linkage that Ojemann reports between language and motor systems at the thalamic level. On the one hand, stimulation of ventral lateral thalamus, which is important to motor function, has clear, identifiable, disruptive effects on verbal memory. On the other hand, examination of event-related potentials provides evidence that thalamic-activating circuits are critically involved in cortical processing of language. One wonders if these circuits might be implicated in the intrinsic readying mechanism that was proposed earlier.

In many ways the data presented here provide evidence for what educators have known for some time: It is the active learner who learns; passivity characterizes the child who does not learn. Consider the efforts teachers make to attract and sustain children's interest, to motivate them to learn, and to provide opportunities for active participation both in the classroom and in work that is assigned to be done at home. One implication for education is, then, that there is strong support from neuropsychological research for specific educational practice.

A second implication stems from evidence that internal, constructive activity is more crucial for learning than overt behavior. The dyslexic boys described by Denckla appeared to be involved and yet, indices of appropriate cortical activation were absent. These findings present a challenge to professionals in both fields. Is there a way to distinguish, behaviorally, between apparent and actual engagement in a task? What might be external signs of an internal "idling" brain?

A third implication is related to the first two. Despite the fact that active participation is recognized as critical to learning, many factors militate against providing appropriate opportunities for children in today's schools. Overcrowded classrooms yielding a high teacher–student ratio, pressures placed on teachers to develop test-taking skills in children, and the emphasis, for a variety of reasons, on maintaining order and quiet have led to the development of educational practices that may not be conducive to learning. Teaching materials that keep children busy with paper and pencil tasks; tests designed for rapid correction that rely on recognition memory rather than recall; homework assignments that take time but do not require purposeful, integrative thinking on the part of the student; electronic devices that place the learner in a reactive rather than in an active mode—all of these can be found in today's schools. They need to be reevaluated in the light of the evidence that learning is an active and constructive process rather than passive or reactive. Let us at least question whether the multiplication of workbooks and paper and pencil tasks are effective means for learning or whether the sheer repetitiveness of the tasks has a dulling effect and diminishes active involvement.

Bradley points out in Chapter 11 that 7- and 8-year-olds devote almost 20% of the school day to copying information from various sources and that poor readers are often given additional work of this nature to keep them occupied. Many poor readers have difficulty with this type of task. They are slow and inaccurate; rather than organizing the material around meaningful units such as words and phrases, they copy letter by letter. The benefit derived from spending time in this way is dubious at best. Bradley's work demonstrates that poor readers copy more accurately when they use a marker. It may be that by directing children's attention to meaningful units, a marker supplies the organizational strategy that is necessary to carry out this type of task efficiently. Bradley's work also shows that these children profit from directed teaching that links motor activity to reading and spelling. For these children, the motor component appears to be critical to learning.

Another theme that runs throughout this book focuses on the dynamic properties of the developing system as the growing child acts on and is acted on by the environment. It is well established that the behavior of young children is highly variably and that, with development, more consistent patterns or profiles of abilities begin to emerge. Equally recognized is the view that behavioral changes evident over time are the outcome or product of both maturational and environmental influences. What is less well appreciated is the dynamic character of the developing but damaged or dysfunctional system. Indications of this dynamism can be found in the evidence presented in this book that symptoms of language and learning disorders change with time. In a manner that is consistent with the performance of normally developing children, two features stand out: a high degree of variability characterizes the performance of young children with some form of learning disorder; and the signs or symptoms of the disorder become increasingly specified with age. In the discussion that follows, although some allusion is made to normal development, the emphasis is placed on age-related symptomatic change in the behavior of children with a variety of problems related to languge, reading, and spelling.

Tallal and Stark in Chapter 5 ascribe the difficulties of dysphasic children to an inability to process brief and rapidly changing sequential information. What is of interest here is to note that at ages 5 and 6, this deficit can be demonstrated across all modalities: visual, tactile, auditory, and cross modal. At ages 7 and 8, the deficit appears to be specific to the auditory realm. This deficit is evident in the children's performance on auditory–perceptual and auditory–memory tasks. These findings suggest what what appeared behaviorally as a global deficit in younger children has become more specified with age. Tallal and Stark point out that the deficiency may persist only in those children who originally showed severe auditory processing deficits. Alternatively, they suggest that the problem may stem from a more general left-hemisphere dysfunction that is expressed across modalities in young children but is restricted in its expression to one modality in older children. Tallal and Stark comment that longitudinal rather than cross-sectional studies are needed to investigate the changing patterns of temporal processing deficits in these language-disordered children.

Rourke in Chapter 10 identifies changing patterns of disabilities in learning-disabled children. His findings show that the performance of 5- to 8-year-olds is so variable that neither the patterns of relationships among measures of verbal, auditory–perceptual, problem-solving, and visuospatial abilities nor the level of performance attained can be used to identify clear cut subgroups. Consistent with the developmental perspective that early variability gives way to differential and consistent performance, Rourke finds that 9- to 14-year-old children with learning disabilities demonstrate clear cut differences. Subgroups can be identified on the basis of patterns of relative strengths and weaknesses and on the level of performance achieved.

Denckla discusses the paradoxical changes that can occur in the neuropsychological profiles of children with learning disabilities. She describes a child who appeared to be severely anomic at age 6 but showed no signs of dysphasia at age 14. Instead, marked deficits were evident in "nonverbal" areas such as those measured by the Ravens Progressive Matrices. Denckla speculates that this dramatic reversal in profile may be due to subtle deficiencies in selective attention, coding, rehearsal, sequential organization, and the ability to infer and generalize rules. She suggests that because deficits in these capacities interfere with new learning, their effects will be most obvious on tasks that require problem-solving rather than practiced skills. Thus the "paradoxical" shift in profile evident in this child may have been due to the disruptive effects of these subtle deficits on tasks that require new learning: language at one age and academic skills at another.

Rourke points out that, in a similar way, attentional deficits in young children can mask the presence of specific learning problems. He notes that in the young child, attentional problems are often expressed in hyperactive and distractible behavior. It is only later, when the child has become capable of attending, that more specific deficits begin to stand out. In this way, he proposes that the influences of attentional deficits in children is analogous to the effects of edema on brain-damaged adults.

Rourke's investigations of children with spelling disabilities illustrate both factors that have been discussed up to this point: symptomatic change over time and the possibility that one dimension of a problem can mask other, and possibly more critical problems. These studies suggest that children who are equally poor spellers (as measured by level of performance) may make characteristically different errors (as noted by qualitative rather than quantitative analyses) because of very different clusters of cognitive competencies and deficits. According to Rourke, children who misspell in a phonetically accurate way demonstrate basic linguistic competence. They tend, however, to rely on their phonemic knowledge without going beyond the particulars to make use of the visual gestalt. Moreover, they have difficulty in working with novel information. Phonetically inaccurate spellers are deficient in carrying out linguistic operations and in developing the rules and strategies for learning. What is important here is the indication that the measures used to identify learning problems can either limit or extend our knowledge. Use of a performance level alone can mask the presence of underlying strengths and weaknesses that can be teased out by a qualitative analysis.

Both kinds of information appear to be important to our understanding of age-related symptomatic changes. Although the young children were classified into distinct groups on the basis of spelling error type, their performance on a variety of cognitive measures was so highly variable that few measures distinguish between the groups; at age 13, many differences were evident in the cognitive functioning of the two groups. Error type did not differ across age groups, but the specificity of associated cognitive deficits changed with age. Rourke notes that the prognosis for the two groups is not the same: phonetically accurate misspellers tend to catch up with time and exposure to the written word; phonetically inaccurate misspellers not only fail to catch up, the performance gap in reading and spelling increases with age. Surely the differential outcome cannot be ascribed to the type of error per se. It must be related to different constellations of deficits that culminate in specific ways of misspelling.

In their discussion of developmental language disorders, Rapin and Allen identify similarities and differences in normal and disordered development of language. Just as variability stands out in the behavior of young normal children, so too variability marks the behavior of young language-disordered children. Both the capabilities of normal children and the symptoms of language disorder change over time. Rapin and Allen point out that some of these changes may actually represent the "recovery" of the developing system from an insult that originally resulted in a more global dysfunction. Although similar stages can be identified in the development of language in normal and some language-disordered children, there are striking qualitative differences in the content and use of langue. Misarticulations are common to both groups of children, but children with phonological–syntactic difficulties produce unrecognizable phonemes that never occur in normal speech. Similarly, language-disordered children, who proceed through the one-word and two-word stages, use single words and word combinations that differ radically from those produced by children whose language is developing normally. In addition, language is used for many purposes by young children: They label, request, and comment on their experiences. Language-disordered children use language for the first two purposes but not for commenting on their own or other people's behavior.

The evidence presented up to this point highlights the dynamic properties of the developing system as it is reflected in behavior. Ojemann's findings provide some grounds for the often cited speculation that the damaged nervous sytem undergoes dynamic reorganization over time. He reports that although electrical stimulation mapping discloses the presence of discretely localized language mechanisms in all patients undergoing surgery for intractible epilepsy, the exact locations of these sites vary across patients. Moreover, the pattern of the localization of sites in posterior language areas differed in patients with verbal IQ above and below 95. Stimulation of the parietal operculum disrupted naming in 75% of the patients with a verbal IQ below 95; this effect was noted in only 22% of those with a verbal IQ above 95.

Whether the variability observed among these patients is due to the influence of recurrent epileptic foci or whether it reflects the more general property of cortical variability that characterizes the undamaged human brain cannot be determined. Nevertheless, the very consistency of the variability is suggestive of dynamic reorganization over time. On this point, Ojemann notes that patients whose seizure onset is early in life have an increased probability of unusual lateralization of language. In addition, he reports a case that illustrates a change in cortical representation of the leg as a consequence of injury at birth. Electrical stimulation mapping in adulthood revealed that the leg was not represented in motor cortex but in the middle of lateral parietal lobe.

The evidence reviewed here has specific implications for the evaluation and remediation of language-related disorders. However valuable early identification is for intervention, it is clear that for children with subtle disorders, the risk of making an incorrect diagnosis is high. Thus the research that is presented is both reassuring and alarming. On the one hand it is reassuring to have some insight into the unpredictability of early predictive measures. The variability that characterizes the performance of all young children, makes it difficult to single out children who, because their variability is compounded by some subtle or not so subtle functional imbalance, will be disabled learners from those who will not show learning problems at a later stage of development. On the other hand, it is alarming to consider the possibilities for misdiagnosis in a society that seeks to label children at an early age. The difficulties confronting the diagnostician and the educator are many: Without a label, special services cannot be provided; given the problems associated with changing or removing a label, it may be impossible to alter an inappropriate educational placement or to modify instructional approaches. Moreover, because the number of children evaluated each year is so large, decisions with far reaching effects are often made on the results of a few tests administered at a specified point in time. Research in neuropsychology warns us: Look for and expect changing symptoms over time; and, recognize that the presenting problem in young children may mask more subtle deficits that will become manifest at a later time.

A second important implication for education is the evidence that performance is not the only measure that can provide information about learning. In fact, it may be the least helpful measure. Knowing that a child succeeds or fails is not as informative as knowing how the success or failure is achieved. If careful observation of the way children approach a task is coupled with error analysis, it may be possible to devise more appropriate instructional procedures and to make more accurate predictions about the eventual outcome. Bradley's work clearly demonstrates that children of different ages and at different stages of learning to read and to spell rely on different strategies to approach these tasks. Young children, who are at the beginning stages, make use of phonological strategy for spelling but not for reading. By the age of 7, they apply both a phonological and a visual strategy to these tasks. Older children, who read and spell at the same level as the young beginners, do not use both strategies spontaneously. Bradley shows that, given specific instruction, they can begin to do so. Thus, observation of the way normal children learn can suggest procedures for teaching children for whom learning is difficult.

Another implication for diagnosis and instruction concerns the concepts with which we work. Unitary constructs such as the "dysphasic child" or the "dyslexic child" must yield to multidimensional concepts. Dichotomies such as receptive and expressive disorders or thinking in terms of nature or nurture must give way to an approach that views symptoms as the outcome of many interactive factors. Finally, to the degree that subtle deficits can be identified and evaluated in relation to a child's overall performance in and out of school, educators may be able to restructure both teaching methods and assignments for independent work in a way that supplies from without what the child, at a given point in time, cannot provide from within.

A book focused on the neuropsychology of language, reading, and spelling would be incomplete without some consideration of the question of cerebral dominance or lateralized function. What stands out in this volume is the absence of this issue as a focal point of discussion. Although evidence of left hemisphere competence for the production and comprehension of connected discourse is presented, the what and how of lateralized function are not argued. For these researchers, the question of cerebral dominance appears to be a nonissue. The more compelling concern is the specialized contribution that each hemisphere makes to the complex cognitive activities of speaking and listening, reading and spelling. The focus is the integrated rather than the lateralized brain.

Molfese's work in Chapter 6 demonstrates that important cues for speech perception are mediated by different regions of the brain. Mechanisms specific to different cues begin to operate at different times during development and they mature at different rates. The evidence that some mechanisms are bilaterally represented whereas others are lateralized to specific cortical regions suggests that even apparently simple discriminations require complex multimodal processing. Molfese states, "language perception can no longer be described solely as 'left' or 'right' hemisphere tasks. Perhaps rather than continuing discussion concerning the presence or absence of hemisphere differences, it is time to turn our attention to the fundamental nature of the processes . . . "

The impetus to study lateralized function came from demonstrated differences in the capabilities of the disconnected hemispheres of commissurotomy patients. Frequently it is inferred—but not directly stated—that the normal system operates in a somewhat similar way, using the left hemisphere for language and the right hemisphere for nonlanguage tasks. What is rarely discussed is that only in the split-brain patient—and then only under controlled experimental conditions—can specified and limited amounts of information be directed to one hemisphere to the exclusion of the other. Under normal conditions, information from multiple sources is available. Within milliseconds of entering the system, it is processed simultaneously at multiple cortical and subcortical levels. In the intact brain with its reciprocally concerned structures, its callosal and noncallosal commissures, its multiple feedback loops, its downstream and upstream gating and recruiting mechanisms, information is not directed selectively to and confined to one hemisphere to the exclusion of the other. The leap from what the disconnected hemisphere is capable of doing to how the integrated brain functions is unfortunate and unwarranted. It might be more informative to examine the plethora of split-brain data for evidence of what each hemisphere contributes to complex cognitive functions than to persist in describing what each can do in isolation—a situation that does not exist in the intact brain.

Trevarthen points out that the disconnected right hemisphere can match objects and pictures rapidly and effectively when the task does not involve naming. Naming objects or pictures is the forte of the left hemisphere. When the task involves learning to name nonsense shapes or unfamiliar figures, however, neither hemisphere is competent. The isolated left hemisphere cannot distinguish the stimuli well enough to apply the correct label; the right hemisphere recognizes the stimuli with ease but cannot generate the verbal tag. Clearly, each hemisphere requires the specialized contribution of the other in order to be successful on this type of task.

Dennis' studies of the reading and spelling capabilities of children with early hemidecortication are of interest here. More important than the evidence that the single left hemisphere provides a better substrate for language and the right for nonlanguage tasks is the finding that each hemisphere processes written material in qualitatively different ways. The child with only a left hemisphere relied on linguistic, syntactic, and semantic information whereas the two children with only a right hemisphere used a logograph-based reading style. Despite these stylistic differences, Dennis found no evidence of hemispheric asymmetry on measures of comprehension unless the task demanded that many details be recalled or that information be gleaned from several sentences in the text. Interestingly, the difficulty the children experienced with understanding this more complex prose did not seem to be a simple function of left and right.

Dennis reports that M. W., with only a left hemisphere, took advantage of the morphophonemic and grammatical structures of English to decode and extract meaning from the text. A discrepancy was observed in the performance of the two left-hemidecorticate children. C. W., using a strictly logographic approach, read single words fluently and understood simple sentences but had difficulty in understanding complex passages. S. M. relied less on a logographic and more on a phonological strategy. Although his decoding skills were poorly automatized, he read complex prose accurately and with more understanding than C. W. It would appear that simple sentences could be decoded and understood whether a logographic or linguistic approach was used but that both styles contributed to the ability to read fluently and with understanding. When only one hemisphere was involved, the left was the better, but not the only possible substrate for linguistic processing; the right was the better substrate for logographic processing. It is likely that, under ordinary circumstances, both hemispheres are involved in reading and that each makes a different contribution to the task.

Research has also demonstrated that left and right brain-damaged adults make characteristically different errors on constructional tasks. Both groups are unsuccessful on these tasks, but their productions are faulty for very different reasons (McFie & Zangwill, 1960; Patterson & Zangwill, 1944; Warrington, James, & Kinsbourne, 1976). These findings support the view that skilled performance is associated with integrated rather than with one-sided functioning.

These findings have important implications for education. First, the popular but unwarranted inferences about normal function that have been drawn from split-brain research must be set aside. Second, there is no evidence to support the current view that education can be directed to one side of the brain and that, for the most part, it is "left brain" that has been taught. Both hemispheres are engaged in learning in the classroom. Short of callossal agenesis or some other form of damage that alters the dynamic function of the system in some dramatic way, it is impossible to involve one hemisphere selectively. Third, Bradley and Dennis provide evidence that learning style differentially affects the degree of proficiency that can be attained. Hence, close attention should be given to qualitative analysis to children's preferred approach to learning. This is not to suggest that one style be emphasized to the exclusion of the other. It is the integration of both styles that makes for proficiency. Integrated function also appears to be necessary for successful performance on nonlanguage tasks.

Finally, in normally developing children, cognitive style must not be confused with the presence or absence of functional integrity. Research has shown that measures of peripheral laterality such as handedness or eyedness and measures of perceptual processing such as dichotic listening or tachisto-scopic viewing cannot be used as indices of central organization. In a similar way, a preferred style of information processing is a preferred style and not an indicator of cerebral function or dysfunction. Because, however, particular styles appear to be differentially effective for specific kinds of tasks, the educator may be able to facilitate learning by using strategies associated with a proficient outcome to introduce children to new cognitive tasks. Alternatively, for those children whose persistence in using a less efficient strategy interferes with learning, the educator may be able to capitalize on the preferred style while calling attention to and gradually incorporating another approach to the task.

What conclusions can be drawn about the relationship between neuropsychology and education? From the suggestions offered in this chapter, it should be clear that, at this time, neuropsychological research has many broad implications for education but few direct applications to practice. In some instances, research findings provide support for approaches to teaching. In others, the evidence sheds light on the puzzling and seemingly paradoxical symptomatic changes that occur over time. In still others, the implication is to be cautious. Research findings can be misunderstood; inferences from limited data can be misinterpreted as factual information.

What stands out in this book is the potential for reciprocity across these disciplines. Insight into the processes involved in reading and spelling can extend the conceptual framework of research. Analyses of the acquisition and proficient use of skill can modify research paradigms. An awareness of the educational dilemmas that confront the teacher can generate new questions for investigation. One conclusion that can be drawn, then, is that collaboration contributes to advancing the understanding of brain–behavior relationships in general and of the neural bases of language, reading, and spelling in particular. A second conclusion flows from the first. For collaboration to occur, professionals are needed who are in a position to understand, to work with, and to interpret the theoretical constructs and empirical findings of related disciplines. An educational neuropsychologist might well take on this role.

A major responsibility of such a professional would be to bring order out of the divergent and often conflicting information derived from basic and applied research. By identifying areas of convergence, it may be possible to open up new lines of inquiry. Another responsibility would be to sift and clarify research findings so that misinterpretation and oversimplications are not translated into educational practice. A third responsibility would be the definition and formulation of research questions that are of particular concern to teachers. Eventually, an educational neuropsychologist, at the interface between the two fields, might be able to suggest to the clinical neuropsychologist intervention techniques derived from an understanding of educational practice, and propose to the educator modifications of the content and timing of instruction based on a knowledge of the differential capabilities of the brain at different stages of development.

It is not surprising that an examination of the multiple factors involved in the production and comprehension of oral and written language leads to the conclusion that collaboration across disciplines is essential. In order to understand the neuropsychology of language, reading, and spelling, multi-leveled systems must be studied from many perspectives. To interpret the results of neuropsychological research for education and to communicate knowledge that can be gained from teaching requires the voice of a professional who is conversant with both fields.

REFERENCES

McFie, J., & Zangwill, O. L. Visual-constructive disabilities associated with lesions of the left cerebral hemisphere. *Brain*, 1960, *83*, 243–260.

Patterson, A., & Zangwill, O. L. Disorders of visual space perception associated with lesions of the right cerebral hemisphere. *Brain*, 1944, *67*, 331–358.

Warrington, E. K., James, M., & Kinsbourne, M. Drawing disability in relation to laterality of cerebral lesion. *Brain*, 1976, *89*, 53–82.

Subject Index

EDUCATIONAL PSYCHOLOGY

continued from page ii

Jean Stockard, Patricia A. Schmuck, Ken Kempner, Peg Williams, Sakre K. Edson, and Mary Ann Smith. Sex Equity in Education

James R. Layton. The Psychology of Learning to Read

Thomas E. Jordan. Development in the Preschool Years: Birth to Age Five

Gary D. Phye and Daniel J. Reschly (eds.). School Psychology: Perspectives and Issues

Norman Steinaker and M. Robert Bell. The Experiential Taxonomy: A New Approach to Teaching and Learning

J. P. Das, John R. Kirby, and Ronald F. Jarman. Simultaneous and Successive Cognitive Processes

Herbert J. Klausmeier and Patricia S. Allen. Cognitive Development of Children and Youth: A Longitudinal Study

Victor M. Agruso, Jr. Learning in the Later Years: Principles of Educational Gerontology

Thomas R. Kratochwill (ed.). Single Subject Research: Strategies for Evaluating Change

Kay Pomerance Torshen. The Mastery Approach to Competency-Based Education

Harvey Lesser. Television and the Preschool Child: A Psychological Theory of Instruction and Curriculum Development

Donald J. Treffinger, J. Kent Davis, and Richard E. Ripple (eds.). Handbook on Teaching Educational Psychology

Harry L. Hom, Jr. and Paul A. Robinson (eds.). Psychological Processes in Early Education

J. Nina Lieberman. Playfulness: Its Relationship to Imagination and Creativity

Samuel Ball (ed.). Motivation in Education

Erness Bright Brody and Nathan Brody. Intelligence: Nature, Determinants, and Consequences

António Simões (ed.). The Bilingual Child: Research and Analysis of Existing Educational Themes

Gilbert R. Austin. Early Childhood Education: An International Perspective

Vernon L. Allen (ed.). Children as Teachers: Theory and Research on Tutoring

Joel R. Levin and Vernon L. Allen (eds.). Cognitive Learning in Children: Theories and Strategies

EDUCATIONAL PSYCHOLOGY

continued from page iii